TONY HILLERMAN

Tony Hillerman. Photo © Barney Hillerman.

TONY HILLERMAN

A Critical Companion

John M. Reilly

CRITICAL COMPANIONS TO POPULAR CONTEMPORARY WRITERS
Kathleen Gregory Klein, Series Editor

Greenwood Press
Westport, Connecticut • London

PS
3558
I45
Z8
1996

Library of Congress Cataloging-in-Publication Data

Reilly, John M. (John Marsden)
    Tony Hillerman : a critical companion / John M. Reilly.
      p. cm.—(Critical companions to popular contemporary
writers, ISSN 1082–4979)
    Includes bibliographical references (p.) and index.
    ISBN 0–313–29416–X (alk. paper)
    1. Hillerman, Tony—Criticism and interpretation. 2. Detective
and mystery stories, American—History and criticism. 3. Leaphorn,
Joe, Lt. (Fictitious character) 4. Southwestern States—In
literature. 5. Chee, Jim (Fictitious character) 6. Navajo Indians
in literature. 7. Police in literature. I. Title. II. Series.
PS3558.I45Z8   1996
813'.54—dc20   95–50459

British Library Cataloguing in Publication Data is available.

Library of Congress Catalog Card Number: 95–50459
ISBN: 0–313–29416–X
ISSN: 1082–4979

First published in 1996

Greenwood Press, 88 Post Road West, Westport, CT 06881
An imprint of Greenwood Publishing Group, Inc.

Printed in the United States of America

The paper used in this book complies with the
Permanent Paper Standard issued by the National
Information Standards Organization (Z39.48–1984).

10 9 8 7 6 5 4 3 2 1

for
Janet Louise Potter

Placetne, magistra?

Contents

Contents

Series Foreword

The authors who appear in the series Critical Companions to Popular Contemporary Writers are all best-selling writers. They do not have only one successful novel, but a string of them. Fans, critics, and specialist readers eagerly anticipate their next book. For some, high cash advances and breakthrough sales figures are automatic; movie deals often follow. Some writers become household names, recognized by almost everyone.

But novels are read one by one. Each reader chooses to start and, more importantly, to finish a book because of what she or he finds there. The real test of a novel is in the satisfaction its readers experience. This series acknowledges the extraordinary involvement of readers and writers in creating a best-seller.

The authors included in this series were chosen by an Advisory Board composed of high school English teachers and high school and public librarians. They ranked a list of best-selling writers according to their popularity among different groups of readers. Writers in the top-ranked group who had not received book-length, academic literary analysis (or none in at least the past ten years) were chosen for the series. Because of this selection method, Critical Companions to Popular Contemporary Writers meets a need that is not addressed elsewhere.

The volumes in the series are written by scholars with particular expertise in analyzing popular fiction. These specialists add an acade-

mic focus to the popular success that the best-selling writers already
enjoy.

The series is designed to appeal to a wide range of readers. The general
reading public will find explanations for the appeal of these well-known
writers. Fans will find biographical and fictional questions answered.
Students will find literary analysis, discussions of fictional genres, carefully organized introductions to new ways of reading the novels, and
bibliographies for additional research. Students will also be able to apply
what they have learned from this book to their readings of future novels
by these best-selling writers.

Each volume begins with a biographical chapter drawing on published
information, autobiographies or memoirs, prior interviews, and, in some
cases, interviews given especially for this series. A chapter on literary
history and genres describes how the author's work fits into a larger
literary context. The following chapters analyze the writer's most important, most popular, and most recent novels in detail. Each chapter
focuses on a single novel. This approach, suggested by the Advisory
Board as the most useful to student research, allows for an in-depth
analysis of the writer's fiction. Close and careful readings with numerous
examples show readers exactly how the novels work. These chapters are
organized around three central elements: plot development (how the
story line moves forward), character development (what the reader
knows about the important figures), and theme (the significant ideas of
the novel). Chapters may also include sections on generic conventions
(how the novel is similar to or different from others in its same category
of science fiction, fantasy, thriller, etc.), narrative point of view (who tells
the story and how), symbols and literary language, and historical or
social context. Each chapter ends with an "alternative reading" of the
novel. The volume concludes with a primary and secondary bibliogra-
phy, including reviews.

The Alternative Readings are a unique feature of this series. By demonstrating a particular way of reading each novel, they provide a clear
example of how a specific perspective can reveal important aspects of
the book. In each alternative reading section, one contemporary literary
theory—such as feminist criticism, Marxism, new historicism, decon-
struction, or Jungian psychological critique—is defined in brief, easily
comprehensible language. That definition is then applied to the novel to
highlight specific features that might go unnoticed or be understood differently in a more general reading of the novel. Each volume defines two

or three specific theories, making them part of the reader's understanding of how diverse meanings may be constructed from a single novel.

Taken collectively, the volumes in the Critical Companions to Popular Contemporary Writers series provide a wide-ranging investigation of the complexities of current best-selling fiction. By treating these novels seriously as both literary works and publishing successes, the series demonstrates the potential of popular literature in contemporary culture.

Kathleen Gregory Klein
Southern Connecticut State University

1

The Life of Tony Hillerman

Looking back on the time and place of his childhood, (Anthony) Tony (Grove) Hillerman sees in it an augury of the career as Southwest storyteller for which he is now best known. Born on 27 May 1925 in Sacred Heart, Oklahoma, where the population at the time was about sixty, he grew up in a culture without television, and what's more in a town without a library and without a movie house. The nearest movie house was in Konawa, Oklahoma, open just once a week for those who could afford to attend. For Hillerman's family, movies were too expensive, and sometimes even batteries for the radio were beyond the budget. Such a background was hardly promising for a writer, it might seem, but, as Hillerman remembers it, being deprived of modern tools for communication encouraged the skills of oral storytelling. "People sat on front porches, or on the benches which lined the front of my dad's general store, and told tales. A lot of value was attached to being good at it. In Sacred Heart, Oklahoma, being a storyteller was a good thing to be" (Winks 129).

If hard times do encourage people to dig deep within themselves for resources to withstand poverty and adversity, then Tony Hillerman had plenty of motivation. Sacred Heart sat within the western dust bowl impoverished by soil erosion. The Hillermans—mother Lucy Grove Hillerman, father August Alfred Hillerman, three children of whom Tony was the youngest—lived on a farm without indoor plumbing, electricity, or a tractor to work the land. The general store run by the elder Hillerman and his brother during the 1930s drew its business from the traffic of the crossroads, which constituted the town of Sacred Heart, where a filling station and cotton gin were the other commercial establishments. Hillerman gives a telling sign of how different the world of his youth was from present-day expectations in a recollection about telephones. The store, which was also the Sacred Heart post office, had a telephone installed, but "I never used it, because I didn't know anybody to *call* on the telephone. I honestly believe the first time I ever used a telephone I was twenty-one years old when I got back from overseas, from the war. . . . The Red Cross gave you a free telephone call. And I thought, well, 'I'll call my mother.' My first telephone call" (Herbert 95).

Immaterial things, those resources that allow people to manage their adversity, loom largest in Hillerman's memory of his childhood. In an interview with Rosemary Herbert, he summed up his thoughts about his parents this way: "I think I had a very happy childhood . . . I got nothing but a lot of love when I was a kid." In the same passage he conveyed the regard he has for the way his parents lived their lives. His mother, he said, was a nurse, and his father had been farmer, schoolteacher, miner, blacksmith, horseshoer, cowboy, "he'd done whatever he could do to make a living. A very interesting man. Both of 'em. My mother was a great storyteller" (Herbert 94). There is a lot of affection in the way Hillerman characterizes his parents, both "very interesting," and his mother "a great storyteller."

In growing up, maybe there is always a tendency to classify the world into groups, those like "us" and "them." For Tony Hillerman, "us" were country kids; town kids were "them." Town had the theater and banks, a main street, drug store, pool halls. Its young residents dressed in clothes other than overalls, went to barber shops, used the telephone (!), and seemed so sophisticated. The rural kids were ill at ease around such suavity, although they were superior at riding horses, shooting, and hard physical work. The country boys, and probably the country girls too, seemed to be the outsiders. Although as he writes about it now Tony Hillerman realizes that the town wasn't all that much either, the attitude formed by the youthful sense of difference stays with him, providing another biographical foreshadowing of his career as a novelist (Winks 128).

Significantly, the split between "them and us" for Hillerman did not fall along ethnic lines. Young Seminoles and Pottawatomies as well as German-American Tony, together all were "us." Later when he met Navajos, he recognized them as "kindred spirits. Country boys. More of us. Folks among whom I felt at ease" (Winks 128). This lesson of experience seems also to have been taught by Hillerman's father who showed his contempt for the Nazi racism, about which he felt sensitive because of his German origins, by instructing his children that people are all basically alike. In impoverished rural Oklahoma that instruction was true enough: Native Americans like the European Americans were "trying without success to make a living on a worn-out landscape" (Holt 6).

Hillerman received his formal elementary school education at St. Mary's Academy, a boarding school for Seminole and Pottawatomie girls run by the Sisters of Mercy. In an amusing recollection, Hillerman indicates that experience also encouraged thoughts about similarity and difference. "The nuns forgave us," he recalls, "for not being Indians but they never forgave us for not being girls" (Herbert 86).

August Hillerman died from heart disease in 1941 when Tony was sixteen (*Current Biography* 258). In a family meeting meant to plan the family's future, it was determined that Tony should go to college when he graduated from Konawa High School. As he describes the decision, Hillerman says he was selected for further education because he was more of a scholar than his brother Barney who would stay at home and run the farm, while Tony went away to Oklahoma State University in Stillwater to study what seemed to him the romantic discipline of chemical engineering. The move also represented escape, for he recalls that he might have done "anything to get out of Pottawatomie County" (Herbert 101).

The first semester at Oklahoma State was difficult. Tony was badly prepared for the mathematics courses required by his planned major; moreover, he needed to work at three jobs to pay his bills, and even then he could afford only the barest shelter. Except for an A in English, his grades were uniformly poor, and by the time the semester ended Barney had enlisted in the Air Force, leaving the family farm in need of Tony's supervision.

World War II, disrupting so many other lives, brought irreversible changes to the Hillermans. Not long after his return home, Tony followed his brother into the military, and the family auctioned off the farm with everything on it.

After enlisting in the United States Army at the age of eighteen, Tony Hillerman became an infantryman, spending two years in European combat with C Company of the 410th Infantry, of whose original 212 men, only 8 finished the war alive. He received the Bronze and Silver

Stars for his service and suffered the trauma of a severe wound. A concussion mine or a hand grenade—he isn't sure which—blew him into the air, broke both legs and partly blinded him. It was an experience enforcing the feeling of death as an oddly continuous part of life. "It was the middle of the night in the winter, and by then I'd seen enough wounded people to know how quickly they die . . . when it's cold and they bleed." He lay there in shock, knowing surely he would die and having a sense of "falling away . . . relief, and comfort, and kind of joy. . . . And I remember when I came out of it, when they were putting me on a jeep, I remember being kind of faintly disappointed" (Herbert 106–107).

Two chance events—but, as they turned out, auspicious ones—marked Hillerman's return from Europe. The first occurred when he was on convalescent leave after seven months in the hospital. Having made his way to the Navajo Reservation in New Mexico, he picked up a job driving truckloads of oil drill equipment. One day he came upon a party of Indians horseback in ceremonial attire crossing the road in front of his truck. Asking around, he found out that the party was conducting a ritual known as the Enemy Way, which was designed to bring people back into harmony with their universe, in this case Navajo Marine veterans undergoing a purgation of the bad influences acquired during their war service. What he had seen on the road was the "stick carrier's" camp making the ritual delivery of the "scalp" to the patient (Winks 128–29). Hillerman was seized by interest in what he saw. He got a familiar feeling about the Indians who in some ways were like the Oklahoma companions of his youth, but he also recognized that they were doing something different, something cultural. Twenty years later he would use this ceremonial in his first mystery.

First, however, he would follow a writer's apprenticeship, and this began as a result of the second chance event associated with his homecoming. During the war he had written home regularly. Beatrice Stahl, a feature writer, heard about the letters and wrote them up in a story for *The Daily Oklahoman*. When Hillerman met Stahl later at the newspaper, she told him he should be a writer (Herbert 102–103). Believing that was a lot better guidance than he had followed when he first went to college to major in chemical engineering, he went back to school, first at Oklahoma State and then at the University of Oklahoma in Norman where he completed a B.A. degree in journalism.

While at the University, Hillerman met Marie Unzner, whose outstanding attainments as a student of bacteriology earned her membership in Phi Beta Kappa, the nation's best known academic honorary. They married on 16 August 1948 (*Current Biography* 259).

Equipped with a degree certifying to the world that he knew something about writing and provided with a companion who would prove to be a dear friend and staunch supporter, Hillerman set out to earn a living with the art of language. The first job he got was writing Purina Pig Chow commercials for the radio in Oklahoma City. He had to be ready with three commercials every day for the 6 A.M. broadcast, and each of them had to be entirely different from the others. Not surprisingly, he lasted just a few weeks in this employment that he has called "the most taxing writing assignment I have ever had" (*Current Biography* 259).

Making a quick shift, Hillerman next began working for newspapers. First, he worked as a police reporter for the Borger, Texas, *News Herald*. That was followed by positions on the *Morning Press* of Lawton, Oklahoma, and in the United Press International (UPI) bureaus in Oklahoma City and, in 1952, Santa Fe. The experience as a reporter and news writer in those two state capitals stirred thoughts about fiction that eventually would appear in Hillerman's novel *The Fly on the Wall*, but before he would begin the writing of fiction, he served eleven years on the Santa Fe *New Mexican*, rising from political writer to executive editor of the capital city daily newspaper, the dream of many a professional newspaper writer.

Hillerman's next career change showed how engaged he had become by the craft of writing rather than by the income or status to which writing might lead. "Working with facts, as a journalist must, is like working with marble," he has written. "Truth has its beauty but it doesn't bend. In the seventeen years I spent covering crime and violence, politics, and that 'deviation from the normal' which journalism defines as news, the longing grew to take a vacation from the hard rock and move into the plastic of fiction. Instead of spending a laborious week digging out elusive facts, simply make them up. . . . If you need a one-legged Navajo to make an ironic remark, you create the Navajo, strike off a leg, and he says exactly what you want him to say." But there is more to it than the desire to be released from the requirement to report reality. On the contrary, as Hillerman sees it, there is the desire to understand reality in "the headful of material every reporter collects" about people desperate and under stress (Winks 131–32). So, Marie Hillerman, who no doubt had listened to talk like this for a while, said to her husband that, since he was nearing, or already, forty and always had wanted to be a novelist, he had better just do it (Herbert 103).

The getting started was not immediate, however. First, Hillerman returned to school, at the University of New Mexico in Albuquerque, to study literature and writing, supporting himself with part-time work for the university president and, after he completed an M.A. in 1965, as a faculty member in journalism. The thesis for his graduate degree, which was a collection of experiments in descriptive prose, includes treatment of a seriocomic episode in New Mexican history that became the lead essay in a volume of Hillerman's essays published in 1970 under the title *The Great Taos Bank Robbery and Other Indian Country Affairs.*

At the same time as the essays were being prepared for publication, Hillerman was completing his first novel. He wanted to do a "big book" about the world of politics he had studied so avidly while a capital newspaper reporter, but he thought maybe he ought first to try something that sounded easier—a mystery. The episode in 1945 when he encountered a Navajo ceremonial party came back to him, and he decided to write a book about an anthropologist studying Navajo witchcraft who accidentally finds himself becoming a detective. In "Mystery, Country Boys, and the Big Reservation" (1986), Hillerman describes his slow pace on the book (Winks 127–47). In preparation for his writing, he tried to outline, from the beginning and then from the end. It didn't work, nor did the original idea of making the anthropologist the chief detective in the narrative. After three years' work during the time when he wasn't working on his thesis, writing papers as a faculty member, or working his part-time job, and after some periods when he set the whole thing aside, he had a nearly complete manuscript for an agent's examination.

The agent was the same person who had advised Hillerman not to write a novel, since he was an accomplished writer of nonfiction, which probably would earn him more money. This agent was just as discouraging when Hillerman called her a month after mailing her his novel. It wouldn't do, she said, but if he insisted on rewriting it, what he should do is "get rid of all that Indian stuff" (*Current Biography* 260).

The book we know now as *The Blessing Way* went next to Joan Kahn, a famous editor then at Harper & Row. Almost immediately she agreed to publish the book, provided that Hillerman made some revisions, but none of them had to do with deleting any Indian material. Curiously, the title was a revision introduced by the publisher. Hillerman originally named the book *The Enemy Way*, which is the accurate name for the ceremony he had witnessed in 1945 and introduced into the plot of the novel. There is no Blessing Way in the book at all.

Nevertheless, the novel was a critical success. It was a finalist for the Mystery Writers of America award for "Best First Novel" (Lawrence Sanders' *The Anderson Tapes* won the prize), was optioned for screen production and paperback publication, and above all gave Tony Hillerman the confidence to pursue a career in writing fiction.

Hillerman continued to teach at the University of New Mexico, until recent retirement, where he was chair of the Department of Journalism as well as assistant to the president. In the 1970s he published three works of nonfiction about the Southwest region, a children's book, and the collection of essays. Today, however, he is fully occupied, and, of course, he is best known as the author of the lengthening series of Navajo detective novels.

The novels draw consistently on themes evident in Hillerman's biography. Probably the chief of these themes is the respect for tradition and spiritual life shown by his treatment of Navajo culture. Hillerman is Roman Catholic, but he values as highly the ways Navajos, Kiowas, and Pueblos live in accordance with what they believe to be the answer to life's mysteries. The well-developed spiritual sense in his novels becomes further manifested in their expressed attitude toward material possessions. Hillerman recalls that his brother counseled him once against coveting wealth (Herbert 107). He found the counsel to be wise and respects its central place in the beliefs of Native American people.

The natural companionship Hillerman feels with what is termed the Navajo "way" is reflected in his novels' preoccupation with evil, its definitions and particularly its expression through avarice. Because the zone of sympathy in Hillerman's work is so broad as to accord respect to several cultures, it is equally natural that his writing constantly revolves around episodes of culture conflict and assimilation, presenting themes recognizable today for their relevance to all of American society, probably the world.

As authors achieve success, their lives become dominated by the work of drafting their texts. We wonder not only what they will write next, but also how they will compose that book and so what their workday is like. Hillerman tells us that he rises fairly late, that is, about 7:30 A.M., drinks coffee, reads the paper, eats breakfast with Marie, gets ready for the day—and then he is tired. So maybe he plays some solitaire, or reads his mail, turns on his computer, or maybe not. And then he starts to go through what he has written (Goodman 77).

Hillerman's routine may not suit anyone else, but for him it is the product of experience. From his first attempt at a novel he learned that outlining accomplishes nothing for him. Instead, he starts a book with a thematic idea, never knowing where the book as a whole is going. Individual chapters are another matter. These he composes carefully, starting with deep thought about setting and scene, pondering the weather that will appear in the chapter, the landscape, characters' moods—everything until he gets it right. It is "an old reporter's conditioning," he says, which results in his never having to do much rewriting (Winks 139–40). Then each day looking again over what he wrote yesterday, he yields to the temptation to make changes. This cumulative procedure results in manuscripts that never go beyond one draft (Goodman 78).

Hillerman has rules about narratives which he is ready to share. One rule is that the active part of a story should occupy as few days as possible, which is a conviction leading to a craft that weaves narrative tightly together. Another rule is that there should be no "footnotes," by which Hillerman means simply that he keeps the story moving. The ethnographic material—information about customs and ceremonies and beliefs—must be functional to the narrative, and not laid in as though the book were "teaching" about Navajo life (Winks 142–43). A reader familiar with Hillerman's works can extend this rule to add that no information, and especially information about the personal lives of the characters, will appear unless it serves an evident function in moving the story along.

Characteristically, Hillerman is constantly alert for material that may make an effective story. He offers two examples that make the point. Once at Mass he watched a man taking the collection, an elderly, thin, "Don Quixote-looking fellow." Later while writing *Talking God* he needed to describe a body lying by some railroad tracks, and the appearance of the usher returned to his memory. Hillerman put him in the book, and eventually it changed the direction of the narrative, because the corpse seemed most probable if he were an exiled South American political leader. A second illustration of this process of using "found material" relates to the description of the hired killer in *People of Darkness*. Hillerman needed a credible portrayal of motivation in a psychologically damaged personality. Then he remembered the last execution he covered as a reporter when the felon had told Hillerman he hoped his mother would read about his death and come to get his body. "What was his mother's name? He didn't know, because he hadn't seen her since his eleventh birthday. She was living in a trailer with a drunk who beat her and chased the boy off. He had hoped his mother would let him come home again, but when he returned the trailer was gone. He had been looking for her ever since" (Goodman 80).

The imaginative power to adapt material that Hillerman has come upon in his life, from the troop of Navajos crossing a dirt road to the motherless felon, accounts in large measure for the effect of his narratives. In a way it also explains why we may be so curious about the biography of the writer who can create such effects.

Yes, Hillerman is a real person, today living in Albuquerque where he writes full time in a comfortable office in his home. Marie remains his life's collaborator. They have six children now grown. The oldest daughter is editorial page editor for the *Albuquerque Journal North* and has published children's books. Their middle daughter is an artist who illustrated Hillerman's children's book, *The Boy Who Made Dragonfly* and a full-time mother. The youngest daughter is a homemaker with four daughters of her own. One son is a pharmacist, another a cable installer, and the third works for American Airlines (*Companion* 67).

Tony Hillerman has plans for future books and works at them more or less daily. In an interview in 1990, he indicated that he had two manuscripts underway—one a novel about "coming of age" during the Great Depression, sort of a Southwestern *Catcher in the Rye,* and the other a novel placed in the Philippines (Bernell and Karni 49). The Philippine novel was published in 1995 as *Finding Moon.* Another, more recent, source claims that the Navajo detective series was completed with *Sacred Clowns* (Sobol 113–16), but "An Apology" at the opening of *Finding Moon* promises that the author's "next book will bring Jim Chee and Joe Leaphorn of the Tribal Police back into action" (ix). During their careers, writers entertain many thoughts about many projects, often more than they complete. Future published books will be the conclusive evidence of the directions Hillerman's creativity is taking.

Perhaps we can hazard one prediction, however. Since Hillerman has rarely received a poor review for any of his books and new readers "discover" the pleasures of his books every day, there is every likelihood that works to come will find success. If they do, it will be because Hillerman writes out of a life's experiences, none of which fails to enrich his writing.

2

Tony Hillerman and the Detective Fiction Genre

Authorities all agree that the father of detective fiction is Edgar Allan Poe and that his first-born was "The Murders in the Rue Morgue," which appeared in the pages of *Graham's Magazine* in April of 1841. There had been forerunners of Poe's detective Monsieur Dupin. The British detective writer Dorothy L. Sayers claimed that the romances of James Fenimore Cooper relating the pursuits of Leatherstocking in the American forests constitute a variety of detection fiction. Other critics, noting the emphasis in detection fiction on revelation of evil design, allege that the roots of the family tree lie in biblical tales. Poe retains his priority, however, because he assembled motifs previously employed for describing crime or its detection into a narrative structure centrally concerned, rather than incidentally so, with presentation of the criminal problem, examination of the evidence, and a process of reasoning toward solution of the problem.

In three short stories—"The Murders in the Rue Morgue," "The Mystery of Marie Roget" (1842–43), and "The Purloined Letter" (1845)—Poe created the formulas and model that have prevailed ever since. The formulas include use of a sidekick to narrate the story; the application of analytical reasoning by a "great" detective, whose accomplishment appears to be a consequence of his eccentricity and his position as an outsider in contrast to the mediocre insiders in the official police; and the thematic indication that the mental powers of the detective can correct the disruption of seemingly unnatural and apparently inexplicable events, such as murder, and reestablish order and control.

Despite his parental role as creator of formulas and model for detective fiction, Poe did not pursue his narrative experiment beyond the three short stories. Nor was his precise delineation of the new form immediately adopted by other writers, although it won admiration appropriately enough in Paris, the setting of Monsieur Dupin's detective investigations. In 1866, the French author Emile Gaboriau took up Poe's lead, created his own consulting detective, Tabaret, and extended the example of investigative narrative to the length of a serial novel, which he titled *L'Affaire Lerouge* (known in English as *The Widow Lerouge*). When it was reprinted in 1873, *L'Affaire Lerouge* made Gaboriau famous and created an eager audience for a series of new novels he published in the 1870s and 1880s featuring Monsieur Lecoq of the French Sûreté.

In a curious repetition of Gaboriau's experience with the first publication of his detective fiction, Arthur Conan Doyle also had to wait a time for the acclaim that has made his detective a world hero. *A Study in Scarlet,* issued in 1888, introduced Sherlock Holmes and Dr. John Watson to an indifferent audience, but as their adventures began to appear with regularity in the *Strand* magazine during the 1890s, they found a never-diminishing readership that has made the name of the odd inhabitant of 221B Baker Street synonymous with genius and the case narratives inscribed by the doughty John Watson among the most popular examples to be found of entertaining literature.

That stories of villainy should prove not only entertaining but also comforting ought to make us pause. Why is it, we might wonder, that motives of greed and envy resulting in crimes of violent destruction hardly shock a reader when they occur in the frame of detective fiction, while in real life violence is so shocking and threatening? An explanation of the paradoxically satisfying effect of violence and disorder in detective fiction is to be found in a simple comparison.

A metropolitan daily newspaper reports the slaying of a young woman. A recent arrival to the city, she had come, according to those who knew her, with hopes of finding work suitable to her talents and her new college degree. Probably adventure and the allure of urban life also motivated her, but that would be natural for youth. People who met her in the apartment building where she found affordable housing found her manner pleasant, although none of them had become well acquainted with her or with the other young woman who shared her flat. She hadn't yet found the job best suited to her, but being resourceful she had sought and taken employment in a small shop while she got settled in the city. Her killer entered the apartment during an evening when she was alone and asleep; he was probably intent on burglary, for some items of value were missing. Surprising his victim in bed, the killer had attacked her, although first reports did not indicate whether the assault was sexual, and then he stabbed and beat her to death.

The newspaper account stresses the representativeness of the young woman. We, too, move about frequently and perhaps have relocated to find new employment and certainly to seek the work for which we feel best suited. Reports of friends and other residents of the apartment building indicate that the young woman was a decent, fine person. Allowing for differences in age or gender, she could be our sister, daughter, or even ourselves. Yet, despite her model behavior, she was vulnerable to violent, mindless assault. So far as the news reporters indicate, no motive explains her death; no reasonable purpose or justice can be found in it.

In keeping with the conventions of newspaper crime reports, this crime is brought close to readers. Through characterization of the victim as someone readers identify with, her behavior as admirable but unremarkable, the story encourages affinity. Then, as circumstances of the killing are related, the story taps into widely shared feelings about the city, its anonymity and danger, the idea that in a place so immense and diverse everyone may be vulnerable and anything might happen—happen to you. The newspaper story becomes the bridge to an unfortunate stranger; distance is erased, so that we may sense the terror the victim felt as she died. The effect is startling and shocking, but not what we think of as entertaining.

By contrast there is Edgar Allan Poe's story "The Mystery of Marie Roget" based on the historical case of the death of Mary Rogers, a clerk murdered and thrown into the Hudson River. Materials found in contemporary reports are Poe's sources, but his strategy is to reverse the practice of newspaper conventions. While Marie/Mary seems to be representative in the possibilities open to a young working woman of the nineteenth century, and perhaps attractively spirited besides, the evidence of her fate—that is, the information available to criminal investigation—is more important than the fate itself. And while Marie/Mary is the victim, she is supplanted as the story's subject by Monsieur Dupin who examines evidence in order to reason his way toward the probable motive and circumstances of the crime. Decentering the crime, Poe replaces the shudder one feels at its occurrence with the satisfaction that is possible when an astute investigator subjects violence to reason and normalizes it as one more event the mind can explain. The conventions of newspaper reporting lead readers across a bridge to vicarious participation in the terror of crime. In contrast, the formula of fiction that makes plot from detection invites readers to move away from terror and to share instead the pleasure to be found in the process of problem solving, which is, of course, the means by which we reduce the terror presented us by the world.

Paradox disappears, having been dissolved in our recognition that narrative invention and technique, not simply the sensational matter of crime, accounts for the astounding success of Poe, Gaboriau, Doyle, and others in creating a form of writing yet unrivaled in its popularity.

Still, it remains to consider how a form so unquestionably universal in its appeal to present-day readers took so long to emerge. We can appreciate the celebrity of detective fiction by asking what was necessary for stories of criminal detection to emerge into a fully developed and distinct genre at the hands of such nineteenth-century Western authors as Edgar Allan Poe, Emile Gaboriau, Arthur Conan Doyle, their contemporaries and successors. To begin with, there had to be the problem of crime before there was the need to seek its solution. Wrongdoing seems to be eternal; it is as prominent in stories of the Creation as in the latest best-selling mystery novel. But, in fact, such is not the case. Violation of divine commandments and evil trespass, as recorded in ancient literature, are plainly disobedient acts demanding swift punishment but requiring no explanation, for there is none to be taken into account. Motive is an irrelevant issue: the means of committing the deed is unimportant beside the fact that the deed was done.

Conditions in the nineteenth-century Western city were quite different. Power had become abstract, present in the trappings and symbols of political authority, but invisible in economic life and glimpsed from a distance in social life. The complexity of an industrializing society multiplied the possibility of offense and violation. In place of ten or a dozen commandments and decrees to respect the nobility and church, opportunities for theft, deceit, and fraud increased and objects of violence became practically innumerable among the thousands of strangers clustering together. The scale of the economy defied the power of a squire or mayor, a single rich person, or a bishop to conceive of all the violations that might occur in realms of activity about which a divine voice had never spoken, let alone released a commandment. The size of the population displaced from agriculture and arriving in the city to do the work of industry had become so massive as to assure virtual anonymity to those with a mind to do wrong. On the one hand, scale, and, on the other hand, expansion of economic activity, commerce, and wealth transformed what once had been an important but evidently limited question of punishment for evil into a larger problem. Writings in law and jurisprudence began to fill volume upon volume meant to codify acceptable practices and to determine necessary evidence and acceptable contingencies in the case of offense. Thus crime became a characteristic and compelling issue.

With the appearance of crime as a problem came specialized efforts to deal with it. The legal profession was insufficient to control crime even as it sought to define it. Owners of property, unlike nobles of old, could not personally marshal the troops or physical force needed to protect their wealth. Banks, commercial partnerships, or manufacturers dealing in large sums of money, great numbers of products, and far-flung operations might dominate the economy but could not prevent crime. Privately employed guards and organizations such as the Pinkerton Detective Agency partly met the need for ways to address the new problem of crime, but by far the most significant development, and the one that confirms the great change in social organization and thought was the invention of official police forces sponsored by government. The Sûreté in France, Scotland Yard in England, and metropolitan police in American cities—together they represent the institutional evidence of an environment that would find its popular literary expression through the genre of detective fiction.

Our interrogation of necessary conditions for the appearance of detective fiction now leads us to an examination of the market and audience for the popular genre. The operative word here is "popular" as distinct from "elite." Readers of the form belong to all social classes, any age, and both genders; they require no special knowledge for comprehension of the narratives, except, of course, literacy. Beyond that, what readers of detective fiction have in common is the universal appreciation of stories and probably some feeling that stories written about the solving of crimes tell us something about the world in which we live. We have already seen that the problem of crime broadly engages people as an issue characteristic of modern society, and experience confirms the power of story for us all. We tell anecdotes all of the time, we know our past through an accumulation of personal stories, and we avidly share all manner of tales from local gossip to accounts we have heard about events beyond our community. Evidence of the disposition to tell stories is so overwhelming as to show that stories are the means by which human beings have always understood their world. The acquired ability to use written language simply extends the range of stories, making available vast stores of additional narratives to feed human interest.

Despite the similarity of popular literature to commodities in the consumer market, it would be a mistake to think of popular literary genres as bottles of soda pop, a momentary fizz irrelevant to nutrition, unnecessary to life. The commodity market enables production and distribution of detective fiction, but it has evident serious connections to life in modern society. The genre might even be said to nourish the ability of its audience to comprehend modern life, because to those who choose to read detective fiction, it offers commentary on the modern problem of crime.

The genre embeds its commentary within the accustomed ways it presents narrative, which is to say that authors of detective fiction work with a system of conventions inherent to the form. The name we assign the genre—detective fiction—denominates its leading conventions as the portrayal of a protagonist, or chief character, methodically examining a criminal problem. That provides the frame for a protocol of choices through which the writer moves selectively to determine what sort of crime will present the problem, what motive and means will characterize the crime, the sort of actor who will commit the crime, and, most important among the genre's requirements, the qualities and nature of the detective.

The combination of conventions in detective fiction works to deploy the narrative as a confrontation of disrupted social order. The reason for this is not hard to see, for it seems inevitable that a genre of fiction accompanying the rise of modern society and speaking of the endemic occurrence of crime will embody a popular hope for security from the harmful threat of volatile change. In this regard, detective fiction makes its every example a parable of social order.

That the popular hope for security would be expressed through the optimistic agency of a brilliant detective seems equally inevitable, if we reflect that the nineteenth-century birth dates of Monsieur Dupin, Lecoq, and Sherlock Holmes coincide with an era of great faith in the powers of the individual intellect. Criminal detectives, either privately consulting or officially employed by a municipal or state government, are the natural expression, then, of hope and faith. At least in fictional narratives they came to reflect this optimism, because while actual police work is often routine and full of drudgery, in the imaginative experience of fiction, the figure of the grand detective is an economical and memorable personification for the parable of social security. An author's assignment of peculiar traits of personality, manner, and speech to the fictional character creates the means by which readers can identify with the investigation. Equipping the detective with a method of reasoning superbly applied in the narrative and akin to abilities that may be developed through education conveys the attractive idea that the mind of anyone, including readers, has within it the potential for treating social disorder as a practical problem that, however daunting or terrifying, is ultimately soluble.

In the century and a half since the detective genre sprang from the ground of the nineteenth-century industrial city, it has undergone considerable change, most of it related to ingenious innovation within basic conventions. Because stories must occur in sites with some semblance of truth to them (i.e., verisimilitude), authors of detective fiction have adopted all sorts of settings, including many that are decidedly not urban. Because the genre requires that the detective be adequately challenged, writers have created many clever schemes for the perpetration of murder and other crimes. And because both the essence of the genre and verisimilitude call for the detective to be a fully fleshed character, writers have ascribed a host of peculiarities and special abilities to their protagonists.

Historians of detective fiction have produced an elaborate record of detective story development. Among the sources for studying the history of detective fiction are such works as Howard Haycraft's *Murder for Pleasure: The Life and Times of the Detective Story* (1942/1968), Julian Symons's *Bloody Murder* (1984), and the entries in major reference works like *Detectionary: A Bibliographical Dictionary of the Leading Characters in Detective and Mystery Fiction* (1977) and *Twentieth Century Crime and Mystery Writers* (1985/1990/1993).

Through all the historical changes, however, the larger conventions of the genre have remained generally stable. Tony Hillerman is well read in those conventions. Among the writers he has studied carefully are Raymond Chandler and Dashiell Hammett, creators of the distinctive American detective type known as hard boiled, and especially Arthur Upfield, whose detective character is an Australian Aborigine bearing a resemblance to Hillerman's own Native American detectives (Holt 6–7). In fact, Hillerman yields one of the best examples of the inherent vigor of a literary form with fixed conventions. In basic respects, Hillerman writes classic detection stories that open with highly dramatic descriptions of a puzzling crime; introduce a detective carefully detailed in person and method throughout the narrative; follow this detective's investigation through scenes introducing numbers of intriguing secondary characters and uncovering an abundance of information, some of which becomes useful and pertinent evidence for solving the crime, and some of which does not; embellish description of the physical and social environment; and come to closure with a plausible accounting by the detective that explains what is possible to know about the criminal problem.

That classic scheme serves the same function that an armature does for a sculptor—that is, as the skeletal framework on which the artist molds clay or plaster to form a uniquely expressive figure. For Hillerman, the unique expression of each of his novels results from intuition as well as his knowledge of form, convention, and Native American culture. He says, for example, that he does not outline his stories before writing, and perhaps he cannot outline them because he depends on serendipity. A character he introduces in one portion of a narrative may emerge in his thought as an appropriate part of a later scene. A chance observation, a memory, can take the narrative in an unforeseen direction (Winks 143–45).

With the armature of his stories established by the initial choice to write in the detective genre, Hillerman's creative decisions are centered on the way he will model the narrative upon that armature. With an intuition of genius—and as he tells interviewers it seems decidedly more intuitive than calculating—he usually places his stories among Reservation Navajos and other Native American tribes. From that first intuition there flows a stream of generic innovations. The grand spaces of the Southwest United States, sacred land to Native Americans, but land requiring irrigation and development in the eyes of Anglo settlers, become a setting for fiction that enables Hillerman to explore themes of cultural difference. It also enables him to dramatize the contrary attractions for Native Americans of assimilation to modern, "white" life versus a deeply seated desire to be nurtured by the indigenous traditions of "Indian" ways. This likely theme provides the functional occasion for filling the narratives with illuminating information about Native American beliefs, customs, and historical experience.

Most notably, the stream of innovations includes Hillerman's creation of two Native American detectives, nearly the first ever to appear in written literature. Hillerman tells an anecdote indicating that at first he may have treated their characters more as cast for the stories than as persons exemplifying varying expressions of Navajo experience. The in-

cident he relates occurred shortly after he created the character of Jim
Chee to replace temporarily the character of Joe Leaphorn. While signing
his book for a woman during a publicity tour, she asked him why he
had changed the name of his detective. He replied, "It's a different character." She said that "she couldn't tell them apart" (Goodman 77). If
there was a lesson to be learned from that remark, he quickly absorbed
it. He put both detectives in his next book, and since that time he has
worked diligently to exploit character differences between Joe Leaphorn
and Jim Chee. They now represent poles of response among university-
educated Navajos to the mingling of experience from the inner world of
indigenous people's beliefs and life with the experience they have acquired in school and from their roles as tribal police officers.

As we follow the publication of Hillerman's novels in sequence, seeking a record within the texts of the lines of development he has found
most important to pursue, two paths figure most prominently. The first
leads through craft. In his first books Hillerman was uncertain about
what his body of work might be; indeed he was uncertain that he would
even prove to be a novelist. His first detective was an Anglo professor
of anthropology who happened to have a Navajo friend working as a
police officer—a friend, by the way, who got his name of Leaphorn not
from Native American sources but from an allusion in the novel *Bull
from the Sea* by Mary Renault (Bernell and Karni 47). In revisions of that
first novel, Leaphorn moved to the center of the story, but the professor
also remained an active sleuth. Following this opening, Hillerman
dropped Native American themes and material altogether to try his hand
at an ambitious "big novel." That long-planned work *Fly on the Wall* had
critical success but not staying power. Hillerman then returned to his
Navajo subject and set about the careful development of characters and
a range of further experiments with narrative perspective and voice that
have resulted in a maturely supple narration.

The second path of development observable in Hillerman's detective
fiction leads to an increasingly careful exploration of spiritual and social
themes relative to both Native American and general American culture.
Notably, these themes center on evil and acquisitiveness as they play out
at the meeting places of tradition and changing culture in a geography
of overlapping worlds.

As markedly advanced beyond their origins as Hillerman's detective
narratives appear in comparison to founding works of the genre from
the nineteenth-century, his stories of skinwalkers, talking gods, and listening women, Navajo police, and villains both Indian and Anglo belong

firmly in the family lineage. Adapting conventions of the genre and innovating his designs upon the armature of detective fiction, Hillerman demonstrates that the genre is a powerful instrument for knowing reality. All it takes is some fine writing, and that will be the subject of subsequent chapters.

3

The Blessing Way
(1970)

The novel that begins Tony Hillerman's series of Navajo mysteries offers a convenient glimpse of the author's creative process. In the dominant role it gives to Professor Bergen McKee, it suggests that Hillerman originally associated the adventure of his plots even more closely with the "romance" of anthropology than he would in the subsequent development of his saga of the Reservation. At the same time, *The Blessing Way* deploys scenes and episodes, and entangles the lines of the plot, in the fashion that has become the hallmark of the Hillerman invention in the crime and mystery genre. Thus, this first novel has unusual value beyond its immediate attraction as an exciting tale of distorted ambition.

CHARACTER DEVELOPMENT

The narrative opens on the Navajo Reservation in Arizona but within a few pages shifts to Albuquerque, New Mexico, 400 miles to the east, where Bergen McKee procrastinates instead of grading the eighty-four final examination papers submitted by his Anthropology class at the state university. Part of the reason for his delay is a mood of nervousness and distraction. A larger cause is his preoccupation with a letter he expects from his friend Joe Leaphorn, an officer with the Navajo Tribal Police stationed at Window Rock, of whom he had inquired about the currency of witchcraft reports on the Reservation. Case studies of contemporary instances of the acts of witches in their characteristic guise of wolves form the basis of McKee's research. He expects this work to result in a book demonstrating his theory that the Navajo belief about witches is representative of the scapegoat procedure familiar to anthropologists whereby the explanation of calamity is simplified by locating its cause in the willful action of an evil agent.

Like his ungraded final examinations, McKee's book has been delayed by preoccupation. His research has been blocked by the collapse of his self-esteem following his wife's elopement with another man. The curt note she left telling him she would not contest a divorce looms in his memory as a sign that "he was less than a man." At the same time, the alternate responses of people in his university department—concern about his evident need for companionship or, conversely, the assumption that he no longer needs to meet the demands of a personal life—he receives as either unwelcome pity or careless disregard. As a result of his pain, his professional work has lost its savor. Thus, it is with more of a sense of release and nostalgia for old times with Leaphorn than with enthusiasm that McKee decides to accompany his academic colleague Jeremy Canfield to the Reservation.

Considering the circumstances Hillerman provides to motivate and move McKee to the site of the narrative's main action, the professor of anthropology does not seem to stand very tall as a hero of Western science and Western action. He is not even an Indiana Jones, who is so likably self-deprecating but confidently superior in his dealings with villains and so-called primitives. That, however, is exactly the point of Hillerman's characterization. Rather than being a projection of a cultural ideal—handsome, athletic, masterful, definitively Caucasian on the model of the protagonists of empire adventures from Sherlock Holmes to James Bond—Bergen McKee is a realistically representative figure. He happens upon the crimes in *The Blessing Way* accidentally rather than because he is part of an elite presumed always to be center stage. His motives are complicated by conditions of mind, such as indecision and doubt, which are common to us all. Yet, he knows well what is good even if he does not pursue it with the single-mindedness of a knight.

Bergen McKee appears to be representative in his characterization rather than idealized, above all because of the way Hillerman has equipped him with a profession. As an anthropologist, McKee practices the science that purports to chart and interpret the complexity of human social organization. Anthropology carries the promise of a unitary explanation of human behavior, but the thrill of anticipation is leavened by practical limitations and sheer complexity. One may be an observer of a society—the interchanges of its markets and communications, its rites and rituals, its customs of association and institutions—but participants in the society can see their activities differently, subjectively perhaps, but no less accurately. Articulation between observation and participation is a vexed procedure to say the least. Add to that difficulty the very multiplicity of social formations, varying among ethnic and geographic groups, classes and genders, ages and linguistic groups. Consider those factors, and there is cause for humility about the possibility of fulfilling anthropology's ultimate project. The science of anthropology can never be complete, it seems, but in its hopes, as much as in its limits, it is work on a human scale. It is never to be transcendent but is always aiming to be; always constrained by practical problems but nonetheless engaging because of the problems. Anthropology is just the sort of work for a representative figure.

This kind of reasoning may have led Hillerman to give Bergen McKee the largest share of the sleuth's billing in *The Blessing Way*. Another motivation may have been an expectation that Anglo readers (in Navajo usage, *Belaconis*) could most readily identify with someone like themselves. For that matter, McKee also would seem to be a natural creation for the Belaconi author himself, who like McKee is an outsider who has grown closer to the Navajo through sympathy and involvement but must always remain the observer.

In interviews, Tony Hillerman has indicated that in first draft the book was primarily about McKee, "in whose viewpoint I felt fairly comfortable." Furthermore, he says that he placed the story on the Reservation because he thought the Navajos were so interesting and that their homeland "would make a captivating setting for a mystery novel, which otherwise might not be very good, because I didn't know if I was going to be a good mystery writer" (*Companion*, 53). In revising the draft for publication, with the assistance of an editor's comments but acting also on his discovery that Leaphorn had potential for a larger part in the story, Hillerman enhanced the role of the Navajo police officer. As a result, Leaphorn and McKee are co-equal in the earlier sections of the novel.

Still, the final version of *The Blessing Way* clearly retains the shape of the original conception as McKee focuses criminal inquiry by interviewing informants, following leads, testing solutions, and, in the late stages of the book, directly experiencing the conflict and showdown with the conspirators. On a secondary level as well, the book remains McKee's story, for the move through the adventure of the stalking of McKee and his captivity with Ellen Leon in the Anasazi ruins is underwritten with an account of McKee's personal recovery—the reawakening of the nerve and initiative that permit him to survive conflict with the character known as Big Navajo and his collaborators. Even the implication of developing affection between McKee and Ellen in the last pages of the novel points to the original assignment of the lead to Bergen McKee.

Joe Leaphorn, referred to in the novel as an employee of the Law and Order Division, or to Navajos a "blue policeman," is, in his own way, also a representative character. Early in the novel his orientation is made clear when it is related that he cannot fully accept McKee's thesis that witchcraft is a scapegoat process. To Leaphorn there is truth in the Navajo Origin Myth: some people do deliberately turn antisocial and choose the evil way. Recalling their differences on the matter, McKee feels regret that he has not been able to persuade Leaphorn to adopt his opinion. The memory of their debates, however, is suffused with fondness, which suggests that Leaphorn has the capacity to bridge cultures described by W.E.B. Du Bois as "double consciousness." One may feel rent by duality, both American, by which Du Bois means part of the majority white culture, and black, or part of an ethnic minority. In feeling "twoness," however, one also has access to both cultures, to make of them what one can. In a positive way what one makes is a modern self (*Souls of Black Folk*). Like Du Bois's modern individual, Leaphorn retains a subjective conviction of the rightness of Native American beliefs and what Navajos affirm as the way of nature. Yet, we find as the narrative progresses that since Leaphorn was schooled in anthropological science at Arizona State University and was familiar with the ways of white people, he has two lenses for viewing experience.

Some might call Leaphorn acculturized; that is to say, they would describe him as having adapted to the majority white society. That assessment is too simple. Luis Horseman and the Big Navajo are examples in the novel of Navajos who have adapted, but Leaphorn describes them as lost souls in limbo between the values of the People (Navajos) and the values of the whites. The old-fashioned expression, "He acted like he had no relatives" (99), captures the difference between them and Leaphorn. They have uprooted themselves from a community of mutual responsibility in order to assume the behavior of a culture in which they cannot become rooted. In contrast, Leaphorn stays rooted not only through residence and elective work, but also through the nourishment he derives from sharing the intangible realm of the "Navajo way."

Leaphorn's remark about lost souls implies that Luis Horseman and the Big Navajo are products of the upheavals of modern life who fail to sustain a "double consciousness." The idea can be extended as well to Ellen Leon's fiancée, Jimmy Hall. Having lost emotional affiliation with their "home"—their native community of shared values—and having no interest in making a new "home," they center their attention selfishly to serve only themselves.

Disregard for community, disaffiliation, and self-centeredness, however, are just the negative ways of coping with the physical and intellectual mobility characteristic of contemporary society. In a positive fashion, Du Bois's formulation can be a model for many others besides African Americans or Native Americans. It describes the consequence of movement from country to city, from town to college, from school to job, as well as a more profound duality of general American citizenship and membership in an ethnic or a religious subculture. In *The Blessing Way* the model defines Joe Leaphorn as Navajo and as American, thus making him Hillerman's second representative character in the novel.

As we have seen, McKee is the dominant sleuth in the novel. Leaphorn appears early in the narrative, follows a line of inquiry parallel to McKee's, and then is absent from the scenes of confrontation and adventure. In another indication of the relative prominence Hillerman assigns the two, McKee's behavior is given biographical motivation (the information about his failed marriage), but Leaphorn's is not. This does not mean Leaphorn is without personality. After all there is the engaging formulation of his double consciousness. In addition, there is provision for readers to measure the emotional investment he has in his job when he expresses the fear that by talking unguardedly in Shoemaker's store he has caused Horseman's death.

Secondary characters, as distinct from those in supporting roles like Leaphorn, typically appear in narratives without much qualification. They are as developed when we first meet them as they will ever become, and they are denominated by a singular trait. The Big Navajo seems puzzling in his first scene, but that is only because as yet too little information is available to contradict the evidence of his physical appearance, which Southwesterners call Tuba City Navajo, meaning without any genetic inheritance from other tribes. Eventually, when the evidence attaches evil purposes to him, it also becomes known that he is a Relocation Indian, the object of forced removal from the Reservation in a failed government experiment to foster acculturation. The facts about the Big Navajo are always the same, but in aid of the story line the narrative retards their revelation.

Jimmy Hall, who designed the entire plot to eavesdrop on the Army missile guidance system and sell the results, is even more circumscribed in characterization. As far as readers know, through most of the narrative Jimmy merely plays an enabling part. His association with Ellen Leon, and through her with Jeremy Canfield, brings Leon and Canfield into the investigation. Mention of Jimmy's ambition to get a million dollars, and of his general frustrations too, could just be items in Ellen's conversations with McKee. When his key role as instigator and director of the crime becomes evident, Jimmy has only been present for a few pages of the novel. Almost faceless, undefined in personality, and practically absent from the story, Jimmy Hall attains the position of an unmodified principle of evil, an alien intruder into the Navajo world of moderation.

PLOT DEVELOPMENT

The Blessing Way immediately places readers in Indian Country. A solitary man, said to be Luis Horseman, appears in the landscape. Description focuses tightly on his preparation of a device that seems to be for trapping. He removes a lump of turquoise from a leather pouch, places it on the ground, and over it intones a song of the Talking God. We are not limited to visual observation, so we follow Horseman's thoughts of the uncle who taught him the song, his immediate plan to finish here and get back to the rimrock. The way in which Hillerman controls description so that readers gain access to Horseman's thoughts and see in their mind's eye what he sees almost converts the writing into a direct expression by Horseman himself. But the writing remains in the third person, and we realize that the storyteller Hillerman has subtly lent his voice to rendering the way Horseman might tell the story, if he were the author. But, of course, Horseman is not the storyteller, so what we have is indirect entry into his consciousness. That accomplished, we see that the lump of carved turquoise is a bear, which Horseman replaces in the pouch. We move with him, gracefully and silently, through the landscape; we look out of the corner of his eye at dust in the distance, and think of it first as a sign of the mythic Hard Flint Boys, then as the track of a truck. We follow in his mind while he wonders further about the raised dust, begins to prepare a meal over a fire, plans a sweat bath, and again feels a dread that evidently he has been trying to escape.

Passing the night with Horseman, the narrative then follows his seemingly random thoughts in the morning while he checks the traps he had set the day before. Suddenly, without a sound a Navajo Wolf has appeared, smiling at Luis Horseman. Frantically, Horseman runs, with the Wolf laughing.

The narration moves back from Horseman, relates the time of events in the Navajo calendar, and rejoins him as he searches his pouch for a charm to protect him against the Wolf. The attention to Luis Horseman ends, and shortly we find that so has his life. But first the narration looks in on Joe Leaphorn in Window Rock, and then at Bergen McKee in Albuquerque.

Like a collage, the narrative selects a piece of the life of Horseman, the end of his life as it happens, a scene featuring Leaphorn, and yet another scene to display and explain McKee in his lassitude. All of it is framed by the "voice" narrating, as though to make it whole. But readers don't yet know the form of the whole, where the narrative will take them, how the parts will fit together, or what additional parts there will be. The mystery narrative, it seems, is itself a mystery.

Experienced readers of Tony Hillerman will recognize that the way he begins *The Blessing Way* foreshadows his practice in the entire Navajo series. Time and again he thrusts his readers into the impressive setting, gives them partial access to the significance of a character's activity in the scene—enough to cause further wonder—and, as he develops a mood of suspense, introduces violence, often murder, and then departs the scene, leaving the crime inexplicable. It is an effective way to introduce locale and to provide clues for later explanation.

More than that, however, Hillerman's characteristic narrative opening, which is as ably used in this first series novel as in later ones, provides cues along with the clues. The first cue identifies the genre of the narrative as detective investigation. As though reading were the counterpart to investigation, Hillerman gives his readers a suggestive episode. It has to be read carefully before it will become entirely clear, and the reading requires additional information, an hypothesis, a testing of the evidence. Such assistance comes as the narration moves along.

In the meantime, another cue is contained in the opening of the Hillerman narrative. This cue tells us about the relationship of investigation to events. Unlike the storyteller who demonstrates total control of a tale's reality by beginning, "Once upon a time," and concluding that, "They all lived happily ever after," Hillerman takes up a story in progress, *in medias res* as the commentators on the classical works of Homer and ancient dramatists put it—"in the middle of things," which implies continuous action, some of it perhaps related in another story but not in this one. Unlike the storyteller who has bagged up all the tales and releases them in completed form with a "Once upon a time" and a final assurance, the narrator *in medias res* relaxes control. The world of action out there is large, and the story to be told is a brief look at just part of the world. Still, control is not entirely gone. The narrating "voice" is selecting the information to present readers, selecting it perhaps as good readers select information to produce an interpretation, and, more to the point for detective fiction, selecting data and clues to create the correct explanation of the crime.

All of this is to say that Hillerman's narrative method is organically expressive of the investigative story it relates. In other words, the story follows the pattern of investigation. The interrogations conducted by McKee and Leaphorn trace the leads arising from their informed reasoning about clues and from their need to process their findings.

Investigative leads need not be as dry as the dust they sometimes kick up on the Reservation. Witness the rising tension as Chapter Fifteen dramatizes Joe Leaphorn's puzzling over the tire tracks left by the Land-Rover. Time seems to be running out while Leaphorn thinks (thinks hard, the book says) about the motive for a Navajo murdering a Navajo. From his familiarity with his native culture, he knows that Navajos don't kill lightly. There must be something he is overlooking or of which he is still unaware. What could it be?

The mental adventure of an unsolved puzzle is more than matched by the physical adventures of Bergen McKee injured eluding one trap, contending with potential rebuff from Ellen Leon, fleeing pursuit again, employing his specialized knowledge of Native American domestic architecture to find a way out of the Anasazi ruins, becoming prey for Eddie, and, again, the Big Navajo, and finally Jimmy Hall. Taking up more than a third of the entire novel, the narrative of McKee's physical adventure advances the plot by bringing the villains into the open and providing readers a breathless chase on their way to a final explanation that comes from Leaphorn after he has rescued McKee and has seen him with Ellen Leon safely to a hospital.

The adventure element in the plot can be regarded as an enactment of the meaning of the villainous design to steal Army secrets rather than a revelation of the design. While Leaphorn and McKee are reasoning through a trail of clues, the impact of the criminal plan is maintained as a puzzle that has fostered new reports of witchcraft and the single killing of Luis Horseman. The plan is a mental challenge, a puzzle to be read as the structure of the narrative cues readers. When, however, they make progress in deciphering the puzzle, they encounter perils—chases and flights, threats and violence—that directly expose them to the unmitigated evil that actively dominates the entire terrain of their story. The criminal plan is no longer an intellectual challenge only. Now it threatens the imminent demise of Leaphorn who representatively is the modern Navajo law keeper, and of McKee, who representatively is the ordinary man constrained but also enlarged by his science. Their ethics and other values are on the line with their lives, and, thus, Tony Hillerman directs our attention toward the significance of theme in *The Blessing Way*.

THEMATIC ISSUES

Function tests a writer's use of social setting and, to a lesser extent, physical setting. The place where the story occurs can be interesting, but could the events just as easily have taken place in Princeton, New Jersey or Columbia, Maryland? Are the detectives, and for that matter the criminals, at home in their setting, or might they be transferred somewhere else, somewhere more familiar to the reader perhaps, and go about their business of breaking laws and sleuthing the same? Many mystery stories entertain us with their settings, and many have satisfying characters. Much rarer are the mysteries and detective narratives that employ a setting that is unusual for most of the readers and that people the setting as well with characters who would act as they do nowhere else.

For the readers of Tony Hillerman who are not themselves Navajo or Native American, his novels meet the test of function. The social order of the Reservation in some way explains the occurrence of the crime, perhaps as cause or, alternatively, because the traditions of the Reservation Navajos provide the insight necessary to comprehend the significance of the crime. Furthermore, special knowledge gained either as participant in Navajo life or its skilled observer presents the detectives with an opportunity to solve the crime.

During *The Blessing Way* an eighty-two-year-old singer named Sandoval conducts an Enemy Way sing, a ceremonial meant to purge a Navajo of a witch's influence by turning the evil back upon the witch. The ritual appears in enough detail to inform readers of a Navajo custom. It also gives Joe Leaphorn a chance to find a large assembly of Navajos whom he can observe and interrogate as part of his investigation. But the ceremonial observance becomes yet more integral to the story when the narration briefly assumes Sandoval's point of view, incorporating his thoughts and comments about the increasing ignorance of tradition among the *dine* (Navajos) as well as appreciation for Leap-horn's understanding of Navajo manners, the way decorum of respect by younger for elder demonstrates values.

Keeper of social order, akin in that regard to Joe Leaphorn, Sandoval is given a role in the narration that extends to presenting the foundation of theme—namely, the issue of finding an identity that preserves the integrity of inherited tradition while permitting individuals to accommodate to new conditions of their life. Disregard of collective values and, as we have seen before, adoption of an either/or approach to life—one is either ethnic or not—turns people away from community and toward riches gained at any cost. This is the condition of evil intimated first by Sandoval, reinforced by the sense Joe Leaphorn has of lost souls, and finally demonstrably present when the criminal plans of the Big Navajo and Jimmy Hall can be explained.

In a way, Joe Leaphorn and Bergen McKee serve as interpreters for the Navajo. What Sandoval concludes from his ministering among his people receives application in Joe's and Bergen's discovery of the source of the new outbreak of witchcraft. Extending the conception of witchcraft into contemporary experience, they reveal a new form of antisocial behavior in the treasonous plan of Hall and the others to betray the secrets of the American army. This plan is originated by men who can be described, as Sandoval would do, as those who have lost their social moorings in their respective communities.

Recalling McKee and Leaphorn's difference of opinion about the correct explanation of witchcraft among the Navajo—are these instances of scapegoating, or are they instances of a deliberate turn to evil—it becomes evident that the Navajo Leaphorn's speculation is the one that holds true in *The Blessing Way*. Evil is a term we tend to save for the perpetrators of especially horrific deeds—for example, slaughter on a scale so massive it defies comprehension, because offenses on a smaller scale so often seem explainable by the circumstances that have victimized the perpetrator and made him select violence as his means of coping. Tony Hillerman, however, seems to be reviving the sense of evil, not in any melodramatic way that prophesies doom for our society, but in a way that can claim wisdom for the value of social integration found in traditional societies such as the Navajo. The exclusive pursuit of one's personal benefit, Hillerman makes his narrative show, whatever the cause of the selfishness, can harm the group. The community has the right to protect itself. That's why there are officers of Law and Order on the Reservation. That's why the community can call the offense an evil.

A MULTICULTURAL READING OF *THE BLESSING WAY*

The multicultural approach to American literature originates from the fact that the United States is a pluralist nation. The fact is verified, for example, by popular forms of music where Rock and Roll, deriving from performances once called "race music," includes percussive sounds and voicing traceable to Africa along with singing styles echoing Country and Western. Everyone who watches the NCAA Final Four or the NBA knows that on the basketball court identical rules yield distinctive styles depending on whether the competitors are male or female, Black or White. And food? What is American food? It comes from Italy and China and Vietnam and Mexico and France and Germany and the Caribbean, from wherever Americans have come.

These thoughts may not seem profound, but what is evident in popular consumption carries over. American English might be called, more accurately, American englishes, since it includes many regional dialects, borrowings from many other languages, varying levels of usage, and styles associated with young urban residents, middle-aged rural people, as well as a host of other permutations. What is true for language also applies to, say, religion. The United States is home to all of the world's major and smaller religions along with ways of worship developed on the native soil.

E. pluribus unum, we say, out of many, one. Often, however, one is not so much a synthesis of contributing American cultural forms as it is the dominance of a majority in a position because of wealth and social power to impose its preferences. The academic study of literature was long an example of that sort of dominance. Taking settlers of the North American continent who came from England as though they were the exclusive representatives of advanced culture, scholars created classroom anthologies that began, perhaps, with Captain John Smith and the Pocahantas story. They presented writing from the Colonial period and then followed with works by authors who were European by origin, mostly English-speaking, almost exclusively male, and, until the anthologies came to the twentieth century, nearly all from the Eastern seaboard.

Analysis and criticism of this approach to the study of literature is not associated with any single name, in the same way, for example, as Marxism is known to be the theory of Karl Marx. Those who dispute the practice of representing American literature as the product solely of Anglo Americans come at the task from many perspectives. Some raise the question of the absence of African-American, Asian-American, and Native American writers from the formal canon of important American writers, at least as they had been defined in academic study. Others point out the lamentable omission of women writers from formal academic study of American literature. All the critics agree, however, that what can be called the hegemony (i.e., repressive dominance) of male Anglo-American writing in academic study is categorically unsound on historical and intellectual grounds.

The omissions from the canon (the selection of major authors) incorrectly imply that ethnic Americans and female Americans have had no voice in literature. The records of publishers, the files of periodicals, the first-hand accounts of reviewers, and the holdings of research libraries show this to be false. Furthermore, the literary history presented in formal study, so say the critics, follows only Anglo-American writing as it proceeds from explorers' accounts through political writing toward a stress on production of the novel. For many reasons, groups other than the Anglo American have directed their literary energy elsewhere—into autobiography, song, oral story, and so on. In brief, critics of the "monocultural" way of treating American literature contend that, because of its false assumptions about the centrality of Anglo writing, it blocks our ability to understand America's literature(s).

The work of multicultural critics has been carried on by organizations such as the Society for the Study of the Multiethnic Literature of the United States (MELUS) and by scholars who have made their way into the pages of professional journals and then convinced publishers that there is a need, and a market, for a new, plural approach to our national literature. The popularity of Tony Hillerman's Navajo fiction confirms the claim.

Of course, multicultural criticism cannot be content with argument against what once was the prevalent way of studying literature in the schools and colleges. It must have positive content, too, and when it comes to that, the multicultural approach seems self-evident. If, as the evidence indicates, the general society of the United States comprises people of many cultures, then our attention must be given to the meeting of those cultures. Cultures may clash, but they also may meld. As the formulation from W.E.B. Du Bois about double consciousness indicates, a single individual can well participate in multiple cultures.

The Blessing Way serves as a natural subject for multicultural criticism. McKee and Leaphorn provide good illustrations of both cultural differences, as in their dispute over the meaning of Navajo witchcraft, and cultural synthesis, as in their mutual engagement in a science of human organization. The thematic exploration of evil brings to the forefront the importance for everyone of finding and understanding a "home" that will sustain common values. That is a multiculturalist's theme inasmuch as it respectfully embraces cultural tradition while it calls for adaptation to change.

Multicultural reading of *The Blessing Way* must be inevitable and certainly is natural. Some further observations are in order, however. The first is that the Navajo way is a *Native* American way. Not everyone comes from immigrant stock, which politicians sometimes forget. So-called Indians predated Europeans and Africans, and, of course, other Asians, on the continent. Sense of that fact, along with battle with European settlers, relocation, betrayals, treaties made and broken, successive experiments at the hands of the Bureau of Indian Affairs, and so on comprise the Navajos' entry into the American nation. For everyone, the distinctive past of their Americanization serves as historical background—no less so in *The Blessing Way*.

Obviously, multicultural criticism has been influenced both by anthropology and by democratic beliefs. The Enemy Way sing related in *The Blessing Way* appears with the detail that anthropological observation yields, and we note that the detail is contained within a sympathetic accounting. Leaphorn seeks understanding; the novel yields its voice for a time to the singer Sandoval, and the reader who is not Navajo gains momentary intimacy with Navajo subjectivity, gaining ability to see almost as a Navajo does.

Here we are at the core of multicultural study and multicultural writing. Narrative techniques offering readers the chance to identify with characters are hardly novelties, but their use in the context of such a novel as *The Blessing Way* does have its novelty. Think of contrasting ways that some other novelist might have presented such a story. A different Anglo novelist might have presented the Navajos as hopeless wretches, or might have given a voyeuristic tour of the "exotic" Reservation life. That other novelist might possibly have resurrected a savage image. Hillerman, however, has crafted his narrative so that readers cross a bridge of sympathy. He has imaginatively projected his creative thought into the condition of Navajos, sharing for the brief span of the novel both the outlook of Joe Leaphorn and of the legitimately curious Bergen McKee. Recognition lies on the other side of the bridge of sympathy. Hillerman can hardly expect his readers who are not Navajo to yearn to become Navajo. He does not feel such yearning himself, and despite the fact that once upon a time this country's policy was to make Navajos, and everyone else, yearn to be white Anglo, Hillerman knows that is not a way to create a just society. Nor is the outlook of this novel uncompromisingly relativistic in a way that would sever connections among cultures. Informed as it is by a multicultural consciousness, *The Blessing Way* employs the principle of mutual respect to find common ground and unifying themes among the differences evident in culture. When Joe Leaphorn translates the Origin Myth so that evil can be seen in contemporary dress, we see the hand of Tony Hillerman inscribing a belief that the human story can be told in many ways.

4

The Fly on the Wall
(1971)

Hillerman's second novel in the crime and mystery genre now appears unusual among his works. Unlike most of the novels that to date have followed it, *The Fly on the Wall* contains no Native American material. Instead, it draws on Hillerman's fourteen years' experience as a political reporter, writer, and editor to create the story of a journalist working against time and mortal danger to complete an investigation of government corruption.

According to Hillerman, the order of publication for his first works confuses his original idea. His plan, when he first decided to write a novel, was for "a big, important book," a mystery on the subject of *The Fly on the Wall*. Not sure of his talent for mysteries, Hillerman tried out first what at the time he thought was easier to do, which it is surprising to realize was *The Blessing Way* (*Companion* 55). In any case, the tryout proved he could manage the genre's requirements, and so he resumed his original plan.

Compared to the popular reception Hillerman has won for the Navajo books, *The Fly on the Wall* has not, in fact, turned out to be his "big" novel or his most important. It is, however, an excellent example of suspenseful, puzzle-based detection fiction displaying a high order of narrative skill.

GENERIC CONVENTIONS

For the milieu of *The Fly on the Wall*, Hillerman has selected the office of an afternoon newspaper in the capital city of an unnamed middle western state. It seems to resemble Springfield, Illinois, but it might be Des Moines, Iowa, or Jefferson City, Missouri. The exact location is immaterial to the story. Crucial, however, is the political atmosphere in which John Cotton and other reporters serving in their papers' capital city bureaus work to find newsworthy significance in parliamentary maneuvers of the legislature, the press releases and public statements of officeholders, conversations off the record, and the lode of public documents within the files of government agencies. Each day's cycle of news becomes the occasion for a competition as morning papers vie with evening papers to be first with a story, and reporters from all the dailies hustle to fill out the coverage and dig for new leads. Although the reporters act independently for their employers, they also share a bond of experience, making them colleagues, if not collaborators, in keeping their readers informed. They can grow weary and become dismayed with what they see, but in their best moments they are public representatives. They are as necessary to popular government as the representatives who are directly elected to govern.

The capital newspaper milieu therefore presents an institutional environment that in some ways resembles those environments to be found in stories of law enforcement and the legal system. Each of these types of stories within the crime and mystery genre features systems of operation: how a homicide squad investigates the crime scene, interrogates suspects, researches background, and more or less cooperatively assembles the information that might solve the case; how lawyers develop a defense or prosecution case, call witnesses, evaluate evidence, and conduct themselves in the courtroom. As the narratives follow the steps of the police and lawyers, the formula of their procedures provides the basic line of the plot. Because of the prominence of the special operations carried out by law enforcement officers and officers of the court, the narratives that feature them have come to be called, of course, procedurals.

Tony Hillerman has suggested a useful comparison of *The Fly on the Wall* to the stories of police and lawyers, as he reportedly terms his novel about capital news reporting a *journalistic procedural* (*Companion* 55). Following the suggestion, we can see that, although John Cotton comes by chance upon Merrill McDaniels's notebook, his efforts to decode its entries follow a well-established routine of record checking, documentary comparisons, background survey, interrogations, and reasoning. Other reporters would repeat those steps, just as Cotton repeats McDaniels's steps center stage in the novel and Leroy Hall seems to be doing at the same time off stage, because it is the professional procedure of investigative journalism.

Drama inheres in the procedure as information collected in pieces from scattered sources falls into an assembly of meaning producing a journalistic scoop. That is one of the satisfactions in reading this narration of news reporting. It simulates the experience of successful journalism, the creation of a report that reveals a truth.

Reducing journalistic procedure in *The Fly on the Wall* to its basic presence, we arrive at the perhaps curious observation that this is a story about the discovery of a story. John Cotton's pursuit of the facts encoded in McDaniels's notebook occupies the foreground, but as he tries out explanations for the evidence he gathers he is testing alternative tales of meaning for the evidence. The story of his investigation throughout the novel shows Cotton trying to compose the story he must eventually write to explain all that has happened, including the perils he meets while collecting the material for his news story.

This curious observation shows the essential connection between *The Fly on the Wall* and the mystery genre, for in some way or another most mystery and detection stories draw upon the immense satisfaction found in making sense of things. Some critics approach the point by emphasizing the occurrence of puzzles in mystery and detective fiction, and from there, they talk about the quality of a puzzle, whether or not the author of the fiction presents all the clues and allows a plausible solution to the puzzle. More important than the appearance of a puzzle, however, would seem to be the fact that it is processed by some agent in the fiction (a private detective, a police officer, a lawyer, and, so we see, a journalist) who is seeking to relate the evidence, whatever form it may take, as an explanatory narrative that tells who committed the crime, how, and why. When the investigator of the puzzle is Agatha Christie's Hercules Poirot, or Dorothy L. Sayers's Lord Peter Wimsey, Earl Derr Biggers's Charlie Chan, or some other "great detective," the sleuth's explanatory narrative may constitute the final chapter of the novel, becoming then a story within a story.

Creation of the story within the story—the sleuth's explanatory narrative—follows the sleuth's process of reasoning and can include application of specialized knowledge in the examination of physical or psychological evidence. In procedural fiction, the sleuth's method of solving the crime and creating the "true" story is distinguished as the common practice of a profession or occupation. In Tony Hillerman's *The Fly on the Wall*, it is the recognizable practice of professional journalists. Functional in all mystery fiction, in procedural fiction representation of the method of investigation becomes the dominant convention for the type.

With the dominant convention comes further implication. The procedure has been collectively developed and is commonly shared by all law enforcement officers, all practitioners of law, or all writers working as newspaper reporters. In contrast to tales about exceptional detectives (the singular figures like Arthur Conan Doyle's Sherlock Holmes or Rex Stout's Nero Wolfe, where the power of the investigative method seems attributable to individual genius), in procedural fiction the method is evidently available to everyone who undertakes an apprenticeship or some occupational training. The procedural method is institutional.

Moreover, in applying the investigation convention, procedural narratives also show that there is an institution at work on the criminal puzzle—the responsible police force, the court officers with jurisdiction over a case, and, in works such as *The Fly on the Wall*, what became known in the eighteenth century as the Fourth Estate, which today is more commonly thought of as part of the Media. Consequently, by terms of the conventions of their variety of mystery, investigators like Hillerman's journalist John Cotton share their billing with colleagues in their profession. They may be singular protagonists, but while readers follow the narrative of their procedure, the readers sense that the story also comes with comment about the ability of a society's institutions to maintain order.

PLOT DEVELOPMENT

Hillerman evokes tension in his journalistic procedural through three mutually reinforcing strategies. The first of these is a handling of time. Even though Hillerman includes a period when Cotton leaves the scene of the state capital entirely, it is only briefly, and events seem to occur in the length of a week or two. The sense of constricted time increases with the indication that the news story Cotton is following has something to do with whether or not the incumbent governor enters the primary election to challenge a rival Democrat for the party's nomination as candidate for the United States Senate. The time seems ripe now; it may not be opportune later.

Hillerman's second strategy for heightening suspense arises out of the odd circumstances by which he has presented the journalistic puzzle. Merrill McDaniels said he was working on a big story before he plunged to his death in the capitol rotunda. Data for the story were entered in a notebook McDaniels had thrown among the papers on his desk. An unidentified man in a blue topcoat scrambled to find the notebook among the papers minutes before McDaniels died an ostensible suicide. The possibility of connection rather than coincidence increases when Cotton discovers the lost notebook that has fallen behind a desk (42), begins to decipher the entries, and, as he retraces McDaniels's investigation, receives threats. All news stories seem important to a reporter, but this one quickly becomes a matter of life or death. He could abandon the story, and for a brief time he tries to do so. When he finds it impossible to give up the story, he also finds that he is in a race against the mysterious figures who want to prevent publication of the story. If they kill him, they will kill the story, as Cotton realizes was the purpose of the faked suicide for McDaniels. As he comes to find out, this was evidently also the intent of a faked accident that destroyed Cotton's car while it was being driven by another reporter, William Robbins. The only escape route for Cotton lies in completing the investigation, publishing the story, and, thus, removing the motive and incentive for his death.

But the escape route is hardly clear, because McDaniels entered the notes in his book in a personal abbreviation and shorthand system meant as prompts for the story he would write. Cotton's quandary about the meaning of the notes brings into play Hillerman's third strategy for heightening narrative tension. Faceless killers know the story McDaniels's notes could tell, but Cotton does not. The notebook is like a collection of signs he must place (or replace) within their significant contexts, so that the abbreviations will have reference and the jotted details will reveal what they signify.

Locating the narration within the consciousness of John Cotton, who is mentally running for his life, Hillerman displays the pressure of time on the journalist's procedure. In this way, he perhaps gives a new meaning of grim irony to the idea of working against a *deadline*. With the three interrelated strategies for heightening tension at his command, Hillerman plays out the suspense with two chilling episodes of Cotton on the run from hired killers. The first of these episodes begins with Cotton's discovery of his vulnerability in Chapter Twelve. Without leaving signs of entry, someone has placed a strange package in his apartment, a cigar box that pops when Cotton opens it. It could have been a bomb instead of a macabre joke as a mysterious voice on the telephone tells him. Unnerved, Cotton accepts the advice of the telephone voice and leaves town for a fishing trip in the New Mexico mountains. In a show of the way menace enters the most mundane circumstances and heightens terror, Hillerman introduces Cotton to the hit man who is pursuing him. At first, Cotton takes him as an engaging fellow traveler, his seat mate on the airplane to Santa Fe, chatting idly about good spots for fishing. Relaxing enough to start enjoying his trip, and almost cool enough to think reasonably about the events that spurred his flight, Cotton journeys expectantly high into the mountains above any place normally frequented by other people. Then his security collapses. A vaguely familiar man appears, dressed for hunting. It is the genial traveler who had identified himself as "Adams." Cotton's mind and heart race as he realizes he is being stalked. The narration remains closely centered on Cotton's consciousness while he scurries away like the hunted prey he has become. Focusing on spontaneous action, immediate physical detail, the elemental responses of Cotton's body, and his desperate plans for escape, the narrative excludes all distraction in order to take readers along on a headlong flight. Only when he has slashed the tires of his hunter's truck and driven away in his own rental car does Cotton turn to making plans to carry forward rather than drop his investigation.

Hillerman presents the second episode that exploits the possibility for high tension in his narrative in Chapter Twenty. Arriving at the vacant capitol building at three o'clock in the morning in response to an anonymous letter promising access to files he needs, Cotton enters a scene Hillerman has prepared to frighten readers. In the darkness familiar things, such as an odd taxidermist's exhibit, become sinister. The architectural scale of the building designed for crowds but now empty becomes daunting. In the quiet every possible sound is strange. With part of his mind, Cotton wonders how the evidence he seeks will fit the puzzle, but another part of his mind is apprehensive of danger, which comes when Cotton discovers he is again being stalked, this time by two men. Once more Hillerman adjusts the focus of narration, so that all description and all exposition concentrate on Cotton's feeling of peril and the anxious haste of his contriving an escape.

The narrative strategies for tension and suspense might be considered the sensational portion of plot, for they introduce the surges of feeling that rise and fall in accompaniment with John Cotton's investigation. The counterpart to Cotton's sensations is provided by the connections among the "facts" he discovers and the revelations to which they lead. As we have seen, Hillerman constructs this portion of the plot in *The Fly on the Wall* in accordance with journalistic procedures, emphasized by Cotton's need to retrace McDaniels's inquiries in order to decode the entries in the notebook. Starting with an enigmatic chart in the notebook, Cotton goes to the files of the highway department. From there he proceeds to contractors' records, interviews with engineers, and corporate records. Progressively, each step broadens the scope of the inquiry and extends the reach of the scandal until the original case of dubious purchases of cement on a road project becomes the thread that unravels a scheme of maneuvers at the top of the state's political establishment. The final purpose of the scheme of finance and business favors is to covertly raise funds for the governor's run for the Senate nomination. Since we have all been well schooled about the costs of political campaigns and the importance of timing in raising the necessary money, the scheme in *The Fly on the Wall* seems entirely plausible. Moreover, the complex arrangements that John Cotton uncovers for his newspaper story are no more convoluted than those we read about in major newspapers.

Hillerman adds to the realism of the factual portion of his plot by presenting the agents of political chicanery, all except possibly the hit man, as accessibly human as we know public employees and politicians to be. Governor Roark joshes reporters familiarly. The Speaker of the House, Bruce Ulrich, plays cards with the reporters and shares confidences with them. The little guys, the patsys in the scheme, are weak and wily; and Joe Korolenko, the political boss, has a credible history of understandable resentments that have diverted his political ideals into the ruthless drive for revenge that is finally revealed to have set the whole factual portion of the plot in motion. For all of them politics offers personal opportunity—a field for their ambition, or possibly some financial security, then again maybe gratification for their egos in the workings of power. At the same time, however, none is insensitive to the fact that politics is also public service. Ideally, we might wish for more than this messy mix of motives, but that would require an entirely different plotting of the facts and would lack the authenticity Tony Hillerman achieves in *The Fly on the Wall*.

CHARACTER DEVELOPMENT

In procedural fiction, the method of investigation tends to overshadow other elements, but if readers are to care about the methodical assembly of information, the author of procedural fiction must put the investigation into the hands of a character who generates interest as an individual, somebody with a life in addition to his or her exercise of a professional routine. Tony Hillerman attempts to invest his protagonist John Cotton with such additional interest by drawing upon three familiar techniques of popular storytelling.

An important technique is the provision of the leading character with a unique past that suggests a source for personality and motive in the influential or challenging experiences the character has undergone. John Cotton's unique past concerns the friends of his youth Charley Graff and Alice Beck. Cotton's memory of the critical moment in their relationship is triggered in Chapter Three by the odor of the police interrogation room where he goes to check the personal possessions left by McDaniels. The "faint animal smell, the universal odor of all jails" (34) causes him to recall his being questioned by a juvenile division officer after he had viciously beaten Charley. They had been friends throughout boyhood, so close they knew each other's thoughts, all their hopes. They built a treehouse together, a private enclave, and when they were older they worked for three years, pooling their earnings to buy a car to drive from New Mexico to Canada in celebration of becoming grownup men. Among their shared thoughts and hopes was John Cotton's expectation that he would marry Alice, so when he found Charley making love to her in their automobile, Cotton snapped. He struck Charley repeatedly "as if to kill something within himself by killing it in Charley" (35). Only Alice's screams stopped Cotton. Now, years later he pieces together the meaning of the violent events. Part of it is that Alice did not really mean as much to him as he thought. Another part, something he realized only when he was in Marine boot camp, was that his fury "had been based in self-contempt for his own weakness" (35). Finally, the narrative shows Cotton recalling, he had concluded that Charley's offense "had simply completed a lesson he had been too slow to learn . . . that each human spirit must travel alone, safe only in isolation" (36).

Hillerman probably intends the peculiar reading Cotton gives his experience to explain his being a loner and to equip him with the guarded detachment that the conventions of detective fiction deem to be requisite for private eyes and other investigators. If so, then another technique for personalizing Cotton seems equally derivative from the conventions of private-eye fiction.

The association of characters who surround John Cotton in *The Fly on the Wall* loosely forms a community whose affinity has developed from their practical interest in the mechanics of politics. Besides capital news reporters, who also have a mutual commitment to their craft, the group includes some seasoned politicians and one notable member of the legislative staff—Janey Janoski, executive secretary to the Legislative Finance Committee. Their bond is their familiarity with "inside" information and sources, their social interaction, shop talk and gossip. Since evidently Janey is the only woman in the group (*The Fly on the Wall* was published in 1971), the gossip about her not surprisingly involves sexual speculation. Maybe she is the governor's mistress, a lesbian, a mournful war widow. Still she is not entirely objectified by the men, or the novel. Cotton goes to Janoski to consult her expertise in reading the financial entries in the mysterious notebook, and stays to talk with her about the eventual implications of his quest for answers. Such talk occurs as conversation between the two becomes increasingly a communication of affection, at first flirtatiously on John's part, franker on Janey's.

Love affairs have varied importance for characterization in mystery fiction. In the fiction of Dorothy L. Sayers, the love between Lord Peter Wimsey and Harriet Vane develops into a parallel plot that transforms the stories of crime into pleasing comedies of manners. Robert L. Parker makes the love between his private eye Spenser and the psychologist Susan Silverman a collaboration that redefines the character of the hard-boiled detective. More often, however, the conventions of American detective fiction with its stress on the lonely, individualistic sleuth guarantee that love will be ill-fated, as when Dashiell Hammett's Sam Spade is compelled in *The Maltese Falcon* to send Brigid O'Shaugnessy to jail. The love between John Cotton and Janey Janoski in *The Fly on the Wall* hardly reaches even the level of the star-crossed convention. Instead, it is an apparent device indicating that Cotton has a fuller definition than simply a heroic journalist with a past. More importantly, the inclusion of an element of emotional intimacy gives Cotton a haven of sympathy, as in the chapter when he uses Janoski's typewriter to write his story. In addition, the novel includes a dramatic articulation of the ethical issues surrounding investigative reporting when Cotton debates with Janoski how to use the information he has gathered.

By far Hillerman's most effective technique for developing interest in Cotton's character has been outlined in the discussion of plot development. Through a narrative point of view tightly centered on Cotton, Hillerman brings his subjectivity to the foreground. Allowing readers vicarious participation in the cycle of Cotton's feelings—heightening and relaxing tension, self-doubt, and excitement—and linking those feelings plausibly to descriptions of events, the narrative gives life to John Cotton.

Nearly all of the other characters in the novel play instrumental parts that involve little development. Some, like McDaniels and Robbins, appear only to provide impetus to the plot by their death. Some give information as clerks or officeholders like the governor. Some frame the issues, as in Cotton's exchanges with the project engineer H. L. Singer and the rival reporter Leroy Hall. Joe Korolenko is the exception among the secondary characters. He functions instrumentally on a large scale as instigator of the fraud, but during his appearance in the novel he also develops into a broadly representative figure. His distinguished career shows him to be a person who manages power well. That he retains power through the years without holding public office demonstrates his continuing reputation and political power. It seems natural that Cotton should go to him for the counsel that a senior politician, and one who knows how to repay a political debt, may be expected to give. What Cotton gets instead is an autobiographical revelation of Korolenko's aggrieved soul and startling knowledge of the ends to which personal grief and political grievance can lead.

In the comparatively brief circuit of Chapter Twenty-two, which fittingly concludes the novel, Korolenko becomes the agent to meet the demands of narrative convention and logic. His exposition of his personal experience and the party's history gives background to the central investigation, and in an ironically economical move by Hillerman, Korolenko, playing expositor of the plot, also reveals himself as the prime mover of evil doings and the dominant actor in the plot's final scenes. He seeks first to prevent exposure of the crimes by threatening Cotton's life. Then when he learns that the story of the crime has been published, he takes the drastic step of removing his political enemy by assassination so that John Cotton's front-page stories of the scandal involving Korolenko's political protégé Governor Roark will be overshadowed by the more notorious news Korolenko creates with the vengeful killing of the smooth opportunist U.S. Senator Eugene Clark. Although their respective positions as reporter and politician and, more significantly, as sleuth and culprit, place Cotton and Korolenko in opposition, they conclude in symbiosis. Appropriately for a relationship in which Korolenko counter-points the detective's role by dissolving mystery into explanatory discourse, the book concludes as Cotton looks for a telephone he can use to offer Korolenko help.

THEMATIC ISSUES

Hillerman's realistic conception of character in *The Fly on the Wall* helps to complicate further the always vexing issues surrounding the practice of journalism and politics and to turn the novel toward a dramatic examination of journalistic ethics. Janey Janoski, who merits respect as a sensitive political observer along with the personal affection Cotton develops for her, presents one viewpoint about the publication of damaging news when she points to the effect it can have on people's lives. Singer has a family that suffers his shame; Governor Roark is a politician with genuine prospects for doing good. Perhaps, she contends, abuse of position can be corrected without public exposure. Clearly, it is not suppression of information Janey Janoski wants, for she works diligently with Cotton to gather information and provides him sanctuary to write the story when he has been staked out as a victim for hired killers. Instead of a coverup, Janoski's idea of using information selectively seems to recommend working within the imperfect political system by alerting the governor to the mess he has to clean up. For her, the lives and careers of people she knows and has learned to like figure more importantly than the abstract value of the people's right to know all the truth about their government all the time. Thus, in the exploration of theme, Janey Janoski stands for a humanistic interpretation of principle.

John Cotton is not immune to Janey Janoski's argument. He, too, knows and likes the people he investigates, with the obvious exception of the hit men who threaten his life. In testimony to his divided feelings about full exposure of the results of his investigation, he leaves the completed draft of the news story with Janey Janoski while he goes to see Joe Korolenko, telling her to decide after she reads it whether or not to deliver it for publication. Possibly because she reads in the draft how extensive the scandal is, and perhaps because of her feeling and respect for Cotton and the values he holds, she sees to it that the story sees print.

But Hillerman does not permit Janoski's decision to resolve the matter completely. There is a sense earlier in the narrative, when Cotton thinks over the hurt that public exposure can cause, that he has become hardened to the hurt by practice (249–51). The first time he faced someone with exposure it was hard. It was less troublesome the second and third time, and now it is likely to be even easier, except, of course, we know from Cotton's sympathy for Korolenko that he still puts concern for other people into the equation of his journalistic ethics. In examining Cotton's ethical position, some attention also must be given to occasions when he drops his argument and lapses into silence when challenged. One occasion involves Janey Janoski when she says Cotton is playing the game much as her husband, a Navy fighter-bomber pilot, did before he was killed on a mission for which he volunteered after his required tour of duty had finished. "He didn't hate anybody," Janey reports. "The bombs didn't really hurt anybody. It was Dick against the antiaircraft guns. It was a game you played." In fact, however, she continues, people do get hurt. It could be Cotton getting killed, and Roark ruined, and Singer's family shamed (286–87). Cotton yields to the emotion, thinking that reasoning will not change her view that he is quixotic. He stays silent but hardens his resolve, telling himself that perhaps Janey ought to see that her own motives are more self-interested than she can admit. Complicated and inconclusive as this conversation between Janoski and Cotton is, one thing is certain. His reasoning voice, the medium we use to announce and advance our principles, is of no use to him. He is reduced to an unreasoning impulse, a private resolve.

A similar result obtains when Joe Korolenko accuses Cotton of ignoring the difference between facts and the truth, of wanting to print an account of the mess without saying, "on the other hand," compared to what Roark's rival Clark has done, "this mess is relatively minor." Korolenko accuses Cotton of "playing God." This provokes Cotton to relate complete details about the killing of McDaniels and Robbins, which shocks the political boss but does not alter his resolve any more than Korolenko has altered Cotton's. They are deadlocked, with readers sympathizing with Cotton's position, but having a sense of regret for Korolenko's (304–306). Nothing more can be said in this debate, and it seems the thematic problem of journalistic ethics may prove insoluble. As though fortuitously, but, of course, actually by the design of Hillerman's plot, news arrives that the story is in print. The issue has been resolved, not by Cotton but by Janoski, who has delivered the story to the newspaper; resolved not by mutual agreement in Joe Korolenko's home study to an ethical principle, but moved to a new stage of action as a practical effect of a nonethical event outside of the house—publication of the story in Cotton's newspaper.

The reporter Leroy Hall presents another perspective on journalistic ethics that at first seems to be similar to Janey Janoski's. In conversation one day, he describes Cotton as a coldly detached observer who studies politicians as though they were laboratory rats (128). Allowing for a change in the named species, this is an allusion to the title of the novel which is explained as an application of Walter Lippmann's idea of the reporter as " 'the fly on the wall,' seeing all, feeling nothing, utterly detached, utterly objective" (45). The concept has been memorialized in the capital newsroom by a large ink drawing on the wall of a housefly. The drawing oppresses Cotton with a sense of loneliness and isolation. His professional work might appear to embody the behavior of Lippmann's fly, but the access to his subjectivity provided in the narrative, and in the scenes with Janey Janoski, show that Hall is wrong in his characterization of Cotton. For real detachment, one must turn to Leroy Hall himself who, despite claims that he has genuine feelings about politicians he knows, expresses the most extreme cynicism about the public for whom he writes. They know nothing, he says. They grant credibility to the candidate with the best teeth; they get political wisdom from disc jockeys on television. Why not realize the public is not going "to digest the facts and come to an enlightened conclusion"? So, why not, Hall says, select the facts you think they can handle, the facts that are good for them (129)? Hall's views on journalistic practice are easy enough to disregard, because they are products of disillusion, not reasoned deliberation, but their lack of ethical content poses a threat that Cotton must consider while he knows that Leroy Hall also is working on the scandal story. Who can imagine what he might do with it? So Hall's position, rather than representing an ethical alternative for Cotton in the narrative as Janoski's views do, instead becomes an incentive to get all the facts and to assure their publication.

The mixed rendition of ethics in *The Fly on the Wall* parallels Hillerman's representation of the political world. In neither journalism nor politics do right and wrong occur in allegorical distinctness, with clearly labeled champions garbed in their moral traits, purity on the one side, a mottled appearance on the other. In the realistic portrayal of Hillerman's novel, character can be uncertain. What is the real Governor Roark like? For that matter, what will John Cotton do about his affections? Similarly, it is a struggle to follow a course of action confidently in Hillerman's capital city, since there are dangers in any case, mortal and moral, and consequences regardless, many of them painful, others unforeseeable. That this is the impression we have of *The Fly on the Wall* is evidence that Tony Hillerman has thought seriously about his experience in political journalism. More to the point in our interpretation of his novel, this impression demonstrates that, despite his original doubts, Hillerman really is good at mysteries.

A MARXIST READING OF *THE FLY ON THE WALL*

Marxist literary criticism derives from the theories of Karl Marx and Friedrich Engels, whose most famous collaborative work is *The Communist Manifesto*. Marx elaborated his theory in the multivolume study *Das Capital* whereas Engels served as a popularizing exponent of the theory in studies of the institution of the family and other publications. Of course, these thinkers have also earned notoriety along with fame owing to the insistence in the former Soviet Union and in communist parties throughout the world that their political strategies and systems were an enactment of Marxist theory. Certainly, it can be argued that the writings of Marx easily lent themselves as justifications for the policies that have marked history until recently in Eastern Europe and continue to serve as the underpinning for government in the People's Republic of China and Cuba. Yet, the essence of Marxism is to be found perhaps more in intellectual method than in political action.

That method can be inferred from the doctrine that social being determines the consciousness of people. This is to say that cultural formations, legal systems, religions, and ideas in general are produced by material relationships. In particular, the economic interests of a dominant social class in society will determine how people see their existence. From this foundational doctrine the rest of Marxism flows. Ideology and politics, which Marx termed a superstructure, rests on the base of production relationships, which in modern times have been capitalist, but in earlier periods, and in places other than the West, might be feudalistic. Moreover, human history, in accordance with Marxist theory, can be read—in fact, must be understood—as a process of evolution through a struggle of socioeconomic classes that will lead to complete human liberation. The capitalist class, known as the *bourgeoisie*, once performed a liberating role by destroying the power of monarchies, but in turn that class has subjugated industrial workers, known as the *proletariat*, to their power.

When applied to literature, Marxist theory can create controversy. All

Marxists would agree that literature is a social product and that literary values, enforced in schoolrooms and book reviews, not to mention publishers' lists, embody the outlook of the dominant social and economic class in a society. Some Marxists, however, discern a special quality in literature that sets it apart from other cultural products of the *bourgeoisie*. Such quality might be found, for example, in classic works of tragedy, possibly in Shakespeare. Other Marxists, however, assert that literature is a weapon in the conflict of classes. It should and must be created and interpreted in terms of what it might contribute to advancing or retarding the social revolution that will lead to ultimate liberation of humanity into a way of life that will be truly communist. The latter position informs the demands by some Marxists for "realistic" literature advancing a party line in literature.

Despite the turns Marxism has taken in the political world, the insight it retains for the study of culture continues to attract adherents. A critic seeking to apply a Marxist method to *The Fly on the Wall* might generalize by observing that the novel takes a "reformist" view of politics. John Cotton's preoccupation with journalistic ethics and the public's right to know about the scandals in their government does not reach to the fundamental relationships within society, which amount to a system allowing a privileged class to appropriate the labor and minds of the working class for *bourgeois* profit. The system of appropriation, the critic might continue, rests on an inequity that is much greater than that involved in sleazy manipulations of contracts, for the government is *really* the oppressive arm of the ruling class.

By this reasoning, then, disputes about who gets a contract for road building amount to a battle among parties whose interests are all on the same side—against any change that would allocate control of public facilities and the economy to the people whose labor creates the wealth confiscated through business profits and *their* government's taxes on working people.

This rendition of a Marxist reading of *The Fly on the Wall* presents a danger of becoming simplistic, and a danger even of being unfair to the Marxist critics. Within it Marxist theory has a tradition of appreciation for heroic action before the project of human liberation is complete. In the *Manifesto*, Marx acknowledges the accomplishments of the commercial and mercantile classes, even as he details the destructive consequences of their supremacy in society. Those classes might be thought of as heroic in their original time, though oppressive later. By analogy, literature, which as surely as anything else cultural is a product of class domination, can embody impulses that are heroic in their original expression.

For example, under a Marxist aspect Tony Hillerman's novel about John Cotton could be said to embody a progressive content to the extent that it exposes the machinations of political bossism and to relate a heroic career to the extent that Cotton acts in a way that can grant some power to the public through the information he will provide in his newspaper stories. Still, however, the novel is limited in its effect by the very fact that it is an expression of prevailing power relationships. Hillerman, and his surrogate character John Cotton, may argue through their novel for reform, but they stop far short of advocacy for genuine reconstruction of society, because they do not envision a more just arrangement of power.

That's correct; one might say that Hillerman's fiction does not seem to imagine a radically different organization of political power in society. By the evidence of this novel, the author appears contented with democratic politics and generally favorable about the role a newspaper can play in those politics. Exactly, the Marxist critic will reply, Hillerman remains rooted in his historical time and culture.

As a practical matter, however, one expects no more of writers than that they express their time and place. What Marxist criticism has to offer about that is a deeper sense of the roots from which writing springs. In the case of *The Fly on the Wall*, Marxist literary criticism reveals those roots reaching deep into the philosophy that inspires the Bill of Rights in the Constitution of the United States.

5

Dance Hall of the Dead
(1973)

In its version of Hollywood's Oscar, Broadway's Tony, and television's Emmy, the Mystery Writers of America (MWA) bestow annual awards on the works they judge to be the best of each year. Appropriately named for Edgar Allan Poe, the reputed father of detective fiction, the MWA's award, known familiarly as the "Edgar," represents high critical praise. It is coveted by writers, because it amounts to an endorsement of their craft by professional peers, and publishers vie for the Edgar in the expectation that it will help promote their product.

The winner for 1973 in the category of "Best Mystery Novel of the Year" was Tony Hillerman's *Dance Hall of the Dead*, his third novel in the detective fiction genre and the second outing for the Navajo police officer Joe Leaphorn. In honoring *Dance Hall of the Dead*, the MWA selected a work constructed on the model of classic detection. The lean narrative wastes not a word as it follows Joe Leaphorn on a search for a missing Navajo boy that leads into the secrets of Native American spiritual beliefs and the archaeological mystery of Native American origins. As functional in the narrative as Leaphorn's detection method itself, these additional levels of mystery attest both to the skill in Tony Hillerman's construction of a detective novel and to the meaning with which he can invest the genre.

WRITING STYLE

During his academic career, Tony Hillerman regularly taught writing to aspiring journalists at the University of New Mexico. In an interview with Rosemary Herbert, he remembers that he encouraged development of a spare style. As he would tell his students:

> Remember always, the adjective is the enemy of the noun; the adverb is the enemy of the verb. If you use an adverb, it almost inevitably means that you didn't find the right verb. If you have to modify a noun with an adjective, maybe you've got the wrong noun.

According to Hillerman, the point of the instruction was that unnecessary words, or sentences, or paragraphs weaken the effect of the writing. Nearly all of the editing he does of his own writing, he explained to Herbert, is cutting, because he senses "that the reader is a busy person . . . and I don't want to waste their time. They're gonna be impatient with me" (Herbert 110).

But it is not only concern for the crowded schedules of readers that explains Hillerman's espousal of a spare style of writing. The principal standard he follows is functionalism: whatever else the writing may accomplish, it must always advance the story.

Landscape descriptions provide convenient illustration of functionalism in Hillerman's fiction. Narratives set in the Southwest Indian Country should be expected to include descriptions of the landscape. After all, the landscape is awesome. In addition to its grandeur which affects every observer, for Native Americans the landscape is the site of supernatural power. As an example, for Navajos the Dinetah (meaning "among the people," or the territory now forming the Reservations) is the place where their holy people emerged to the surface of the earth. A telling historical episode indicates the continuing significance of that site for Navajos. After being driven from their homeland in 1863 by troops led by Kit Carson and confined for five years to territory around Bosque Redondo, near Santa Fe, a Peace Commission headed by General William Tecumseh Sherman offered the surviving Navajos a chance to move to the Oklahoma Territory where land was fertile, to stay in Bosque Redondo, or to return to Dinetah, which General Sherman told President Johnson was worthless wasteland. Dinetah had been created for them by the holy ones, however, so to Dinetah they returned (Hillerman, "Dinetah, If I Forget You" in *Companion* 302). What is true about the Navajo reverence for the land pertains as well to Zunis and other Native American tribes.

In view of the importance of the landscape, it is not surprising that Native American characters in Hillerman's fiction are shown in intimacy with their scene, as when the Little Fire God in the opening chapter of *Dance Hall of the Dead* is presented before "the red sandstone wall of the mesa," over which "a skyscape of feathery cirrus clouds stretched southward toward Mexico," while "to the west over the Painted Desert, [the clouds] were flushed with the afterglow of sunset," and "to the north this reflected light colored the cliffs of the Zuni Buttes a delicate rose" (3). The named portions of the landscape—Painted Desert and Zuni Buttes—the well-established geographical directions, and the specificity of the cloud formation show that the Little Fire God is no visitor, but native to the landscape. But once that point is made, description does not linger. The narrative relates that below the Little Fire God a light goes on at the anthropologists' dig, bringing him back to thoughts about his companion George Bowlegs, with whom he might be, but should not be, angry.

Later in the novel, as Chapter Seven begins with Joe Leaphorn at the place where the body of the Little Fire God has been found, Hillerman presents another landscape description. The perspective of the view is set precisely on a ridge above Galestina Canyon. Morning sunlight, warming the right side of Joe Leaphorn's face and thus indicating the direction he is facing, strikes landmarks that serve as coordinates locating the scene. Again, description of the landscape situates character in the dual terms of geography and nativity. And again the description becomes additionally functional—this time as the narration records the shortening of Leaphorn's vision from the distant buttes to the signs of human settlement nearer by and, then, to the evidence of human violence before him where the track shoe and leg of the Little Fire God protrude from the earth.

One final citation of landscape description makes the evidence of Hillerman's functional approach conclusive. At the start of Chapter Twelve, Leaphorn is with Ted Isaacs at the anthropological dig. The third-person point of view of the description places Leaphorn squarely in the scene; his shadow at sunset forming part of it as the view pans across a vista of stone outcrops, junipers, and Corn Mountain across the valley. It is a moment "of startling beauty," readers are told, of the sort Joe Leaphorn normally enjoys. Now, however, he is preoccupied with other matters. In this case the description satisfies at least three functions. First, it provides a specific and familiar setting for events, which is a requirement if fiction is to have verisimilitude or the semblance of reality. Second, the specificity of the description and the note that Leaphorn normally appreciates the scene once more demonstrate a harmonious relationship between Native Americans and land, while reinforcing the individualized description of Leaphorn as a *Navajo* police officer. And, third, by the subtle twist of indicating that on this occasion the impressive landscape does not get Leaphorn's full attention, the passage directs readers to see that Leaphorn's intense pursuit of a solution to mystery gives plot to the narrative.

Landscape descriptions in *Dance Hall of the Dead* are just one opportunity to find the functional principle of Hillerman's writing style. The way the narrative introduces secondary characters, such as those residing in the Jason's Fleece commune, shows similar economy. Talking about the commune with a young Navajo couple, Leaphorn observes that the group's name comes from a story about a hero hunting across the world for a golden fleece. "I heard of it," the Young Husband said. "Supposed to be a sheepskin covered up with gold . . . I think you're more likely to find scabies on the sheep they're raising" (55). Once Leaphorn is at the commune, with a few words of conversation. Hillerman presents the unequal relationship between Suzanne and Halsey: "This is Halsey," Suzanne had said. "He sort of holds this place together." Under his mustache Halsey grinned, challenging and combative. "I never met a Navajo fuzz before," Halsey had said (60). With those brief exchanges, a contrast is established between the way the Belacani commune dwellers and Native Americans inhabit the land.

Probably the most notable of all ways to observe Hillerman's devotion to functional writing is to reflect on how he weaves into *Dance Hall of the Dead* information about Zuni or Navajo tribal beliefs. As illuminating as that exposition may be, it never appears outside of a dramatizing context. Exchanges between Leaphorn and Ed Pasquaanti, chief of the Zuni Police, are necessary for each to do their jobs. The tone of conversation between the two, however, tells readers that there are less than trusting attitudes between their respective tribes, even as the professional cooperation between the officers helps piece out a solution to the criminal problem. Leaphorn's memory of his Zuni college roommate conveys to readers more information about rituals, but it, too, is conveyed within passages that work at the same time to fill out Leaphorn's characterization.

In an author's note prefacing the text, Hillerman explains that the view of the Shalako religion "is as it might be seen by a Navajo with an interest in ethnology." And that is exactly how the longest disquisition on Zuni beliefs occurs in the novel. In Chapter Thirteen, Joe Leaphorn questions Father Ingles about George Bowlegs. Joe's "interest in ethnology" carries the interview into greater detail than it might otherwise require, but that is because, besides growing out of Leaphorn's need for information to explain where George Bowlegs would be heading, the interview with Father Ingles also helps characterize Leaphorn as the sort of man whose inherent interest in the cultural expressions of religion leads him to tap the priest's encyclopedic knowledge.

The way Hillerman phrases his dedication to a functional style is that he does not like footnotes in mystery stories (Winks 142). The way the 1973 Edgar prize committee put it is through praise for Hillerman's craft. And the way readers of such a novel as *Dance Hall of the Dead* come to appreciate Hillerman is as a writer whose style creates a taut, fast-moving narrative.

CHARACTER DEVELOPMENT

The fourth chapter of *Dance Hall of the Dead* provides a rare opportunity to see Joe Leaphorn as other characters do. Ted Isaacs, working the anthropological dig, notices a truck drive up and stop "a polite fifty feet below the area marked by his network of white strings" (31). Isaacs does not connect the way the truck gradually stops at a distance with the practice of rural Navajos who believe it is good manners to let someone they visit have a chance to get prepared. All that Isaacs recognizes is that the person intruding on his time is not like the boss of the dig, Dr. Reynolds, who always arrives in a cloud of dust. When his visitor emerges from the truck, he is evidently a stranger to Isaacs. He is a man with an Indian face, but too tall to be a Zuni. His vehicle shows him to be an employee of the Bureau of Indian Affairs, so ethnically he could be anything from Inuit to Iroquois. With slight modification, Isaacs seems to suffer the Anglo vision problem that makes all Indians look alike.

For readers, this meeting of strangers holds considerable importance. The conversation devoted to Leaphorn's questions about the missing

George Bowlegs and the young Zuni named Ernesto Cata makes Isaacs uneasy. Leaphorn receives Isaacs's answers with prolonged silences and phrases his inquiries enigmatically. We are to understand this, however, as a Navajo way of speaking representing the cultural divide between Isaacs, the son of poor white Tennessee farmers, and Leaphorn, the grandson of the Navajo wise man Hosteen Nashibitti. When he is doing his police work, it seems, the lieutenant speaks like the middle-aged Navajo he turns out to be, and, in the face of questioning, Isaacs behaves like the insecure younger fellow without established occupation or profession that he turns out to be.

The taciturnity and discomfort disappear when Leaphorn's curiosity about the dig leads them into talk about anthropological theory regarding Folsom Man. Isaacs volubly presents Dr. Reynolds's "modification theory," while Leaphorn eagerly prods for details of the case being built by the excavation for a solution to disappearance of Folsom Man.

Later, this discussion will prove to hold the key to solving the criminal problem of Ernesto's death and George Bowlegs's disappearance. In the meantime, however, it sketches the shape of Joe Leaphorn's complex character. Indian by heritage and continued cultural preference, he seems to have taken to heart the recommended Navajo behavior of adapting to changing circumstances. Later in the novel, we will learn that through his grandfather Hosteen (a term of respect for wise elders) Nashibitti, born in the time of Kit Carson's campaigns, Leaphorn has received vivid instruction in the history of Navajo travail and an extended course in the interdependency of nature underlying the philosophy of beauty and harmony. Through the interview with Isaacs, we have found that Leaphorn also has studied anthropology at Arizona State University, a seat of Anglo-style learning. In a phrase, Leaphorn is a resident of two cultures, not simply acquainted with the Indian and Anglo cultures as anyone living in proximity to the several peoples might be, but instead a person who may be said to have been schooled as a citizen of the two cultures. From his grandfather he learned one way of seeing and interpreting reality; through formal education in social science he acquired an alternative sight. As though they were the lenses of binoculars, the two ways of seeing give Joe Leaphorn a singular, blended view of the world.

Although Leaphorn claims the heart of the narrative in *Dance Hall of the Dead*, other characters hold their own interest. Ted Isaacs, the young graduate student, has streaks of resolve and ambition that help him to rise from poverty and family neglect, but when he is tested by Suzanne's need for a haven and comfort, his rejection of her to accommodate what he expects his superior Dr. Reynolds would want reveals his single-mindedness to be unmodified and self-centered opportunism. In retrospect, the voluble enthusiasm of his presentation of the "modification theory" to Leaphorn seems to have been much less the result of intellectual enthusiasm than of pleasure in the prospect of personal fame. In an article on archaeologists in Hillerman's fiction, John Neary finds practically all of them to be "intruders from academe who sometimes even commit murder to validate themselves and vindicate their half-baked theories." Among these, Neary judges Isaacs to be "perhaps the most pitiful" (Neary 58, 60). Surprisingly, Neary does not mention Isaacs's employer Dr. Chester Reynolds, although Hillerman has created him also in the negative image.

Suzanne of the Golden Fleece commune develops into the most positive Anglo character in the novel. Anything but prepossessing when she first appears, she nevertheless does not seem to be a loser like the men with whom she is associated, because she truly cares for other people. Accompanying Leaphorn on his search for George Bowlegs, she provides crucial information for tracking George and becomes a resourceful protector when Leaphorn is shot.

As is usually the case in Hillerman's mysteries, the Native American characters are the most fully portrayed in *Dance Hall of the Dead*. George Bowlegs provides an excellent example of Hillerman's care in their drawing. Bowlegs never directly enters the narrative, but by the oblique means of commentary on him gathered from acquaintances, family, and friends a picture of a rare boy emerges. He is so inquisitive about the Zuni religion that he wants to become a Zuni himself, and he is so convinced of the spiritual importance he sees in Zuni beliefs that he dreams of transcending the circumstances of his own tribal identity to follow "a concept so foreign to The People [i.e. Navajos] that their language lacked a word for it," a concept of ecstatic immortality in "the dance hall of the dead," where Zunis enjoy an afterlife (147). As Father Ingles states it, George was "about half genius and half crazy. The kind of a boy that if you can make a Christian out of him will make you a saint" (139). In outline, the character of George Bowlegs testifies to a fundamental human wish to be rooted in a system of belief. Because his dysfunctional family failed to connect him to the Navajo way, with its belief in natural harmony, George sought the condition of "being" poetically transcribed in Zuni mythology. The breathtaking leap he tried to make marks him as a boy with extraordinary soul, while the fear he experiences about violation of a taboo and the destruction meted out to him by his much more narrow-minded killer seem the kind of inevitable fate met by what theories of tragedy call an overreacher.

The role of other minor characters actually present in the text can hardly match the offstage career of George Bowlegs. John O'Malley stands in the story for a typical FBI man, as Leaphorn finds them to be: officious and unimaginative. Agent Baker's appearance in the novel signals the possibility of a narcotics investigation, since he works for the Treasury Department. Other officers, including Pasquaanti for the most part, are single-dimensional creations furnishing the novel with the cast that is usually requisite to an investigation that crosses state and federal, county and Reservation jurisdictional lines.

STRUCTURE AND NARRATIVE POINT OF VIEW

One way of appreciating the craft required to write an effective mystery is to consider the competing demands of narrative unity and expansiveness. Actual criminal investigations stretch on in time, jerking to a stop or sliding off track when the police discover that leads arrive at dead ends. The constant arrival of new cases suspends pursuit of unsolved cases. The investigator has to scurry to stay abreast of things or lose track of what's going on. That's the real experience, but the vicarious experience related by fictional narratives needs more coherence than reality provides. The satisfaction in a fictional story *about* reality lies in the way it gets somewhere expeditiously, or, if it doesn't arrive at an end, tells why it doesn't. The satisfaction is doubled with a detective story because it not only goes somewhere but in the process also represents the power of the detection method to make sense from the unpromising materials of violence and, thus, to achieve, with the closure of the case, a semblance of order.

Limiting the time span of a story is a time-tested way of creating unity. Another equally venerable technique is to concentrate the narrative on a single, dominant character and to give that character one problem at a time to manage. Of course, Tony Hillerman adopted these techniques in *Dance Hall of the Dead* and most of his other works. For the length of *Dance Hall*, an italicized note of the date and time of day at the head of each chapter keeps the readers informed of the temporal progress of the story and confirms at the conclusion that the time taken for the events of the novel to occur falls just eight hours and eighteen minutes short of a single week. Moreover, the prominence of Joe Leaphorn in every chapter but the first neatly links these chapters as related episodes in the detective's investigation of a single case.

Unity and coherence are important for a story, but overdependence on these qualities for effect can drain the narrative of interest. Getting the crime solved and the story finished are only instrumental goals without intrinsic interest. Because we want the crime and its solution somehow to appear to be about something besides swift dispatch of evildoers, the writer must find or create material that inserts meaning and interest into the narrative. Some authors of detective fiction locate interest in the peculiarities or eccentricities of a great detective. Others feed the reader's hunger for engaging detail with accounts of exotic settings or unusual crimes or, perhaps, a tone of humor. Still others bend their talents to fostering a discovery of the malice abroad in ordinary life. Whatever techniques a writer chooses to create a partiality for the text in readers, the result is a tension between the pull toward tight unity and the contrary necessity to expand the scope of the narrative.

Tony Hillerman maintains that tension by highlighting Joe Leaphorn's subjectivity. Technically, the means of presenting Leaphorn subjectively lies in his use of a third-person point of view and indirect discourse. The point of view is termed third person because it relates information *about* a character rather than *through* character. It recounts that he or she did this and that, tells that it was sunny (not that "I" saw the sunshine), and so forth. If the author, through this point of view chooses also to be omniscient, then there is also the possibility of giving readers access to the thoughts and feelings of character. Since this interior life is reported in the third-person voice, it is a kind of discourse, but since it presents information that the character is not stating, it is indirect discourse.

The narrative freedom Hillerman gains by selecting this point of view gives him the space he wants for presenting animating motives for Joe Leaphorn's character—for instance, the influence of his grandfather, his conflicted feelings about Zunis, and his estimates of other characters. It also makes possible the *tour de force* in Chapter Sixteen where Hillerman describes for pages and pages Leaphorn's movements in and out of hallucinatory states of mind after he has been shot with an animal-tranquilizing dart.

This remarkable passage includes interludes when Leaphorn lucidly reasons about George Bowlegs's disappearance, thereby indicating that the lieutenant is always at work on his case. In fact, thinking back through the narrative, a reader realizes that the truly essential and ceaseless activity occupying Joe Leaphorn is application of his detection method. It might seem reasonable enough that the detective would appear in a genre story demonstrating his or her method—reasonable enough and conventional enough since the days when Edgar Allan Poe's Dupin or Arthur Conan Doyle's Sherlock Holmes stupified their companions and the police with startling exercises of deduction. In *Dance Hall of the Dead,* however, method provides more than display to the narrative, more even than Poe or Doyle typically wrung out of their set-piece demonstrations of detection power.

PLOT DEVELOPMENT

In Hillerman's novel Leaphorn's detection method provides the framework for both plot and character. The practical displays of Leaphorn's Navajo lore in deer tracking in Chapter Fifteen show his relation to traditional cultural practices, while also showing the applicability of the lore to the police problem of discovering the movements of suspects. If it is true what the story tells us, that Leaphorn is a better tracker than any Zuni or any white man (184), then his tribal heritage must be a source of his skill, although there are additional sources. One of them is experience as a police officer. Another is the interest in cultural differences generated by Leaphorn's formal education in anthropology and his acquaintance with Zunis. As Leaphorn sees his mode of thought, however, Hosteen Nashibitti is its origin, for Hosteen taught him the parables of a Navajo science where "every cause has its effect, every action its reaction. A reason for everything. In all things a pattern" (77). When Leaphorn became a police officer, an occupation without precedence in Navajo tradition but with plenty in Anglo culture, he brought the tools of Navajo tradition with him. Thus, in the execution of police work, as much as in the experience of culture, he remained a Navajo but adapted to new circumstances. Managing adaptation while retaining a sense of rootedness, he became a healthily integrated person, with self and profession indivisible.

So far as its founding of the narrative's plot goes, the framework of the detection method creates dramatic action. In one place (74) Leaphorn has the unpleasant feeling that he is being stymied by the problem before him; therefore, he redoubles his efforts to satisfy the demand made by his mind for answers (80), and two chapters later he realizes that he must redefine the problem. If there are two homicides, he reasons, there must be a connection (96). Every interview Leaphorn conducts, whether with Cecil Bowlegs, with Isaacs, or at the commune, with Father Ingles or with Suzanne, and every examination he conducts while tracking George or puzzling at the meaning of the Zuni ceremonial—each action arises from the rational mind's compelling need to discover an orderly explanation.

To enforce the dramatic centrality of rational method for the plot of the novel, Hillerman brings it all to an end with one of the sturdiest conventions of the detective genre: a wrapup explanation by the detective. With Ted Isaacs as his audience and readers of the novel as his privileged listeners, Leaphorn extracts from the assemblage of evidence built up by his dramatic process of investigation, the story of cause and effects that underlies all the puzzling events. In confirmation of the strength of purposeful reason and the efficacy of Navajo-inspired methodology, Leaphorn presents the solution, though not a resolution. What Isaacs will do about the scientific fraud remains uncertain. Whether anyone else will ever know the solution of the problem seems unlikely. It is enough that Leaphorn's detection method has worked, because that method, and the character who employs it, embody a more important resolution for the writer—a synthesis of narrative economy and engrossing interest.

THEMATIC ISSUES

The discussion of the characters of Joe Leaphorn and George Bowlegs should make evident how important the theme of cultural integrity is for Hillerman. Like the biblical prophet, Hillerman believes that without a vision the people will perish. The acquired beliefs and practices we know as culture provide that vision, allot to us the stories and images that explain the order of the world, and grant us the guidelines for behaving in accordance with the store of culture we share with our kin and community. Yet, as Hillerman's Native American fiction shows, culture can be difficult to sustain. The old stories embodying the values of a culture may lose their appeal to people thrust into a modern economy or attracted by the flash of distant ways of life they incompletely understand. Traditional modes of behavior may no longer seem to have a significant function. One may be, so to speak, no longer at home in the native environment. But as we have seen from the examination of theme in *The Blessing Way* there are both negative and positive ways of relating to one's culture in times of change or crisis. The negative path of abandoning oneself to the allure of novelty may result in the loss of "soul" in weak imitation of alien ways of life. The positive path does not require stubborn adherence to tradition, however. Rather, psychic health results from reinterpretation, making culture accommodate to the new and unique conditions of one's life. Such an effort to reinterpret culture so that it continues to guide and sustain may be seen to be the underlying thematic drama of all Hillerman's writing.

Rosemary Herbert points out that "the solutions to Hillerman's crimes always turn on cultural insights that the author thoroughly understands and conveys to us" (Herbert 86). This is just as true in *Dance Hall of the Dead* as in any other Hillerman novel, and the cultural insights are not exclusively about Native American culture. Often knowledge of avarice or distortions of ambition to be found in Anglo culture plays an important part in solving the crimes too. The significance we can draw from Herbert's remark, however, is that while cultural details help to fit pieces of the puzzles together, the matter of living a culture, making it manifest in one's life, more often than not propels the plots and concerns the characters of Hillerman's mystery novels. The desire to assume a culture motivates George Bowlegs. The wish to figure in his culture made George's friend Ernesto Cata don the guise of Little Fire God. The expression of his cultural self distinguishes Joe Leaphorn's work as a detective. Each of these characters lives or would live his received or adopted culture with dignity and integrity. But what is to be said of Dr. Reynolds or Ted Isaacs or Suzanne or Halsey? They are participants in a culture, because culture really cannot be escaped, but only Suzanne among them demonstrates commitment to the collectivity meant in the term *culture*.

Integrity also provides the keynote of the second large theme in *Dance Hall of the Dead,* namely, the values inherent in cultural practices. Joe Leaphorn's inquiries depend on a method that proves valid by serving to explain all of the events. Just as important as the quality of method is the purpose to which it is put. Skill in tracking could be applied to stalking a murder victim, and, of course, we see that to be the case with the killer of Ernesto Cata and George Bowlegs. We feel that application is a perversion, even though deer tracking does usually result in death for the animal, because tracking to Navajos is part of a conception of natural harmony. The hunter reveres the spirit of the animal and offers prayers of thanks for the nourishment it gives to human beings. The deer, moreover, may become part of the worshipful ceremonials. The remains of the deer slain by George Bowlegs shows that he has taken those parts of the body that have talismanic power and has prepared a fetish to bury by the carcass that Leaphorn finds after he and Suzanne have eaten from the venison (205). Significantly, the ball of tallow and clay forming the fetish made by Bowlegs also contains material clues Leaphorn can use in finding the boy whose goal in life, and imagined death, is spiritual.

The murderer Dr. Reynolds, however, displays no such reverence for the victims he stalks. His aim is destructive removal of the boys from the chain of life, rather than the participatory enactment of the chain of life found in the Native American hunting rituals. For Reynolds, tracking and killing have instrumental value for his own protection, but the actions have no intended resonance for others, no higher purpose.

What is true of Reynolds's actions in stalking the boys is pertinent also to his anthropological work. The investigative methods of science are intended to extend the power of reason to discover knowledge that will serve human beings in society. Scientific training, such as Joe Leaphorn sought in his studies in the university and such as Dr. Reynolds's work as a graduate professor has inherent social value: first because it is conducted by the transmission of skill from one generation to another; second, because trained scientists constitute communities of study to share their data and test and confirm hypotheses; and, third, the collective effort results in theories and formulations adding to the sum of human knowledge, allowing people to understand themselves and their social or biological histories better. In a sense, then, the scientific community is held together by a compact of mutual commitment.

Naturally enough, there are rivalries and jealousies within the community of investigators arising from individual ambition, but the compact of the scientific community, and the procedures of its investigative method, work against abuse and help direct ambition into productive channels. Because he has experienced ridicule from his scientific peers and is impatient for the proof of his theory, Dr. Chester Reynolds, however, breaks the community compact and falsifies his evidence.

By tying Dr. Reynolds's desperate action in salting the site of the dig to his murder of the boys to cover his trail, Tony Hillerman strengthens his ethical theme. The same motive that will lead to abrogation of one's commitment to the community compact of science, Hillerman seems to say, can also lead to the reprehensible action of murder. Intellectual violation is akin to the violation of life because deceit and murder both rend the fabric of social trust.

With awareness of this theme in mind, we see further importance in the attention Hillerman lavishes upon Leaphorn's method in *Dance Hall of the Dead*. Hillerman's emphasis on the sources of Leaphorn's detection method in his deeply felt knowledge of Navajo philosophy indicates that the intellectual method of his detection embodies his essential identity, as well as the technique of his police work. Fidelity to his method amounts to fidelity to Navajo culture. Moreover, by making Leaphorn's use of his detection method and his intellectual approach to the criminal puzzle the thread of the novel's plot, Hillerman inserts the issue of intellectual integrity deep into his narrative's structure.

A PSYCHOLOGICAL READING OF *DANCE HALL OF THE DEAD*

Characterization in contemporary fiction commonly includes what readers and critics think of as psychology. Writers' techniques for presenting the subjective dimensions of characters qualify as psychological techniques, while much of the detail about the personalities of fictional characters is meant to be taken as external evidence of individual psychology. For instance, a curt, dismissive way of speaking attributed to a fictional character suggests an angry inner self, or an unusual fastidiousness may spur the reader to expect that the character feels somehow unclean because of some past experience.

All of that is the psychology of verisimilitude, we might say. It draws on commonly accepted views in our culture, including the concept of an internal life motivating behavior. Although every writer in the detective fiction genre will employ the psychology of verisimilitude as a standard part of characterization, at times a writer feels it necessary to give unusual emphasis to a single dimension of psychological makeup. This is so in *Dance Hall of the Dead* where Tony Hillerman three times repeats a presentation of the relationship between "fathers" and "sons." The quotation marks around those terms means that the characters in question may not be the biological sires and offspring, but rather that the relationship introduces the psychological exchanges and stresses normally found in American culture between the male parent and male child. It has bearing on female children and parents, too, but the cases in *Dance Hall of the Dead* are male. Tony Hillerman does not draw on specified theory for his sketches of parent-child relationships. Instead, his treatment derives from the accumulated store of human experience as it is reinforced through clinical practice and study.

This "knowledge" of parents and children, fathers and sons, is culturally determined, for it is generally accepted in every culture that the role of parent includes modeling for the young. Indeed, the expectation that this will be so accounts, at least in part, for the bonding between parents and children *and* for the tension as well. Distortions of the relationship are familiar to everyone. The possessive and demanding parent is a stock figure in story and life. Just as well known are the resentful and rebellious offspring. The distorted examples, however, simply confirm the dependence human communities place on the directive influence of a parent who can give love and appreciation unconditionally. Not that parental bonding and mentoring must be confined exclusively to the line of genetic inheritance. Communities often use kinship terms (grandfather, grandmother, aunt, uncle) to denote respect for an elder who provides a center of meaning for the group. Priests are called "father," and people pray to God as a father. Yet, once again such practices confirm the importance of a parent figure, a father and a mother if you will, to our growth and development, our sense of belonging in the world.

The first "son" whom Hillerman examines in *Dance Hall of the Dead* is George Bowlegs. As the narrative makes clear, his biological male parent is a loss. His alcoholism makes it impossible for him to nurture or counsel George or provide him models. Put another way, George's biological father can give him no meaning for life. And, of course, it is meaning he seeks with his plan to become a Zuni. It is for what we think of as life's meaning that George dogged Father Ingles with questions. In its comprehensiveness and the warmth of its reverence for ancestry, the Zuni belief system offers place and status to the mind of George Bowlegs. In the Zuni scheme of things, he thinks he could belong in a way he cannot ever belong to his parent, or, it seems to him, among Navajos. If it appears to stretch the point to attribute the role of a comforting parent for George to the Zuni beliefs, think of how he feared reprisal for breaking a taboo—just as one might dread the response of an angry parent. Think, too, of the literal way George seems to receive the Zuni beliefs. They have substantiality for him; they are neither metaphor nor abstract metaphysics.

George's devotion to his friend Ernesto may also be studied within the father-son scheme. Ernesto, achieving the opportunity to be the Little Fire God, has a genuine place and meaning. He is a son of his tribe; that's obvious enough. He also plays a role as intermediary, or even substitute, for George who yearns to gain the same role for himself. His dream of transcending his origins and becoming instead a Zuni indicates the intensity of George's need. He does not just want an equivalent experience to what he sees in Zuni ritual. He wants another parentage that will accord him a different self-identity. The reported devotion of George to Ernesto, his assistance to him as he trained for the ritual role, suggest a desire to be like Ernesto or even to become Ernesto. George gets as close as possible to him, almost making him a totem figure that would function, as totems are meant to do, to transfer the qualities of the original to the one who reveres the totem.

The second pair Hillerman uses to repeat the father-son motif are Ted Isaacs, who plays son, and Dr. Chester Reynolds, the father figure. Isaacs is another character without a natural family to give him position or support. Reynolds, we find out, is extraordinarily helpful to his graduate students. He gives them topics for the dissertations that will qualify them for their doctoral degrees, and he does not care that they get credit for discoveries. In other words, as mentor and transmitter of knowledge, Reynolds also awards identity that adds luster to one's name. After studying with Reynolds, a student becomes "Doctor" and author of a research dissertation that establishes the newly minted doctor in the academic profession. What more can a father give than knowledge, a name, status, and satisfying position?

Ted Isaacs eagerly assumes the son's role to Reynolds, and the child-like ways too. He dislikes the way Reynolds drives up in a cloud of dust but cannot tell him that. He sets aside the young woman of his choice, somebody he would like to marry, because Reynolds will disapprove of her place in his life on the dig. And the enthusiasm in his voice when he describes Reynolds's theory to Leaphorn perhaps sounds a little excessive, a bit like awe.

The father-son relationship between Isaacs and Reynolds makes all the more poignant the revelation of Reynolds's fraud. Ted has been betrayed by the man who played father to him. The situation is fraught with pain and possibility. Will Isaacs cover up his father's misdeeds in order to succeed to his position in the world? Will he repudiate the false evidence at the dig, even though he has nowhere else he can immediately find meaningful work? The problem is a deep one in psychology—how to handle inheritance from your father—but it is not the detection problem of *Dance Hall of the Dead*. It is a problem that provides context to the lives of characters.

Of course, the third parent-child relationship is Joe Leaphorn's and Hosteen Nashibitti. The discussion in this chapter ought to be sufficient to support the idea that Leaphorn's grandfather fulfills the nurturing role of elder guide, and, in doing so, demonstrates Hillerman's point that within the Navajo culture a generation still can hand on to its successor generations a compilation of learning and behavior that can satisfy human needs for human connection and significance.

A psychological reading of the sort outlined here does not require extensive support from theoretical writing, even though it pertains to the views developed by Sigmund Freud and others. More than any other source, it draws on widely held and popular views of the role of parenting. The narrative evidence of Tony Hillerman deliberately presenting and re-presenting father-son relationships as they are popularly understood, demonstrates in yet one more way his abiding interest in cultural instruction and its failure.

6

People of Darkness
(1980)

The popularity of series stories in the detective genre tells us something very important about the relationship between author and reader. Writers become attached to their central characters, seeing the narratives that feature the detective as a set of adventures permitting repeated instances of triumph. Readers become no less attached to fictional detectives. Often readers identify the stories they love by the names of the featured detectives; they admire Agatha Christie's stories of Hercules Poirot or Miss Marple, for instance. And publishers, because of this popular devotion to sleuths who become familiar through repeated appearances, encourage writers on their lists to keep a series alive.

Understandably, then, writers are not going to whimsically introduce a different detective into their fiction. They need a compelling reason to do so. After using Joe Leaphorn in three Navajo crime stories, Tony Hillerman invented a new detective for reasons intimately associated with themes he wanted to explore. In an interview with Jon L. Breen, he explained that he wanted to set his fourth Native American novel on the Checkerboard Reservation, a section on the eastern side of the big reservation where settlements have been carved out to relocate different tribes in a hopscotch pattern. Ethnically, the section includes Lagunas, Acomas, and Navajos, Mexican Americans, German Americans, and others mixed in a way that brings cultures and religions—among them fundamentalist Christian, Roman Catholic, Mennonite, and the Native

American churches—into contact. Hillerman wanted to explore this "total melting-pot situation," but Joe Leaphorn didn't serve the purpose very well. In Hillerman's conception, Leaphorn was too seasoned and sophisticated to display the interest in cultural mingling that the story seemed to demand. There was nothing to do, said Hillerman, but "start me a new guy" (*Companion* 57–58). So out of the necessities of Hillerman's craft, Jim Chee was born into the Navajo detective novels, making his debut in *People of Darkness* (1980).

Easing Chee's introduction was his appearance in the contemporary Navajo environment and the Navajo Tribal Police, already familiar to readers from Hillerman's previous books. In that respect, Chee does not represent a complete departure from the series Hillerman was constructing up to that time, but by directing his attention to the "new guy," Hillerman brought a fresh inventiveness to his narrative.

CHARACTER DEVELOPMENT

When Jim Chee makes his entry in *People of Darkness,* he is poised between the Navajo and Anglo worlds. A sergeant in the Navajo Tribal Police, the agency for which he has worked since graduating from the University of New Mexico in Albuquerque with a degree in anthropology, Chee has been accepted as a student at the FBI Academy in Virginia where he is to report in a month. If he goes to the Academy, of course, he will become a federal agent, but more important than that his work assignments will likely take him far from the Reservation and inevitably he will assimilate deeper into Anglo culture and become more distant from the traditions of the Dinee (a term used by Navajos to mean themselves, the People).

The choice Chee faces reflects in part the situation of many other young Navajos for whom it seems "easy, now, to be a white man," and much harder to follow the way taught by Changing Woman, the primary divinity in Navajo cosmology. For Chee, however, the fork in the road where he stands presents a starker contrast, for he is not only a young Navajo with a college education but also a man with prospects for a significant tribal role. There is reason to believe that he has what the terminology of religious practice denotes as a "calling." From an early age, his talent of memory had caused his family to think he might become a "singer" (*yataalii* or *hataalii*) performing the oral chants and directing the movement of the rituals that sustain the harmony of life revered in Navajo theology. In the narrative of *People of Darkness,* we learn that Chee's Navajo clan, more than any of the sixty others, produces famous singers, including very prominently his uncle Frank Sam Nakai, whom the Navajo always addressed by the title "Hosteen," demonstrating respect. Hosteen Nakai had selected for Chee the "war name" required of Navajos but kept as a secret identity. In Jim Chee's case it is Long Thinker. It is also Hosteen Nakai who remarked to Chee how easy it had become for a Navajo to be a white man. With the wisdom of a venerable elder, Hosteen Nakai counseled Chee to take advantage of the ease and "study the white man and the way of the white man," so that when he understood the white world surrounding the dinee, he could decide whether to follow that new way or to be a Navajo. Combining the formal study of social science and American literature in the university with watchful observation of white ways, Chee followed Hosteen Nakai's counsel, and at the same time began the regimen of learning from his uncle the healing songs "that brought the People back from their sicknesses to walk in beauty" (85–86).

As he enters the adventure presented by *People of Darkness,* Jim Chee's preoccupation with the direction of his life creates tension in nearly every scene between his Navajo cultural identity and the curiosity, even fascination, he feels about the outside, white world. When in the second chapter he goes to the home of B.J. Vines to meet with Mrs. Rosemary Vines, he is intrigued by the design of the house, reportedly the work of Frank Lloyd Wright, and by its fame as the most expensive house in New Mexico. However, when he inspects two small gravestones on the grounds of the house, he feels the characteristic puzzlement of a Navajo at the white man's sentimental burial customs; for the Navajo, corpses have no value worth commemorating. Knowledge of Navajo customs, it turns out, is exactly what Rosemary Vines requires of the detective whom she wishes to recover a stolen box belonging to her husband. The likely suspects, according to Mrs. Vines, are members of a one-time cult in the Native American Church known as "People of Darkness." Most Navajos would not take such a job, or any other, on behalf of B.J. Vines, because he has gained a reputation as a witch. Only a person experienced in Navajo customs, and at the same time freed from the pull of their full significance, can be successful in the case. Jim Chee fills the bill.

Hillerman sustains the impression of duality in Chee's character by making him an expositor of Navajo culture. At different times in the novel, he explains to Mary Landon Navajo secret names, family names, and nicknames (105–107); he tells her the legends associated with the landscape (114–16); and relates parts of the Creation story (219). Acting in the role of a guide in comparative cultures, Jim Chee articulates differences between Native American and Anglo ways in a manner comfortable for Mary (who serves as the reader's proxy in these lessons), since he shows equal familiarity and respect toward her inherited customs.

Chee himself, however, is not entirely comfortable with two cultures; he is too self-conscious for that. Looking for Windy Tsossie, dead or alive, in Chapter Thirty, Chee feels confident of the "purely Navajo" features of the quest, which is "in intimate harmony" with the Navajo "pattern of thinking and behavior." However, he does not understand the thinking of whites involved in the affair that has led to the quest (234). The Navajo way, it would seem, emerges spontaneously in Chee; yet, the technique of narration (known as indirect discourse) reports him consciously reflecting on a prayer taught by his uncle that describes perfect understanding and deliberately summoning to mind the way Hosteen Nakai would advise him to understand the whites (235). Thus, Jim Chee appears to be fundamentally Navajo in all ways, but not intuitively so. His acquired familiarity with Anglos has broken the seamless connection between impulse and thought. It has introduced mental space for reflection and, within the space, an awareness that while he can choose his life, choice will have serious consequences.

To illustrate the freedom for choice, as well as to turn up the pressure on Chee while he ponders the opportunity of attending the FBI Academy, Hillerman introduces Mary Landon into the story. A new teacher at the Crownpoint Elementary School, with a previous term's experience at the Laguna Pueblo School, Mary first encounters Chee at the rug auction held annually in November at the Crownpoint School. At first, her intensive look makes Chee think of her stereotypically as the guilty Anglo who takes Native American courses at the university but is interested "more in Indian males than in Indian mythology" (90). Despite this dismissive male chauvinism he uses at first to characterize Mary, her personality, perhaps her friendliness, attracts Chee. They become easy conversationalists and then fond acquaintances as Chee's invitation and Mary's responsiveness draw her into his criminal case. Soon she assumes the position of sidekick to detective Chee, interrogating him about clues, prodding him to articulate hypotheses, accompanying him on the investigation, and eventually sharing the danger it holds.

With the addition of infatuation to their relationship, Hillerman increases Mary's importance to the story. Comradeship makes it natural for Chee to explain the Navajos to Mary; for her part, fondness makes it reasonable for her to begin acting as Watson to his Holmes, until growing affection makes her a factor in the life choice Chee faces. His happiness with her adds allure to the white world, making it seem possible that intuitive feeling, love, might grow from Anglo soil as well. So optimistic does Chee become about his relationship with Mary, and, one might add, so oblivious of the choices both of them must still make at the story's end, that he asks her to join with him in the ritual Enemy Way that would return them from the sickness of the criminal case to the harmonious way of beauty. Chee's miscalculation of how swiftly Mary can assimilate into Navajo life remains to be worked out in several succeeding novels.

In the meantime, *People of Darkness* introduces one of Tony Hillerman's strangest villains and a figure he considers one of his best characterizations (Parker and Parker 12). Hillerman's experience as a newspaper reporter with the case of a criminal condemned to die in the gas chamber left an indelible impression on his memory. In a short story called "First Lead Gasser," published some years after *People of Darkness*, he took the point of view in the narrative of a reporter trying to crowd the impact of the execution into a 300-word release he means to dispatch over the wires of a press bureau. The short story alternates wording for the teletype, printed in boldface capitals, with passages of memory of the execution scene returning to the mind of John Hardin. The climactic memory presents the doomed man, named Toby Small in the story, pleading with Hardin and his press associate Thompson to include something in the newspaper story about getting word to his mother so she will claim his body for burial. Small behaves restlessly while he tells the reporters how he had been abandoned as a child, how he had hunted for his mother for years, while he was in and out of trouble, and how he wonders about this Jesus the prison chaplain had been talking about. But he offers no direct explanation or motive for the brutal murder of a newly married couple that brought him to the death chamber; he expresses no remorse or particular fear. All he reveals is an obsessive concern about the arrested relationship with his mother.

In a note appended to the story when it was published in *Ellery Queen's Mystery Magazine* (April 1993), Hillerman writes that the real events he relates in the story caused him "to think seriously for the first time about writing fiction," because he could not "report the true meaning of that execution while sticking to objective facts" (quoted in *Companion* 364).

In *People of Darkness*, Hillerman assigns the killer the same background as the man he calls Toby Small in his short story. Like Small, this character does not know the names of his parents or their whereabouts during the nineteen years since they had abandoned him. He has named himself Colton Wolf, perhaps thinking of his preference for living as a loner, and he follows a compulsive routine in his hobbies of building model steam engines and making weapons. In his occupation as a paid hit man, he pursues perfection by keeping his contact with those who hire him to a minimum, preparing for each of his methodical killings by careful research, and living constantly on the move with post office boxes, which he frequently changes, as his sole connection with organized society. Hillerman portrays Colton Wolf as completely without feeling for others, except possibly the mother whose departure years before engendered his life-long self-pitying search for her. Unmodified in his pathology and, thus, inexplicable by normal psychology, Colton Wolf becomes the principle of evil in the novel. His active role accounts for many of the deaths in the narrative. Then, as he stalks Chee and Landon to conclude his assignment, he assumes the position that literary criticism calls the nemesis, or daunting opponent, of the protagonist. Pitted against each other by the plot, their contest comes to signify the struggle of civilized values against the subversion of madness.

In a different fashion from Colton Wolf, B.J. Vines and his wife Rosemary also provide bizarre characterizations in the novel. B.J. is hardly present for the narrative scenes, but even in absence he looms over the story as the legendary figure who made millions of dollars from uranium discoveries, who continues to hold a place in Navajo history as an erstwhile friend of the Charley family (Dillon Charley, Emerson Charley, and Tomas Charley—all of them chiefs in the Peyote Church), but who is now feared to be a witch. He is also known as a hunter whose big-game trophies hold pride of place in his magnificent home, and a person whose sudden rise from an obscure past to the celebrity and prominence of wealth predictably makes him a man of mystery. Rosemary, B.J.'s second wife and hunting companion, conveys her own aura of mystery by the odd action of commissioning Jim Chee to recover a box she says contains merely keepsakes. As characters in the narrative, Mr. and Mrs. Vines must be considered enabling agents. Mrs. Vines sets Chee's investigation into motion and helps bring it to a conclusion in the final pages. B.J.'s past career and past relationships emerge as background causes of the puzzles that must be solved in the story. They do not introduce exposition, but without them the story would neither begin nor end.

Any story set in a sprawling expanse like the Navajo Reservation would have a sizable cast of secondary characters serving a variety of functions. *People of Darkness* is no different from other Hillerman novels in this respect. For instance, Sheriff Lawrence (Gordo) Sena, fixated on the explosion that had killed his brother and jealous of his jurisdiction, provides a negative perspective on Vines and places obstacles in Chee's path that in time suggest important details about the crimes. Discovery of information about the Charley family and their church illustrates social divisions on the Reservation. Other Navajo characters give authentic testimony useful to Chee's investigation, as do Anglo characters such as Dr. Edith Vassa who adds epidemiological reporting to the compilation of evidence for Chee's inquiry. Together the secondary characters also work to create narrative verisimilitude, that resemblance to actuality which authors use to gain credence for their stories.

PLOT DEVELOPMENT

With *People of Darkness* Tony Hillerman displays his aptitude for plot development in a pattern alternating Jim Chee's investigation with Colton Wolf's stalking. The effect is of two lines moving to convergence. Along the one line Chee looks into the Charley family, as Rosemary Vines has suggested, discovering through a meeting with Sheriff Gordo Sena that an explosion years before has motivational importance, although he cannot be certain exactly how it pertains to the seemingly minor crime of the theft of a box. The Chee plot line, instigated by the problem of the burgled box, presents answers to the inquiry that are only tentative because, in fact, they reformulate the problem. For example, when B.J. Vines returns from a hospital stay, he counters Rosemary's commission of Jim Chee to find the box, explaining that really there was no crime at all. His wife may have taken the box, he says, and it contained no valuables anyway. Later, as Chee persists with his investigation despite Vines's attempt to call him off, he confronts Tomas Charley and hears how he took the box to turn Vines's witching around but found only rocks in it (94). By now, Chee's attention has been attracted by the story of the mining explosion that originally had come up, as if by chance, in conversation with Gordo, and again in his talk with B.J. Vines. Once a secondary puzzle, the mining accident of years before gradually becomes the primary object of inquiry, thereby reformulating the detection problem.

Meanwhile, the second plot line emerges in Chapter Eight with the introduction of Colton Wolf who is portrayed in sufficient detail to encourage the reader to believe Wolf will play a major role in the novel. Since that role is not yet clear, however, the reader files the information about his obsessive character for later reference. By Chapter Thirteen, Colton Wolf's plot line has edged close to Chee's. He has been spotted by Jim and Mary at the site of Tomas Charley's killing. In the following chapter, Wolf reclaims center position in the narrative, making it clear that he has begun stalking the policeman and the woman.

Hospitalized after the encounter with Colton Wolf at the *Malpais* where Tomas Charley had been murdered, Jimmy Chee becomes cornered prey for Wolf. The account in Chapter Eighteen of Wolf's arrival at the hospital and his murder of a nurse firmly hooks the divergent plot lines together to generate an atmosphere of terror. Wolf's impersonal hunt for Chee, in the first place, defies any normal explanation of motive. Neither his fright nor accident explains Wolf's murder of the nurse, and when Wolf mistakes Chee's hapless roommate for the detective, another cold execution is added to Wolf's record. Detective fiction is rational: criminal motives are usually revealed to be ones familiar to readers, and the detective discerns plausibility behind mystery. But when the writer relocates crime in the realm of the pathological, as Hillerman does with the acts of Colton Wolf, a reasonable motive and plausible fear are replaced by terror.

As a result, when Chee has left the hospital to resume his research on the explosion and his search for the survivors, the investigation is supercharged with suspense. No longer only a process of interviewing witnesses or authorities and an intellectual engagement of a criminal problem, the course of detection becomes a contest between the good man who has grown so familiar to detective readers that they identify with him, and the killer whose description has shown him to be so psychologically alien to readers as to be beyond their sympathy. To intensify the sense of contest, Hillerman pairs Chee's investigation with Wolf's. Chee displays his method in chapters where he researches news stories of the explosion, questions Fannie Kinlicheenie about the Peyote Church and the Charleys, and interviews Dr. Vassa about the medical mystery surrounding the survivors of the explosion. Then, in a perversion or parody of the detective's search for truth, Colton Wolf appears in Chapter Twenty-nine duplicating Chee's method for his evil purpose of destroying the man, and mind, that has reached the verge of truth.

Hillerman assigns dominance to converging plot lines, devoting a full chapter to Chee's exposition of the criminal design before the action of the novel concludes. Sitting with Mary before a fire after they survive Wolf's last attack on them, Chee explains that Lebeck, the geologist at the oil well, faked his death and returned as Vines; that the unusual series of deaths has been caused by radiation poisoning; and that Vines has hired Wolf to kill Emerson and steal the body. Explanation, however, does not conclude the narrative. Conclusion of the plot, as distinct from the criminal puzzle, requires active closure. To accomplish that, Hillerman gives his plot another inversion, with Chee becoming the stalker (272) and Wolf the victim lured to Lebeck/Vines's house. Moreover, Chee has alerted Sheriff Sena, so that all of the interested parties are on the scene, including Mrs. Vines who shoots Wolf after he has killed her husband. *"El brujo est muerto,"* the Acoma woman house-servant says, "The witch is dead" (277). Is it Wolf Colton or B.J. Vines she means? No matter, both are done for. It isn't courtroom justice that has brought about conclusion; rather, it is the design of plot rendering the verdict and the punishment.

Hillerman's use of converging plot lines has a dual effect. On the one hand, the movement of the lines toward each other laces the narration of detection with the thrills of a manhunt. On the other hand, the transformation of the problem for detection from the routine scope of a small burglary into a broad-scale drama of connivance and deception, with its roots deep in the past and its stakes amounting to a fortune, invests the narrative with the outsized dimensions worthy of a story that might be thought of as a legend of the modern Southwest.

NARRATIVE POINT OF VIEW

Tony Hillerman's plot in *People of Darkness* succeeds largely as a result of his technical decision to employ the alternate points of view centered on Jim Chee and Wolf Colton in the narrative. Throughout his fiction, Hillerman shows a preference for the third-person narrative point of view, that is, the way of telling a story through reporting that "Chee said the following:" or "Then Chee looked up at the bleached white remains of the Anasazi dwelling carved from the walls of Canyon de Chelly." This common means of presenting a narrative usually frees the writer from the limits of character consciousness without prohibiting entry into a character's mind. The writer can describe events that happen without needing to have the leading character present, but still report that when that character heard about the events, she felt puzzled.

People of Darkness is an impressive illustration of some functions that the popular point of view can serve for an inventive writer. First, telling the story through a third-person point of view allows Hillerman to economically set forth the terms of the life choice Jim Chee faces, since he can tell about Chee's background and education (Navajo tradition, Anglo schooling, Hosteen Nakai's counseling) at nearly the same points in the text where he represents Chee's anxiety about his impending decision about whether to stay on the Reservation or to go to the FBI Academy. In addition, when Chee enters the expansive case of the stolen box, third-person narration allows Hillerman to sort conveniently through the detective's activities so as to feature detection method and reasoning as an expressive attribute of the kind of character Chee is—fundamentally an inquiring person with a sense of service that is projected also in what the narrative technique reveals about his ambition to become a singer.

Similar functional purposes are involved in Hillerman's decision to use the same third-person narrative technique in the chapters centering on Colton Wolf. Again, reported thought advances characterization. Devotion to his schedule denotes Wolf's obsessive nature. The repeated thought about finding his mother points to the void in his capacity to feel for others. The third-person narration brings readers within Wolf's orbit, while Chee's plot line is temporarily suspended, and depicts his unswerving pursuit of victims who represent no more to him than the means of completing a paid job. In this way, Hillerman sets up the fundamentals of the plot design. Finally, the provisional entry into Colton Wolf's consciousness adds a chill to the text.

We can understand Hillerman's fix on Colton Wolf as a result of the real experience he had as a newspaper man with a similar killer and the desire Hillerman developed to understand the creature. To appreciate Hillerman's eventual use of the motherless killer, however, we have to note that Wolf's important effect in *People of Darkness* derives from Hillerman's shrewd artistic decision about narrative point of view.

GENERIC CONVENTIONS

When Sergeant Jim Chee meets with Rosemary Vines at the opening of *People of Darkness*, readers can feel some uncertainty. Obviously, Chee is a police officer. In the second paragraph of the interview episode, he glances at the Navajo Tribal Police seal on his automobile, and he is greeted by Rosemary Vines as "Sergeant." Yet, in the subsequent interview she acts as though he is a private detective available to take a case for hire. That Chee has thirty days' leave time during which regulations might permit him to free-lance seems beside the point. The meeting, the house, the circumstances resonate with scenes that open many a private-eye story. For Jon L. Breen the scene is reminiscent of the first chapter in Raymond Chandler's *The Big Sleep* (1939) "and countless of its imitators" (*Companion* 20). To other regular readers of detective fiction, it might suggest the way Ross Mcdonald begins novels about his detective Lou Harper.

When the visit to the Vines home and conversation with Rosemary Vines begins to sketch the character of B.J., the echo of convention becomes stronger. B.J. resembles the rich man in private-eye stories who has built an empire by mysterious means and is reaping the consequences of what he sowed. That, too, echoes Chandler or Macdonald.

And there is more. After Mary Landon enters the narrative, Jim Chee's budding romantic interest in her moves him to invite her company on his case. Soon she effectively becomes his sidekick, which reminds us of such classic coupling of detective and aide as Agatha Christie's Hercules Poirot and Colonel Hastings, Arthur Conan Doyle's Holmes and Watson, Rex Stout's Nero Wolfe and Archie Goodwin, and others. In this case, the detective and sidekick are man and woman, perhaps not unlike Dashiell Hammett's Nick and Nora Charles in the badinage they exchange (see *The Thin Man*, 1934).

Finally, the retrospective element in Jim Chee's case that uncovers past crime in solving recent crime recalls turns of plot marking detective fiction at least since A. A. Milne's *The Red House Mystery* (1922), as well as works by John Dickson Carr, and more recently continuing into the canon of Ross Macdonald. Some of these precedent works employ assumed identity as a feature of the plot, just as Hillerman does when he reveals that Carl Lebeck became B.J. Vines in *People of Darkness*. Because detective fiction is directed closely on the matter of crime, making it the problem, and the solution of the problem the task of the leading character, the chances that readers with some experience of the genre will be sensitive to convention are greater than they might be with the mainstream novel. All the more reason, then, to concede that a writer's originality may often consist in the way he or she presents his version of a story twice-told, at least twice-told. That is why our discovery that Tony Hillerman's Colton Wolf has a cousin in the serial murderer who appears in Lawrence Sanders's *The First Deadly Sin* (1973) whets our curiosity to read about them both, rather than provoking us to swear off reading any more books where we are going to meet a pathological killer. Killers, like detectives and like plots concerned with the solution of criminal problems, are native to the territory of the genre. There is pleasure in learning how the individuals of a species so alike can be so different, but first we identify them as instances with much in common.

THEMATIC ISSUES

Dissection of the plot structure in *People of Darkness* also identifies some of its major themes. The converging lines represented by Jim Chee and Colton Wolf present the age-old conflict of good and evil within modern definitions that allow a workaday police officer's compassion and commitment to service stand for values that civilize society and a dysfunctional killer embody the vicious consequences of alienation that lie within the possibilities of common-day life. Initially, neither figure stands out as other than realistic. As events bring them closer together, those traits that make the characters recognizably realistic seem to enlarge them. Chee's work ethic and his capacity for affection, his trained mind and his curiosity, the ambition he has to be either a singer or a federal agent, along with the conflict he feels between the two occupations—these traits with which readers might readily identify come to seem what the life open to most of us should be about. Colton Wolf's compulsive behavior, which at first is like something out of a case study yet possibly recognizable among people we have seen before, grows sinister when the perversion it represents swings against Jim Chee and Mary Landon in a way that may suggest there are other antisocial Coltons out there threatening civil order.

Similar to the revelation following upon dissection of the plot structure, analysis of the broadening scope of the criminal story leads directly into a prominent theme. The medical consequences to the survivors of the explosion capsulizes the significance of the theme of the past in the story. An apparent set of coincidental deaths turns out to have a common cause in radioactivity, which is invisible and, therefore, discoverable only through specialized investigation and the confirmation of intellectual method. Traces of the ultimate cause, the crimes of Lebeck, appear to be equally the result of chance until the specialized investigation of detective work correctly defines the criminal problem and teases a solution from the accumulated evidence. Without anyone being the wiser, past exposure to radiation and past actions of deception have had continuous consequences. The passage of time has not alleviated occurrences of the past. The past remains active, just as radiation has remained active; both examples show readers of *People of Darkness* that Tony Hillerman conceives of history as a continuum that keeps the past an active force in the present.

Hillerman's emphasis on Navajo inheritance in the story of Jim Chee and his uncle Hosteen Nakai allows one of the lessons of history to be the power of cultural tradition to define and nurture personality. Another lesson is the importance of undertaking a personal study, as Chee has done, of learning how to adapt inheritance to new circumstances, while refreshing the original stock with assimilations from other cultures. In Chee's case, the inheritance and original stock are Navajo customs and spiritual practices, while the refreshment flows from education in the Anglo university and interaction with those who follow the white ways. There can be no doubt that Hillerman allows that the lesson Chee is learning can be applied by any readers of *People of Darkness*.

MULTICULTURAL READING OF *PEOPLE OF DARKNESS*

Multicultural literary criticism, discussed previously in Chapter 3 of this book, develops from the observation that American literature like the United States itself is composed of many ethnic streams. A look at a list of the literary works most often regarded as the "great" American writings from earlier centuries gives the impression that the most important writing was produced in New England or the Middle Atlantic states and ordinarily by white male authors. Multicultural critics point out, however, that such a list (or canon as literary historians commonly term it) reflects the preferences of earlier authorities who had a comparatively privileged literary education, including especially works of literature created in Great Britain. These authorities, the multicultural critics claim, encompassed a comparatively small circle of acquaintance with decided tastes for what they considered higher forms of writing than the popular genres represented in oral folk literature, in widely circulating magazines and newspapers, in performances on the stage of city theaters, or in the inexpensive books of prose and poetry issued by presses serving immigrant groups and ethnic enclaves such as settlements of African Americans.

Multicultural critics also observe that there are definite historical reasons why probably the vast majority of the American population did not participate in the exclusive literary circles of eighteenth- and nineteenth- and early twentieth-century America. For one thing, the first language of many people was not English, so they read and wrote in foreign-language publications for a generation at least. Another cause was economic: small farmers and urban laborers had neither the education to direct them toward Anglo-American literature nor the income to pursue what must have seemed to be an activity of the leisured population. In addition, prevailing social views generally discounted the intellectual abilities of the female half of the population, as well as the mental capacity of most people who were not recognized as "white."

According to multicultural critics, people outside the circle of special literary taste and attainment had their own literature. As the universal human interest in storytelling and experience show us, wherever there is literacy there is also communication. Besides, there is much surviving evidence of imaginative writing among women, immigrant generations, and people of color. It stands to reason, the argument concludes, that American literature should be pluralized.

During the past thirty years, the position of multicultural critics has become commonplace enough to result in extensive publication, and republication, of literature created by Americans who were not especially privileged, white, male, or long-term inhabitants of the country. With the availability of a spectrum of literary works, the critics have turned their attention to comparative study. Finding stimulus for study in such issues as the differences between writing by men and by women, the effect of historical experiences of racial segregation and ethnic discrimination on the subjects authors choose to write about, and the ways they write, and the evidence of ethnic or gender culture in literature, the multicultural critics are developing a large body of critical writing that shows us a broader range of influences that shape a literary work. Readers have always recognized that the personal philosophy, chosen values, and individual experiences of authors affect the works they create. To a lesser degree, readers are also aware that publishers' decisions about what they will retail, and the conventions associated with writing in a chosen genre, have their effect in the finished writing as well. Now, with the assistance of multicultural criticism, readers can learn how the cultural background of the author and the author's audience influences the texts that entertain or instruct us.

As this summary implies, the usual way of treating the subject is to examine a text with an eye to finding what the author has included "naturally" because she or he is a member of a specific cultural grouping in the United States. Thus, a multicultural critic might study Nobel Laureate Toni Morrison's novel *Beloved* in search of elements that can be said to result from her identity as an African American and a woman.

Multicultural criticism offers the possibility of another task, however. That would be examination of a text for its deliberate inclusion of information and themes related to multicultural experience. The application of such an alternative multicultural approach to a novel by Tony Hillerman should be obvious.

Hillerman's knowledge of Navajo culture did not come from personal experience as a Native American because in fact he is German American. He has always lived among Native Americans and, as his biography shows, developed a deep interest in Native American people and their life in his youth. He comes to the subject of Jim Chee's culture, then, as an outsider, just as do most readers of *People of Darkness.* That becomes the important point. Hillerman writes from a perspective he shares with practically all of his audience. This observation leads us to some provocative questions.

First, what is Hillerman's attitude toward Navajo people and culture in this book? Many a writer has written about so-called minorities in a patronizing or hostile way, but if the author makes the leading character in the story a minority and raises that character to the level of a hero whom we admire, as Hillerman does with Jim Chee, then it seems clear that the attitude is respectful.

While respect is one thing, appreciation and sympathy are something else. We might respect, say, the white male King Arthur in a medieval tale, but it is difficult to put ourselves in his place and thereby understand his feelings about Guinevere and Lancelot, because the point of his characterization is that the King is uncommon. As we have noted about the characterization of Jim Chee, he is not a distant imperial presence. He experiences a dilemma about employment in *People of Darkness* that is recognizably like that faced by most of Hillerman's audience. Chee's interest in Mary Landon follows a trail of infatuation likely to make us smile in recognition. And because Hillerman has presented Jim Chee as a sympathetic character, the audience slips easily into the scenes where he is pursued by Colton Wolf and the reader feels rising tension along with Chee.

In addition to sympathy for Chee, Hillerman also seeks to create sympathy and respect for Chee's Navajo culture. That is why the repeated references are made to Chee's bewilderment at the way Anglos feel about dead bodies. Similarly, the scenes in which Chee explains Navajo names to Mary Landon and tells her Navajo myths and legends serve to present information that will allow an understanding of the Navajo outlook on life. Placing those passages of exposition in Jim Chee's conversation ensures that they will appear with familiarity and regard, thus directing Hillerman's readers toward the attitude he believes Navajo culture deserves.

Hillerman has observed that he writes what Graham Greene called "entertainments." Hillerman's first priority is to keep the story moving, because "readers are buying a mystery, not a tome of anthropology" (Winks 142). Surely, however, a serious purpose in Hillerman's writing, as distinct from the priorities for constructing a technically effective narrative, becomes clear under the light of multicultural criticism, for this German-American "Anglo" novelist of Navajo stories is an exemplary multicultural novelist.

7

The Dark Wind
(1982)

Hillerman's second novel about his "new" detective Jim Chee allows a rare insight into its process of composition. The author's notes prefacing the book explain how he came by the knowledge of Hopi beliefs appearing in the text, while disclaiming any pretense to authority on the subject. In an essay about his writing published well after the appearance of *The Dark Wind*, Hillerman mentions the novel as an illustration of his practice of beginning with a thematic idea. In this case, he says, he "wanted to expose Tribal Policeman Jim Chee to a crime motivated by revenge—a white value which has no counterpart in the Navajo culture" (Winks 140). In an interview with Jon Breen, Hillerman states that he was stuck on the plot of the book until he and his wife went out to a Hopi Reservation where he read in the weekly newspaper that somebody had vandalized a windmill. The newspaper story got him moving again by providing a reason he could use to put Jim Chee where he had to be in the novel. Then, when he "began thinking why the mill would be vandalized [he saw] how it could be as important as the plot" (*Companion* 60).

Suggestive as Hillerman's direct comments are, they are less important than the indirect evidence about composition of the novel that can be inferred from two related short stories about Jim Chee. The first story, "The Witch, Yazzie, and the Nine of Clubs," was published in 1981, a year before *The Dark Wind* appeared. The second story, "Chee's Witch," was published in 1986 but is so similar to the first story and to *The Dark Wind* that whether or not it predates the novel becomes immaterial, because together the short stories show Hillerman's preoccupation at the time with plotting a puzzle story. Observing him at work on his plot, we can see that in *The Dark Wind* he draws on the legacy of conventions in his selected genre at least as much as he does on the theological traditions of the Hopis and the culture of the Navajos. The result is a novel Hillerman believes is a high point in the accomplishment of his craft (Parker and Parker 12).

GENERIC CONVENTIONS: THE PUZZLE STORY

During the 1920s a number of writers in the detective fiction genre made it fashionable to think of their short stories and novels as intellectual challenges to the reader. Dismay at the sensationalism of detective adventures in the mass pulp magazines spurred them to launch a campaign to legitimize their use of the genre as art. R. Austin Freeman, the author of fiction about the scientific detective Dr. Evelyn Thorndyke, wrote in "The Art of the Detective Story" that fiction about detection required special talent. Other writers developed the idea that good detective fiction consists in the ingenious use of the principles of intellectual inquiry. In 1928 the pseudononymous S. S. Van Dine (who was actually the art critic Willard Huntington Wright) presented "Twenty Rules for Writing Detective Stories." Van Dine saw the detective story as an intellectual sport demanding fair play and close attention to a worthy problem. His prescriptive definition allowed for no professional criminals, elaborate descriptions, conspiracies, or love interests.

Sometimes the presentation of rules meant to support the idea of detective fiction as intellectual enterprise seemed less than serious, as in Father Ronald A. Knox's presentation in 1928 of a "Decalogue" for detection. These proscriptive commandments forbade poisons unknown to science, inexplicable intuition, unidentified clues, secret rooms, the late introduction of the criminal, and so on. On the other hand, the collaborative authors known as "Ellery Queen" took the idea of intellectualized fiction to heart when they adopted the practice of introducing a break in their stories at the point where readers would know everything the detective, also known as Ellery Queen, knew. This "Challenge to the Reader" encouraged the notion that both the essence of the genre and its audience appeal lay in the puzzle.

Regardless of the motive that led critics and authors to espouse the genre as intellectualized art, and despite the silly way they sometimes put limits on the form, advocates of the puzzle created a continuing tradition. To this day, reviewers of detective fiction can be found evaluating works in terms of the plausibility of the criminal problem and the validity of its solution. They will also speak only vaguely about that solution in order not to spoil the sport for others. Beneath all of the attenuated, sometimes tedious, talk about the puzzle of detective fiction lies an important issue for the craft of writing detective fiction, namely, plot. Whatever else a detective story might do, simply because it is about a criminal problem, it requires the simulation of investigation. Writers can shape their stories variously, even invert them so that readers see events from the viewpoint of the criminal, but the stories require a procession of credible evidence, the execution of an apparently legitimate methodology, and a plausible explanation of the relationship of events. If they accomplished nothing else, the champions of intellectual detection established a standard of plausibility consistent with verisimilitude. The genre claims a real concern as its object—the problem of crime. It can do no less in its narratives than simulate a reality in the presentation and solution of the problem. But the zealous critics of the 1920s did accomplish more. They set for their successors the task of creative manipulation of a puzzle as a source for engrossing plot. A summation of the Jim Chee short stories will help illuminate the relevance of this legacy to Tony Hillerman's fiction.

"The Witch, Yazzie, and the Nine of Clubs" picks up Jim Chee, a corporal rather than sergeant in these stories, at an Enemy Way ceremony being held for Emerson Nez. Chee has been working on a case of theft reported by Ed Yost, proprietor of the Burnt Water Trading Post, who claims that Taylor Yazzie stole $40,000 worth of pawn. Yazzie is nowhere to be found. A character named Cowboy, who is among the horde of people attending the ceremony, updates Chee on the death of an unidentified "John Doe" whose skeleton and dessicated flesh, when Chee had seen it, left little to report except that the man probably died of exposure. Now, however, it seems that a man named Pinto had seen the body fresh, and the skin of its palms had been flayed. To a Navajo this is a clear sign that a witch killed him to get the unique markings of individuality from the fingers and palms and balls of the feet to make the corpse powder skinwalkers (as witches are called) need to spread sickness.

Chee finds Pinto among a cluster of men behind Ed Yost's pickup truck playing stick dice. With a dramatic flair, Pinto tells about his discovery of the body and signs of a hasty departure by the killer in a truck. In a seeming digression at this point in the story, except that we know nothing is wasted in a short story, Yost performs a card trick in which he wagers that he can present a bystander the exact card he thinks of in his mind. The grinning man names the nine of clubs, and Yost pulls an envelope from his jacket pocket containing . . . the nine of clubs!

Moving among the crowd at the ceremony, dancing a bit, and talking a bit, Chee works out how Yost managed his trick: "A simple matter of illusion and distraction." The apparent digression of the card trick episode bears further fruit as "the easy way it had fooled him made him aware that he must be overlooking other things because of other illusions." Reviewing the story of the unidentified body, Chee recalls his experience with the decayed body—the feel of the bones, the leather of the boots. The boots! Why would a witch take the skin for corpse powder from the hands and leave the feet, with their equally useful skin, shod in their boots? In the space of a moment, Chee connects the illusion of Yost's card trick to the distractions and illusions in Yost's reporting of Yazzie's theft. Both had been charades, for just as the innocent victim of the card trick did not imagine that Yost could have envelopes in his pockets holding every card he might name, Chee had missed the fact that Yost had pretended anger at a man he claimed was Yazzie, but that Chee had no real reason to believe was. The body, falsely prepared to look like a witch's killing, was Yazzie himself, probably murdered to cover up Yost's theft of the pawn.

In a flash he goes after Yost, finds he has killed again, orders him to drop his carbine, and though he "thought he would never shoot another human, [shoots] Yost through the chest." When Cowboy rushes up to ask what happened, Chee replies, "The witch is dead" (*Companion* 341–54).

"Chee's Witch" uses language similar to that of the first story to describe the reports of witchcraft that occupy Chee. Here, however, the incident of the body falsely prepared to appear like the work of a witch plays out in conversation between Chee and FBI agent Jake Wells. At Wells's request, Chee goes to Wells's hotel where he learns that the agent wants to talk about Simon Begay, a City Navajo (a descendant of members of the tribe resettled by the federal government forty years before in cities such as Los Angeles). There's lots of gossip about Begay, including charges that he is a witch, says Chee, because, lacking ties to local clans, he is a stranger. Gossip is just what the government did not want, because Begay is in the witness protection program waiting to testify about a car theft ring in L.A.

Explaining the significance of witchcraft, Chee tells Wells about a reported witch killing. The palms of the hands were flayed. Add that in with the gossip, and Begay becomes the suspect witch. For the sake of adding more information to the story, Chee telephones the clinic to have the autopsy report on the unidentified body read to him. The corpse had shoes on. It is not a witch case at all. But in that case, what about Begay, and why the deception?

This version of the story ends enigmatically with Wells saying he will take "my Begay back to L.A. tomorrow" and Chee driving away from the hotel wondering how "they" (whoever they might be) set up the replacement of Begay, whom Chee seems to assume is the victim of the false witch killing, with somebody whose witness testimony will cast doubt on the prosecution's case (*Companion* 366–75).

The brevity of "Chee's Witch" leaves a lot unsettled, such as why Begay's killing was staged as the work of a witch when it will direct attention to the replacement witness. "The Witch, Yazzie, and the Nine of Clubs" includes so much present activity, and activity recalled from the past, that it verges on the cryptic. These faults, however, must be attributed more to the limited scope for development available in a short story than to the puzzle at the heart of the two Chee stories. Since the same puzzle occurs in *The Dark Wind,* the stories may be thought of as test runs.

More than once, Tony Hillerman has said that he is not fond of puzzles in detective fiction, preferring elaborated character instead (Bulow 67; Ross and Silet 128). Yet, together, the stories preceding *The Dark Wind* and the completed novel illustrate the legacy in Hillerman's work of the Anglo-American genre tradition of detection puzzles, perhaps showing him to be more directly an heir than he suspects. In combining plot drawn from that tradition, however, with characterization and setting informed by Native American traditions, Tony Hillerman produces a model demonstration project of literary adaptation and synthesis.

PLOT DEVELOPMENT

The Dark Wind places the material evidence for solution of the criminal problem in front of the reader before he or she is aware of the problem. The opening chapter relating the discovery of a slain Navajo by Hopis on a ceremonial pilgrimage establishes that there has been a witch killing and that for plausible reasons the Hopis suppress knowledge of the killing. In the third chapter, when Chee appears for the first time, that suppression is shown to have effect on the evidence, because by then the body has been stripped of its flesh by scavengers (23). Still, however, there is no indication of what the primary problem of the puzzle text will be.

Meanwhile, readers are privy in Chapter Two to a plane crash that Chee then observes from the ground in the next chapter. The intermingling of scenes from different perspectives in the opening pages of the novel has considerable importance to the development of a puzzle plot. First of all, this narrative technique establishes parity between sleuth and reader. Neither knows more than the other, and they will stay abreast throughout the novel. The parity can be taken as indication of the fair play principle. Like readers of classic puzzle stories by Ellery Queen, readers of *The Dark Wind* gather the evidence at the same pace as Chee. The reasons why the detective and the readers move at that pace are different, of course. The third-person narration presents discovery of the body to readers from the select perspective of the Hopis, while the sequence of events ensures that Chee will see the body only after it is too dessicated for easy analysis. For the airplane crash, readers are confined by the narrative point of view among strangers inside the cabin, so that the crash can only seem a shocking mistake. Chee sees and hears the crash, and a later shot, from a distance that also prevents him from observing any cause. The eventual effect of such narrative management comes while readers enjoy the vicarious sensation of proceeding through the intellectual stages of investigation—accumulation of evidence, the drawing of inferences, and tentative hypothesizing—as a mental companion, maybe even a competitor, with the detective. That was precisely the effect the critics of the 1920s sought in their puzzle theory.

As we have noted, those critics held plausibility to be essential to the puzzle effect. The opening pages of *The Dark Wind* are sufficient to show that Hillerman accepts the requirement. The Hopis' suppression of information about the witch killing has understandable cause, which results in a plausible explanation of why Chee does not see the body until later. Sergeant Chee's presence at the crash site is explained by a narrative flashback to Captain Largo's review of open cases. Chee has been ordered to a stakeout at the vandalized windmill Hillerman read about in the Hopi weekly newspaper.

With the advance of the narrative, all events will be found to have plausible establishment, including the repetition from the short stories of the misleading pursuit of the burglar of the pawned goods from the Burnt Water Trading Post (21–22, 41–42) and the performance of the card trick by the store's proprietor (43–44) that plants a suggestion of distraction and illusion which flowers later.

To accomplish the plausibility verisimilitude requires of a detection puzzle, a writer must only follow the criterion of probability. Events need not be familiar to readers. For many, after all, contemporary witch killings will seem out of the ordinary. But they must be linked to a naturalistic explanation, which is one reason why Hillerman takes pains to inform his readers about the alternative ways of interpreting witchcraft as a scapegoat phenomenon and as a metaphor for someone's turning away from the way of peace and harmony. Spiritual values and immaterial forces can operate in the narrative, since they will serve to make portrayal realistic, but the author of detective fiction puzzles, like any writer seeking verisimilitude, accepts the idea that values and abstract forces work through the world's characters and society.

Provision of opportunity to participate vicariously in the mental process of investigation and the necessity for plausibility do not yet exhaust what the opening pages of *The Dark Wind* can show us about plotting the puzzle story. They also illustrate the importance of what is termed narrative deformation. When all the facts are known, and if one chooses to do so, a story may be presented in a strictly linear way: this happened to cause that to happen, which, in turn, produced a new consequence. That's what students of narrative structure technically call the "story."

The retelling of the "story" in the form we call the "narrative" deforms chronology by moving the point of view from one vantage point to another, for example, from the Hopi's to the reader's to Jim Chee's, or information about events is withheld from the audience, like the information that Jake West, the reincarnation of Ed Yost from "The Witch, Yazzie, and the Nine of Clubs," has faked the burglary of the trading post in *The Dark Wind* in the same way that Yost did in the short story. If the novel were truly speaking after the fact, as the common use of the past tense in the third-person narration pretends, when the case has already been resolved, then the "story" could be presented from start to finish with the aid of the final conclusions. The body in Chapter One would be described as a faked witch killing, and the airplane crash in Chapter Two as an act of deliberate destruction.

It all could be done this way, except . . . and that's the critical word for these observations about narrative, except. We might get the "story" linearly, except that we do not read fiction, or write it, for the "story."

We read and write precisely for the pleasures of narrative deformation, not the least of those pleasures being participation in the puzzles presented through skillful representation of the problem of crime. We read for narrative deformation, and write in it, also because it holds truth. We actually do apprehend life tentatively, a bit of evidence here, another bit there, and we figure out what other people are like and what their actions mean by the same process of increment. So as writers distort and deform for purposes of sustaining a puzzle and moving a narrative along, their craft creates yet another way of experiencing verisimilitude.

Having resolved to deform his imagined "story," Tony Hillerman has to set several processes in motion so as to re-form events in a puzzle plot. One process moves the detection investigation forward with pronounced notice of progress toward defining the problem and finding its solution. In a closely related process, Hillerman also introduces obstacles and blockages to the investigation that will illustrate difficulty at the same time as throwing more light on the problem. In a third process, Chee is shown actively thinking through the puzzle, turning it over in his mind so as to keep the audience current with his progress.

Although Chee always seems to be at work on his cases, the progress of his investigation begins to move steadily in the sixth chapter of *The Dark Wind* when a visit to the Burnt Water Trading Post allows him to listen to witchcraft gossip, conduct an interview about the windmill, and recall the details of the burglary as he observes West's card trick. Two chapters later, the investigation takes a decided step forward when Chee solves the mystery of the plane crash. True to the nature of a narrative centered upon problem solving, Chee's discovery of the cause of the crash introduces new questions and additional lines of inquiry that will lead further along the chain of causation.

With the assistance of Cowboy, Chee is able to question the elderly Hopi man Lomatewa who found the body of the Navajo killed by a witch. Through Cowboy also, he gets a picture of Richard Palanzer, which returns him to investigation of the plane crash and alerts readers to the possibility of a connection among the outstanding cases Chee is pursuing. Later stages of the investigation are marked by Chee's tracking of the missing vehicle at the site of the crash, gathering information at the state prison on Joe Musket, the alleged burglar at Burnt Water, and his looking into the case of the vandalized windmill that put him at the spot of the plane crash.

The first major break in the investigation comes through the questioning of Sawkatewa, the Hopi who found the Navajo body on his spiritual pilgrimage. His exchange with Chee explains the vandalism, while also leading to new information about the plane crash. The reader soon learns that in the world of detection puzzle plots everything connects. All that is necessary to make the connections is to get the detective, and the readers, to the right places at the right times. The final chapters of *The Dark Wind* are written to assure that. Chee and Gail Pauling, whose relationship of reasonable trust has been established earlier, collaborate to find out about an impending sale of the narcotics carried in the doomed airplane. Another visit to Burnt Water puts Chee in a position to witness another of West's magic tricks and to stir new thoughts about deception and illusion. The separate puzzles of the body, the plane crash, and the burglary are fused into a single problem that is now ready for solution.

Progress has not been easy, because, in the second notable process for building the plot, Hillerman has brought into it the lucrative trade in narcotics. The FBI agents take a proprietary interest in the plane crash, trying to dissuade Chee's investigation by bluster and violent threat. Gaines and West figure as blocking agents, too, the one because he wants a piece of the action, and the other because he has bred a plan of vengeance. While these characters attempt to prevent solution of the puzzle, they also aid the detective, who acts in puzzle plots as a person for whom nothing is insignificant or digressive, in piecing together the fabric of explanation.

The activity of preparing the explanation is subjectively dramatized through the third process for building plot, the scenes of Jim Chee's pondering the puzzle. There are passages showing Chee running through questions surrounding his puzzles (56 ff). At other points in the narrative, readers hear him disciplining himself to stick with the detection method he has learned and not give way to confusion or anger (57, 123). Still other places in the narrative present Chee in mental action that makes him seem a model of detection, as when he reasons in Chapter Twenty about the windmill vandal's motive. These descriptions of Chee's thinking work, of course, to relate his uniquely individual method of crime solving that merges Navajo belief and philosophy with police force procedures. For this same reason, Chapter Twenty-seven is given over entirely to the ritual sweat bath that gets him in a state of harmony for the hunt.

Classically, a detection puzzle brings everything together in a final chapter. The lines of inquiry are all completed, and the connections among them are made plain. The villains are exposed and possibly even set up for appropriate punishment, which need not mean a court trial

and prison—death will do. Hillerman fulfills the formula completely in
The Dark Wind. The rain for which the Hopis have prayed since the novel
began with the ceremonial pilgrimage in Chapter One comes down in
torrents. West confesses to Chee his role in the crimes. Chee tells the
crooked FBI agent Johnson why he became suspicious of him. Johnson
knocks West into the flood to drown. West's illusions end with his death
and the rain that soaks the cards he used in his magic tricks. And Jim
Chee throws the remaining suitcase of dope into the rushing water. The
scene, thus, presents a solution to the puzzle, which ties up the plot
logically and neatly, as well as a narrative conclusion demonstrating both
a kind of natural justice at work and a logic of skillful craft.

HISTORICAL AND CULTURAL CONTEXT

Tony Hillerman's skillful plot structures never obscure the rich context
of those plots. His intriguing puzzle in *The Dark Wind* taps deeply into
the cultures of the Southwest to develop significant conflicts and contrasts, while the encounters of Native American and Anglo characters,
which are staples in his novels, germinate themes of commentary that
deserve application in any society facing the inescapable modern condition of living in a multicultural way.

Throughout the novel, allusions are made to the dispute between Hopis and Navajos over title to the territory of the Joint Land Use Reservation. The dispute lies behind Jim Chee's reasoning about the
vandalism of the windmill installed by the Office of Hopi Partitioned
Land "to provide water for Hopi families being resettled along Wepo
Wash to replace evicted Navajo families" (15). Considering the location
of the windmill, the damage might be reasonably thought to have been
done by a Navajo vandal, but maybe that conclusion betrays the sup-
positions Anglos have about conflicts. As the case develops, the reason
for destruction of the windmill has nothing to do with tribal rivalry and
everything to do with the intrusion of an officious governmental force
on sacred land. From that perspective, it becomes easy to understand, as
Chee does, the Hopi's reverence for the spirit of the spring (195).

In one of the fullest references to the Joint Land Use dispute, Chee
reflects about it in the context of ethnic antagonisms. One part of the
antagonism, he feels, is abstractly the result of ancient legends of warfare,
but the recent Supreme Court decision awarding the land to Hopi plain-
tiffs "lent a sort of reality to the abstraction," because now 9,000 Navajos

"were losing the only homes their families could remember" (143–44). It is tempting to point out that the whole matter of lands assigned exclusively and jointly to tribes takes form from white practices of segregating Native Americans. It was the United States Supreme Court, not a tribal nation's court, that reached the decision on land rights based on the precedents of the white man's law. To be sure, the land was traditionally contested. Chee thinks how the San Francisco peaks are sacred to both Hopis and Navajos (144). Evidently, then, there is no simple resolution to be found in the concept of land possession, and the entire dispute reveals a palimpsest (a text where one layer of writing is overlain with other layers) of cultures where ancient differences lie beneath the forms they have been given in modern times. If the image is apt, then the situation is characteristic of the Southwest where history serves vastly different cultures in greatly different ways to support their claims to the same territory.

The days of warfare and conquest, however, have long since ended. In the contemporary time period of Hillerman's narratives, cultures coexist peaceably, though not always harmoniously, through a tacit agreement on the necessity to tolerate differing beliefs. The practical requirements of tolerance may rise to the level of mutual respect, as they do during the conversation between Navajo Jim Chee and Hopi Taylor Sawkatewa in Chapter Twenty-one. There, Chee's statements of approval for the Hopi power to bring the rain, and his declared understanding of the sacred importance of the spring by the windmill, lead to an informal agreement of cooperation. In return for the crucial information he gives Chee through his eyewitness report on the night of the airplane crash, Sawkatewa receives assurance of assistance in protecting the holy site of the spring.

While an intuitive sympathy between Chee and Sawkatewa makes their arrival at an agreement seem easy, collaboration between Native American and Anglo characters can be much more tentative. When Gail Pauling states her desire for vengeance on her brother's killer, Jim Chee hesitates to agree on that motivation for his investigation of the airplane crash. "They're not going to kill him and just walk away from it," says Gail. "But sometimes they do," Chee replies. "No," Gail continues in a tone "suddenly vehement," as she poses to Chee two questions calling for sympathy. "They won't get away with it. You understand that?" is the first. "Do you understand 'An eye for an eye, a tooth for a tooth'?" is the second. These are easy enough questions to answer without temporizing, but not for Chee. "Not exactly," he replies to the first plea for understanding, and to the query about his familiarity with the meaning of the Old Testament teaching, he says merely, "I've heard of it." In bewilderment, Gail Pauling asks whether Chee doesn't believe in justice. But apparently the Judeo-Christian tradition of justice is alien to Chee's traditional Navajo feeling. For the Navajo, the narrative informs readers, harmful behavior by someone means that person is "out of control," because the "dark wind" had entered them. "But to Chee's Navajo mind, the idea of punishing them would be as insane as the original act" (147–48). As the plot turns out, both Gail Pauling and Jim Chee gain circumstantial satisfaction for their contrary views of the treatment the evildoers deserve, but agreement in their outlook, much less respect for the continuing differences between their outlooks, falls short.

Hillerman's presentation of the context of Southwestern cultural coexistence follows upon his use of the narrative to show lead characters both objectively and subjectively. The plot and the dramatic scenes of Jim Chee in conversation with other police and with Anglo characters show him as the investigator prescribed by the conventions of the detective fiction genre. He addresses the puzzle and criminal problem through police procedures that ally him with fellow detectives and police officers in New York or Los Angeles. In that portion of the narrative, however, that enters his inner consciousness, Jim Chee is decidedly different from the conventional detective of the Anglo-American genre.

The definitive illustration of the cultural context as it emerges from management of narration occurs in Chapter Twenty-seven. Removed from the sight of all other characters, and any requirement to compromise or translate his beliefs for them, Jim Chee takes a ritual sweat bath in preparation for the action that will lead to the denouement (final outcome) of the plot. Shortly he will confront the killer, complete the solution of the puzzle, and perform the final duties of a genre character, but now he undergoes a process of transformation and adaptation—transformation of sleuth into Navajo hunter, adaptation of Navajo ritual to detective work. For the space of a chapter, the objective and subjective realities of Jim Chee merge in demonstration of the formula by which he lives the historical and cultural context of his adventures.

CHARACTER DEVELOPMENT

Often we expect fiction to display a change in the leading character as he or she undergoes influential experiences. This is the premise of stories about characters coming of age or gaining practical education in life, death, or sex. The same premise of a changeable personality often underlies stories of war and trauma. In detective fiction, however, character change is more likely to be incidental for the reason that the plot must be devoted largely to an investigation that will change circumstances rather than character, change circumstances from confusion or disorder into lucidity and order, so that characters may resume their "normal" life. In detective fiction, then, when we speak of character development, we refer not to ways the character develops but rather to the ways the author presents character.

In *The Dark Wind* Tony Hillerman presents Jim Chee much as he does in the two short stories, except that the novel gives him greater scope to explain Chee. Within the enlarged scope, the same formula observable as the basis for contextualizing the novel can be seen as the pattern for Jim Chee's characterization. In fact, that formula for alternating and combining scenes of dramatized conversation and actions with passages of indirect discourse revealing the subjectivity of Chee makes every portion of the novel featuring Chee carry the double freight of context and characterization. What provides us context for the novel, whether it is conversation between Chee and the Hopis and Gail Pauling or the sweat bath chapter, tells us about the character of Chee, too. In this respect, he is to be understood as a representative figure, as well as the novel's sleuth. Unlike detectives in the genre who are portrayed by their authors as great because they are not centered in the same way as other characters and, therefore, move eccentrically, Jim Chee draws attention because his mind moves concentrically with the minds of other Navajos. Of course, looked at another way, that is, from the perspective of Anglo characters, Chee is eccentric in his fidelity to the views of an ethnic minority. Typical when seen from within his indigenous culture, unusual when viewed from the outside, an agent of order for the Navajo people employed in a police force designated by the national government, Jim Chee ought to be perfectly suited for his job.

Surely in *The Dark Wind* he is ably prepared for the job, because the economy of this novel dedicates the detective almost exclusively to the criminal puzzle. Undistracted as he was in *People of Darkness* by an impending career choice, Chee has no immediate fear of being marginalized as a minority person. He has his conflicts with the majority culture of the United States, most notably in the expressed bias of an Anglo lawyer (73) and the violent mistreatment by the FBI agents (Chapter Eleven), but these problems occur on his native turf where his specialized knowledge of the cultures gives him a competitive edge in solving the puzzle.

Most of the other characters in *The Dark Wind* gain their individuality from conformity to their function in the narrative. Jake West, who is a reincarnation of Ed Yost in "The Witch, Yazzie, and the Nine of Clubs," is provided the motivation of his son's death for replaying the role of magician and falsifier of the trading post burglary. Captain Largo enters the narrative to explain Chee's assignments and to give him a sympathetic ear. The FBI agents take the roles of villains as they are usually played by corrupt drug traffickers. Gail Pauling, as we have seen, not only speaks for Anglo values, but is also instrumental in revealing information about the drug deal. Cowboy exemplifies the historic distrust between Hopis and Navajos while also becoming a go-between to lead Chee to Sawkatewa, the windmill vandal. None of these characters is without inherent interest. Each adds drama to the scenes in which they appear, while the fact that their functional roles in the narrative can also be readily designated testifies to Hillerman's careful designing of his puzzle.

THEMATIC ISSUES

Time and again *The Dark Wind* refers to the comprehensive system of Navajo beliefs as a way of presenting the theme of alternative value systems. At dawn by the windmill, Jim Chee experiences the beauty that the mythical Changing Woman taught Navajos to attain, the feeling of *hozro,* or harmony, that leads him to greet the morning with a shout and a rite of blessing (55). Momentarily stymied by the puzzle, the memory of Changing Woman's teaching that "all was part of the universal pattern" and his uncle's instruction to "look for the pattern," reassures him that a solution will come (57–58). In confirmation of his confidence, he soon figures out how West had performed his card trick and realizes a connection between the spring and the windmill (61).

Multiplication of such passages throughout the narrative indicates that they are meant to show more than some "local color." What that is emerges most significantly during the conversation between Chee and Sawkatewa in Chapter Twenty-one. When declarations of mutual respect have bridged the distance between Hopi elder and Navajo police officer, the two proceed to talk of the windmill. Chee offers thoughts on motives for vandalizing it: a Navajo might be angry about it, a Hopi might think the windmill is *kahopi* (against Hopi values). The old man responds with a comment about how many Hopis have abandoned traditional ways for the white man's teachings, including letting the Tribal Council run things "instead of the way we were taught when we emerged from the underworld" (193). As the rain for which the Hopis have prayed falls significantly in the scene, Chee states an interpretation of the spring and windmill. Because he does not speak the Hopi language, Chee's remarks have to be translated by Cowboy Dashee, but there can be no doubt that he is speaking in a mode shared by Hopi and Navajo, if not in a common linguistic system, for he speaks of a blessed and holy earth and how drilling for the windmill went against Hopi ways.

With that, the two men reach agreement on essential reality, an agreement that precedes the practical agreement by which Chee will help Sawkatewa close down the windmill permanently. Chee states the basis of their understanding when he says, "There are higher laws than the white man's law" (196). There is a spiritual law that sometimes must take precedence over other laws. The conviction that this is so allows Chee to aid and abet the "crime" of disabling the government's windmill. As the occurrence of their conversation in the first place demonstrates, this conviction also allowed Chee and Sawkatewa to transcend the joint use land dispute that has exacerbated ancient differences between their tribes.

But the existence of a higher law cannot justify everything. One must negotiate distinctions. The higher law will permit Chee to destroy the evidence of drugs that might aid in prosecution of the case, but he is careful to frame that in a way that will meet the orders of his superior to stay away from the case. He can assist the old Hopi in shutting down the windmill, but he must also secure information that he can use in his investigation. Chee can assert the existence of a spiritual realm, but still he has a job to do in the material world. The pounding rain during Chee's interview with Sawkatewa, and in the resolution of the plot in the final chapter, symbolically underlines the existence of a higher law with the physical appearance of the object of Hopi prayer, yet the crimes making up the puzzle of the plot took place in the physical world, and that's where Chee has to resolve the puzzle.

The issue of vengeance espoused by Gail Pauling provides further expression of the theme of alternative value systems. Chee's Navajo view of "the dark wind" filling people who turn away from the teachings of Changing Woman offers a spiritual basis for the prescribed conduct of ignoring such insane people and feeling pleased if they return to *hozho*, but, for that matter, so does Gail Pauling's view of retribution have a traditional spiritual basis. As the novel works out, the difference between the two becomes negligible. The puzzle is still going to be solved whichever view of the evildoer prevails.

By no means a simple issue, the idea of a higher law can illuminate subjective life and give a character like Chee a means of integrating his actions with his beliefs. However, he can no more be entirely directed by a traditional way that in its pure state would have no need or wish for police officers than he can be satisfied by adopting a completely secular view of reality. It is another instance of the continuous adaptation required to live in contemporary society and an indication that there must be a Navajo version of the admonition to render unto Caesar those things that are his and unto God those that belong to the divine.

A POSTCOLONIAL READING OF *THE DARK WIND*

When taken in conjunction with the evidence of the derivation of *The Dark Wind* from the Anglo-American development of the puzzle story, the discussion of the novel's context and its spiritual theme will display a tension within the narrative that lends itself to interpretation with the aid of postcolonial literary theory.

This theory directs attention to the encounter of one culture with others, just as does multicultural literary study, except that postcolonial theory is more thoroughly based on a model of political power. As the theorists argue, Empire and, in the case of North America, racial dominance through the system of slavery and then white supremacy are the most significant determinants of modern life. The demands for rationalizing the system of African slavery in North America and the imperial domination of so-called colonies have infected the entirety of culture with ideas about the relative superiority and inferiority of people and their customs. Moving to integrate colonial possessions into their metropolitan economies, the imperial powers created for the purpose a hierarchical classification of the world's peoples. In this classification, the born leaders were white and were possessed of the heritage of Europe. According to the theory of racial supremacy, those designed by nature for subjugation were the others, usually darker complexioned and possessing the traits of behavior and culture that because of their differences from the European were described as primitive and uncivilized. Intellectually, psychologically, and culturally, the point of distinguishing the European from others was to mark their place on an idealized scale of development, with the top slots reserved for those who designed and employed the scale.

The imperial activity of hierarchical classification was much more than a delusory self-justifying mental exercise. It expressed real power relationships with serious consequences including slavery, colonial wars, and policies of cultural subjugation that would lead to denigration of native languages, erasure of heritage in a history reconceived along colonial lines, dismissal of religious practices as superstition, and imposition of European models as the goals of education and intellectual attainment.

The story is well known. Less easily recognized is the eventual effect of Europe's imperial enterprise in settler colonies like America where the descendants of Europeans replicated colonial practices through generations of subsequent history. Where Europeans establishing colonies on the African continent redrew boundaries and relocated indigenous populations to make their task of control easier, so did the European Americans relocate indigenous people of the North American continent, making of them an internal colony.

If anything, the handling of the internal American colonies, being more thoroughgoing, was more severe than European management of overseas colonies, because the incoming population of Europeans in North America so greatly outnumbered the Native Americans and so completely replaced the original economies with one more suitable to their purposes. Culturally, too, it might be said that domination was more complete over the internal colony, because all formal education and all interchange became regulated by the government of the European descendants.

Once postcolonial critics have established this historical circumstance, they turn their attention to what might be termed the subjective results of the colonial process in the psychology and consciousness of colonial people. To say that a person belonging to a group designated primitive would be subject to discrimination is to state the obvious. It ought to be equally obvious that repetition of the designation undermines self-identity, particularly if replacement values are consistently offered for the so-called primitive ways of belief and behavior.

Native Americans were relocated at will in past years, subjected to school curricula designed to replace Indian ways with white ways, and constantly saw evidence about them of the power of the Anglo government. Under these circumstances, they were placed under the stress of a continuing crisis in belief and values. Shall they live as their elders prescribe or as the Bureau of Indian Affairs wishes? Systematic segregation of Native Americans does create enclaves in which people may reduce the stress. All that is required is willingness to exist on a subsistence level and to curtail contact with the world beyond the Reservation.

But that would be impractical for most people and inconceivable for ambitious younger people such as those Jim Chee represents.

As a consequence, most Native Americans live in a mental and physical environment that was formed by the past of their internal colony. Postcolonial critics typically examine literary texts for evidence of the ways they embody the outlook of colonial mastery: preference for colonial models of social arrangement, assumptions of relative superiority and inferiority of European/white culture, and denigration of the so-called primitive ways. Conversely, a postcolonial text may be one that rejects colonial idealizations and attempts to subvert the cultural dominance of the European through satire or exposure.

At first thought, Tony Hillerman may seem a peculiar candidate for postcolonial study, since he writes about the colonized from a position within the membership of the dominant group. An author's identity, however, is not the sole determining factor in settling attitudes either for or against the colonial models. The theory takes account of the possibility that a writer may be one of the colonized but still an implicit advocate of the cultural subjugation of his or her native group. There also ought to be room in the theory for the reverse condition.

The lessened relevance of authorial nativity makes it clear that the subject for examination is the narrative text, not the author's biography. With that in mind, it becomes evident that *The Dark Wind* is informed by an awareness of the postcolonial situation of its leading character. Jim Chee seems to be highly self-conscious, continually aware of himself as a Navajo. When he refreshes his memory of Hosteen Nakai's teachings of Navajo philosophy, he is thinking in a more deliberate way about heritage than is actually required by an experienced detective. The elevation of his response to bigotry from impulse to principle, as when he tells himself to keep his mind on the puzzle and not get angry at stereotypical statements about "Indians" (73), shows him to be a man who will never get used to racial insult and must think deliberately about it.

Chee's self-conscious nature is associated with his encounters with Anglo characters, as in his thoughts about crime and justice during the conversation with Gail Pauling. Among other Native Americans, he seems to be entirely focused on the task at hand. He feels comfortable with the Hopi elder, even though he has felt uneasy about Cowboy Dasheen's attitude toward him. Chee is capable of pursuing his goals even through the medium of an oral translation, which in other people, or in other circumstances, might make him impatient.

From the vantage point of postcolonial theory, then, the characterization of Jim Chee, as the chapter on the sweat bath illustrates, gives a portrayal of a man working to integrate the heritage of his precolonial culture with the occupation he has taken in the postcolonial world.

That's one part of the text, a major part to be sure, but much remains that a postcolonial critic must think about. There is the genre and the consequent form of the plot, for example. The detective fiction genre arose in a time when colonialism was thriving. One need only recall that the exemplary chronicles of the cases of Sherlock Holmes are kept by a veteran of British imperial battles in Afghanistan, and that he resides with his companion the Great Detective in the metropolitan heart of the British Empire where they meet adventures imported from all over the colonial world. Moreover, Holmes becomes a hero of the empirical science advanced by European technique throughout such intellectual disciplines practical for empire as anthropology, as well as in the more immediately local tasks of industrialization. And he lives with Dr. Watson in rooms decorated with such items from empire abroad as a Persian slipper in which he keeps tobacco and the initial VR, standing for Victoria Regina, that he has put in the wall by firing a pistol in honor of her reign over the far-flung empire. Chee is hardly a Holmes, but readers meet him in a genre that is most hospitable to imperial pretension or Western confidence in the power of a superior mind over the disorder of the world.

Postcolonial criticism illuminates the complexity that is at the core of *The Dark Wind*. Read one way, the novel relates the struggle of the detective to resist being marginalized as an exotic primitive and to make his culture authoritative and relevant to contemporary life. Read another way, Jim Chee is still a detective modeled on the figures who insinuated colonial values into a popular literary genre. Which is the correct reading? The answer is that both readings are relevant because both result from seeing the novel in the context opened for us by postcolonial literary theory.

8

Listening Woman
(1978) and
The Ghostway
(1984)

Listening Woman brought to a close the series of three novels devoted to presenting Joe Leaphorn as a solo detective. After introducing the Navajo detective in *The Blessing Way* published in 1970, Tony Hillerman turned to writing *The Fly on the Wall,* the book based loosely on his practical experiences as a political reporter and editor, which appeared in 1971. Two years elapsed before Hillerman used Joe Leaphorn again, this time as the protagonist in his 1973 detective novel *Dance Hall of the Dead.* Then, while he wrote and published a children's book, *The Boy Who Made Dragonfly,* and works of nonfiction, there was a five-year gap before Leaphorn returned in 1978 in *Listening Woman.*

Hillerman has explained that he dropped Leaphorn for two reasons. One was that he had an idea for a plot in a new book that would work better if the detective were newer to the police force, younger, and with an even more traditional Navajo background that could be used for good effect in a narrative about the Checkerboard Reservation where ethnic groups are all mixed. Another reason was that he had signed a film and TV option on *Dance Hall of the Dead* that included waiver of his television rights to Leaphorn—a disturbing mistake that lent encouragement to his interest in a new detective (*Companion* 57–58).

Once he had conceived of his new sleuth Jim Chee, Hillerman worked steadily on novels about him. Chee debuted in 1980 in *People of Darkness,* had his second appearance as a lone detective in *The Dark Wind* in 1982, and a third outing in *The Ghostway*, issued in 1984. Then this use of an exclusive lead detective also ended. Hillerman's next novel, *Skinwalkers* (1986), published after he had bought back his rights to use Leaphorn for $21,000 (Sobol 87), united his two detectives Jim Chee *and* Joe Leaphorn. Collaborative investigations have remained the rule in Hillerman's fiction ever since.

The symmetry of the two series about Leaphorn and Chee encourages their comparison. Members of the same small police force, the two detectives are subject to similar operational procedures on the Reservation and the same jurisdictional limitations when they are off the Reservation or dealing with federal authorities. Both Leaphorn and Chee have formal university education in anthropology and the ethnology of Southwestern Indian tribes. Each has a distinct interest in beliefs about the supernatural among indigenous peoples of the region and deep knowledge of the mythological heritage and cultural practices of his own tribe. Leaphorn and Chee, each playing the lead in his own series of three novels, seem to be two sides of the same coin.

But, of course, the two sides of a coin, for all they have in common, bear different designs and inscriptions. The same might be expected of two versions of Navajo detective narratives. As a matter of fact, keeping in mind what *Listening Woman* and *The Ghostway* share in general helps to illustrate how they differ.

CHARACTER DEVELOPMENT

Major Characters

In deciding that he would introduce a Native American sleuth, and then two sleuths, into the detective fiction genre practically for the first time, Tony Hillerman also selected a formula for characterization that would not only allow him to use established conventions of the genre but also secure the opportunity to represent Navajo culture authentically. Making Leaphorn, and then Chee, police officers, Hillerman inserted them into familiar genre roles where they would encounter challenging cases in the course of their professional duties. Designation of the detective as police officers, rather than, say, free-lance private eyes was simply good sense for stories set in a rural locality and culture where a private detective might starve before finding steady work. Plausibility also made available to Leaphorn and Chee the specialized procedures associated with police work in detective fiction and made likely the step-by-step pursuit of investigation underlying all the varieties of the genre and receiving particular emphasis when the detective is on the police force.

A further element of Hillerman's formula for characterizing his sleuths was his assignment to each of a past on the Reservation and an education in a university. Indication of membership in Navajo clans and mention of influential elder relatives experienced in ceremonials and learned in tribal history guaranteed that Leaphorn and Chee would be intimately familiar with a Native American culture: able to act naturally in accord with the culture of the people they serve, likely to take cultural practices into account for their investigations, and useful in explaining Navajo ways to readers of their adventures.

This last point, the utility of Leaphorn and Chee for readers, results from Hillerman's establishing that they are both university trained. Police officers generally have formal education, but Hillerman has awarded his officers university degrees and majors in anthropology. This single detail of the common formula of the detectives' characterization accomplishes a great deal. It stipulates, for example, that they have membership in two cultures along with consciousness of duality that can sometimes cause uneasiness about self-identity but that always results in sensitivity. In addition, and just as important for the success of their narratives, as a result of their cross-cultural experiences, Leaphorn and Chee bridge two cultures for readers of their novels. Navajo in their original language and outlook, the detectives have come to possess also the English language of the American majority and, with the language, routine acquaintance with the Anglo majority's way of looking at life.

By placing his detectives in the context of genre conventions, Hillerman makes them at once familiar characters, likely to behave in the satisfying fashion of other police detectives. Giving Leaphorn and Chee literally the language of their dominant audience, and making them knowledgeable about the cultural freight carried by the language, Hillerman encourages the reader's tendency to identify with the leading characters of fiction. With that, he completes his formula for characterization.

Satisfying his need for utility does not cover everything significant about Hillerman's presentation of the detectives in these two novels. The conventions he adopts from the genre and the formula he devises for representing character are the frame Hillerman selects. Within that frame the portrayals are differently executed.

The earliest chapters of *Listening Woman* integrate the characterization of Joe Leaphorn within scenes of his police work. In Chapter Three, for example, his review of outstanding cases with Captain Largo includes reference to his relentless rationalism. There seems to be no handle to grasp in the killing of Hosteen Tso and Anna Atcitty, but Leaphorn believes it has "to fit some pattern of cause and effect. Leaphorn's sense of order insisted on this. And if the case happened to be insane by normal human terms, Leaphorn's intellect would then hunt for harmony in the kaleidoscopic reality of insanity" (28). Later, when Leaphorn reads the case files for his own review, it becomes evident that his reasoning about causation leads inevitably to the psychology behind crime. The record of FBI procedure in the file on the Tso-Atcitty killing meets with his approval, because it had been "a thorough hunt for motive" (56). His own imaginative recreation of the crime confirms for him that "the reason for what had happened at the Tso hogan must have been real—desperate and urgent" (131). The interest in motivation reaches the point of empathy during his reflections on Father Bennie Tso's quandary of faith and affection, when Leaphorn senses the priest's anguish (272–74). Finally, when the narrative moves toward its conclusion, the problem of motivation that the detective has worried about since the early pages yields explanation of the crime, prediction of the criminal's plans for escape, and a tool for Leaphorn to use in trying to turn one of the conspirators against the villain.

The attention to motivation is entirely in keeping with the convention of detective fiction instructing us that a trinity of factors—means, motive, and opportunity—requires explanation for satisfactory solution of a crime. It is an eminently practical lesson for the reader and a guide to points of stress for a writer. Emphasis on the means of committing the crime will focus attention on material evidence, and stress on the criminal's finding the propitious opportunity for the crime will introduce circumstantial considerations, but pursuit of motive can lead into the complexities and uncertainties of the mind. Like Georges Simenon, whose Inspector Jules Maigret is the exemplary detective working by imaginative apprehension of motive, Tony Hillerman decidedly prefers to stress motive in his detection puzzles.

For all of his rationality, Joe Leaphorn hardly seems a dispassionate thinking machine. On the contrary, in *Listening Woman* anger at Goldrims and a desire to get even spurs Leaphorn on to hunt him down (38) and strengthens his resolve to survive when Goldrims tries to burn him to death (228). More generalized, but nonetheless personal, anger arises in

Leaphorn in response to his discovery of what he sees as Theodora Adams's seductive designs on Father Tso.

The vengeful thoughts about Goldrims will seem out of place to readers who think about how Jim Chee suppressed his anger at an abusive FBI agent and barely concealed his criticism of the Anglo belief in the code of "an eye for an eye" in *The Dark Wind*. There readers are informed that such a vengeful code violates Navajo philosophy. In *Listening Woman*, however, no such implication pertains to Leaphorn. Clearly, however, Leaphorn's dismay at the relationship between Theodora and the priest is meant to be consistent with the high value he puts on spiritual conduct.

In Chapter Ten, while the Kinaalda ritual for initiating a girl into womanhood goes on about him, the narrative records Leaphorn's "fierce pride in his people, and in this celebration of womanhood." In that scene, and elsewhere (e.g., 44), he relates his respect for Navajos to the philosophy of adaptation to nature which he shares with the Dinee. A restored sense of adaptation, or harmony with nature, fills him while he joins in the "hypnotic repetition of pattern which blended meaning, rhythm, and sound in something more than the total of all of them" (145–46).

The narrative explains that Leaphorn had stopped believing in the most controversial aspect of Navajo spirituality, witchcraft, while a student at Arizona State University (101–102). Still, his reverence for the spiritual outlook of Navajos no doubt contributes fervor to his investigation of the hidden cave where, during the time of the attacks by the U.S. Army on the Navajos, the wise man Standing Medicine preserved the sand paintings for the Sun Way ritual so that the people could start a new world after cataclysm.

His Navajo inheritance acquires significance also for Leaphorn's investigative method. The scenes where he checks watering places in Chapter Four, withstands the fire in Chapter Fifteen, and conducts his inquiring conversations with John McGinnis at the Short Mountain Wash Trading Post in Chapters Five and Nine are all equally informed by the knowledge Leaphorn comes by naturally as a Navajo. Whether he is pursuing physical evidence by use of the tracking skills that all Navajo hunters have, displaying the resourcefulness of a man used to the outdoors, or conducting interrogations on the basis of the trust he creates as a Reservation insider, Leaphorn is never just a detective, but always a Navajo detective.

Jim Chee in *The Ghostway* shows, as he does in his earlier appearances, a devotion to reasoning out solutions similar to Leaphorn's. A notable example occurs very near the ending of this novel, when the narrative shows that Chee has assembled all the pertinent information available and necessary for solving the criminal problem. While the questions "hung in his mind, unanswered" and there appear to be "no loose ends," he thinks he must be faced with "just a sequence of murderous incidents which seemed to violate reason" (273). Then reviewing events one more time, this time putting on them an ingeniously different interpretation than the facts previously had suggested, he comes up with a new possibility. Testing the new interpretation against his memory for anything that would make it impossible, he finds none. Possibility has become probability, and Chee speeds to a solution. It is as though Hillerman pauses for a beat to allow for an Ellery Queen style "Challenge to the Reader," when Chee reviews the evidence, and then impatiently shifts instead to Chee performing a model demonstration in solving a detection puzzle.

The demonstration fits Chee neatly into the conventions of detective characterization. Hillerman places Chee within his own developed practices of characterizing Navajo detectives, when he introduces Chee's hesitancy about entering a hogan (a Navajo dwelling) that harbors a *chindi* (ghost), and in a continuing way throughout *The Ghostway*, as he interleaves description of Chee on the case with passages of Chee thinking through his relationship with Mary Landon. Introduced as a companion and love interest in *People of Darkness* where her relationship with Chee underscored his dilemma about following a career in the FBI or staying "home" on the Reservation, Mary Landon has risen now to a determining role in the choice. She could make assimilation into the Anglo world worth the difficulty, or she might be a star to steer by, if she would join him permanently on the Reservation. Eventually, the narrative takes the decision about the future of his relationship with Mary Landon out of Jim Chee's hands. Before it does, however, her continuous presence in his thoughts makes it evident that Chee is in a vexatious state between his two cultures.

Like Leaphorn, Chee is a master of Navajo acquired skills, such as tracking and credible interrogation resulting from the trust he inspires as a fellow Navajo. Even more than Leaphorn, however, he is devoted to Navajo practices as only someone who aspires to a spiritual role in the tribe would be. He knows, for example, the great importance of the Four Mountains Bundle he locates in Ashie Begay's hogan, because he had made one himself (231–32). He moves familiarly about the grounds as a Ghost Way is performed in Chapter Twenty-five. Most of all, however, Chee's Navajo reverence is signified in his ambition to become a singer of the ceremonial rites. To choose an occupation, as he would do if he enrolled in the FBI Academy, is one thing, but to feel a "call" to service is quite something else. A "call" portends deep roots in a spiritual system of belief and a desire for fuller integration in the community's life. In the language of developmental psychology, Chee's conflicted feelings about love and vocation represent an identity crisis. He performs a classic detective's role on his criminal cases, but all the while he lives his experiences in the force field between two cultural poles. Such characterization is truly unique in the genre of detective fiction.

Secondary Characters

Hillerman populates these two series novels in his customary way with secondary characters who are illuminating in what they typify within their stories and interesting in themselves. In both novels, the villains seize immediate attention. Goldrims, alias Frank Hoski but really Jimmy Tso, pops up in *Listening Woman* as deceptive and malevolent. He threatens Leaphorn with vehicular homicide early in the book and disappears from the scene only to reappear in further threatening ways. Like Leaphorn's evil affliction, Goldrims pursues him in a canyon maze, attacks him with fire, and traps him deep in the hidden cave. True to his villainous role, he also turns out to be the duplicitous mastermind who conceived the plans of the Buffalo Society for taking hostages under the guise of securing justice for Native Americans, as well as the elaborate design for an explosive Armageddon that would conceal his tracks. The novel reveals Goldrims's motives, but makes little attempt to explain his character, leaving him instead the agent of inexplicable evil that he seems upon his first appearance.

Goldrims's accomplice, John Tull, is given explanation in the narrative. Leaphorn in Chapter Twelve reveals Tull to be a psychotic diagnosed as a paranoid schizophrenic. Believing he has already died and been reborn, Tull lives in the conviction that he is immortal and has become an invaluable risk-taker for the Buffalo Society and an unquestioning subordinate to its leaders. He inhabits that "kaleidoscopic reality of insanity" (28) where Leaphorn's reason tracks him.

In terms of Leaphorn's view of things, Theodora Adams may also be seen as a villain, a *femme fatale* locked in struggle for the soul of Father

Ben Tso. She provokes antagonistic thoughts in Leaphorn, and she provides the occasion for him to gossip with John McGinnis, but her doings are none of his professional business. Considering that Benjamin Tso is a grownup person vacillating about whether or not to leave the priesthood and marry Theodora, he might be thought to partake of a share in the apparently despicable behavior, but that is not the way Leaphorn or, for that matter, the narrative sees him. For them he is a tragic, malleable man waiting in the passages of the plot to become the victim of fratricide.

The most dangerous villain facing Jim Chee in *The Ghostway* echoes the characterization of Colton Wolf in the first series novel, *People of Darkness*. Hillerman allots both of them chapters in their respective books when the third-person narrative viewpoint accompanies their thoughts as they prepare for their work as hit men. Eric Vaggan, the latest of the villains, seems drawn from the accounts of the contemporary militia movement. A racist and white supremacist, Vaggan awaits the judgment day when Los Angeles will be destroyed by hydrogen bombs for its sins and only the strong will survive. Awesomely strong himself in a way that is most often associated in literature with animalistic characters, Vaggan, however, shows sadistic ingenuity. Curiously, he admires the nonwhite Navajos for their philosophy of survival. Because of that detail, the accounts in the novel of his stalking his victims take on the tone of perverted parody in which the positive qualities of Native Americans are bent toward destruction, rather than restoration, of harmony. Besides allotting two chapters to his perspective, the novel also provides a shorthand explanation of his psychotic self through details about his upbringing by a martinet of a parent.

Other characters on the wrong side of the law and Jim Chee in *The Ghostway* are much less elaborated than Vaggan. George McNair, head of the stolen car ring, who hires Vaggan has a set of peculiarities such as a devotion to symbols of British nobility and signs of Scottish background, but he figures in the narrative mostly as the man behind the scenes. The Leroy Gorman, who is identified as Grayson in the novel but who may be Robert Beno, enters the story largely to be observed as a person in the Witness Protection Program and to play a false lead who confuses the case.

Of course, Mary Landon has an important part in Chee's novel as a constant presence in his thoughts and memory, but since she is always filtered through Jim Chee, she is oblique to the action. Of the minor characters playing a direct part in the action, Margaret Sosi stands out.

Largely self-sufficient, skeptical, resourceful, and quick-witted, Margaret is an uncannily strong character who literally saves Chee's life and, through the information she provides him, instrumentally aids in solving the crime. Thematically, she seems to represent a new generation of Navajo adaptability and vitality.

Because the Navajo police force is small, it does not seem surprising that Captain Largo would appear in both of these novels and others besides. Essentially, his presence creates a reason for the detectives to review their cases with him and thus inform readers early in the texts of the general direction the books will take with their investigative processes. Howard Largo also gives the detectives cautionary warnings about FBI and State Police jurisdiction over cases, arranges their leaves and assignments, and, above all, puts a sympathetic Navajo face on the bureaucracy.

In addition to all of these characters, more or less crucial to plot, the novels acquaint readers with an assembly of people formed either by traditional Navajo culture or by their history. Along with the parts they take in the narratives as victims, relatives of victims, gossips, and informants, they also typify the unique conditions of the Reservation.

Margaret Cigaret, the blind Listening Woman, holds the position of diagnostician. Her skill helps determine what ritual treatment an ailing person needs. Anna Atcitty, Margaret's niece, shares her gift for divination and is otherwise a modern young person. She dies because, unlike her aunt, she could see the killer of Hosteen Tso. Emerson Begay, whom Leaphorn has arrested in Chapter Two of *Listening Woman,* is a likable man with an ethical code that can justify stealing sheep, if they are taken from white men, and a skill at escaping the law that generates as much amusement for the Navajo police as frustration. Among these typifying characters in *Listening Woman,* none is more interesting or important than John McGinnis. The For Sale sign on his isolated trading post is laughable because it memorializes his original disappointment with the purchase and now stands in contradiction to a rootedness that would never let him leave. Not himself a Navajo, McGinnis speaks as one entirely familiar with the tribe's ways. He comments to Leaphorn that murder, except as a result of witchcraft, is alien to the Navajo world (70). He knew Leaphorn's grandfather (68) and is Leaphorn's source for the history of Standing Medicine and his preservation of the Sun Way at the time of the Long Walk (80, 129). A natural gossip, McGinnis helps Leaphorn analyze the relationship of Father Bennie Tso and Theodora Adams. A well-placed person to gather information, he also tells the detective about Hosteen Tso's frustrated desire to send a letter before his death (119–20).

In *The Ghostway* Jim Chee encounters comparable characters reflective of Navajo experience in Los Angeles when he travels to see Bent Woman and Bent Woman's Daughter. His narrative also introduces a reference to the Navajos relocated to the cities by the Bureau of Indian Affairs when he ponders the participation of Navajos in the L.A. car theft racket.

Both *Listening Woman* and *The Ghostway* have official law enforcement characters outside of the Navajo police force. Most of them follow the genre's convention of portraying police, other than the lead characters, as hostile or limited in their abilities. Such a portrayal obviously enhances the attainments of the detectives playing the lead and ensures that competition to be the first to solve a crime will be won by the figures readers have learned to like. Hillerman regularly uses the genre convention in presenting federal agents. In these two novels, however, there are exceptions to the norm. In Chapter Eleven of *Listening Woman* Leaphorn and Special Agent George Witover carry on a cagey conversation resulting in their agreement to share information. In *The Ghostway* Jim Chee reaches a similar understanding with Sergeant Willie Shaw of the Los Angeles arson squad when it becomes clear that they share a zeal about tracking down the Gormans.

PLOT DEVELOPMENT

Hillerman found three different models useful in creating the plot of *Listening Woman*. The first of these models derives from the inner logic of police procedural narratives, the second from action stories, and the third from the established practice of fiction about private-eye detectives.

When procedural fiction dramatizes the work of the police, the institution becomes an inescapable subject. The narrative can emphasize the importance of single officers or a squad of officers, but the simulation of reality (verisimilitude) demands reference to the larger agency that employs them. A superior officer, sometimes the police chief, other times a division chief, appears as an executive director of the investigation, and on occasions when the importance of the case requires it, a district attorney plays a role.

Through collective practice, the police amass a fund of technical knowledge about the commission of crime and its patterns greater than any single individual might be expected to obtain. Collectively, the police also create a battery of instruments and methods to acquire the evidence needed to solve crimes and prosecute offenders. Over time the knowledge and techniques become organized into guidelines for investigation. In the manner of all professional agencies, the police share the codified knowledge and the accompanying techniques through the training of new officers and a matrix of organization designed to create a means of cooperation among those who have developed specialties in types of crime or the kinds of possible investigation.

A police force thus takes the shape of a bureau with its own peculiar knowledge base and its own insiders' subculture. When it is replicated in detective fiction, the attributes of a police force mandate narrative progression. The account of the fictional crime must include representation of detection as in some way a combined effort by officers. More important still, the investigation will assume a methodical step-by-step movement reflecting the organization of police knowledge and techniques. Of course, that is why the type of story in the detective fiction genre that uses police officers is called a police *procedural.*

Because Tony Hillerman's detectives are police officers, their narratives embody essential attributes of the procedural. In *Listening Woman* Joe Leaphorn's interactions with Captain Largo and the FBI, the case files he has available to study, and his cooperative arrangement with Special Agent Witover show that the solution of crime is an institutional venture. Moreover, through much of the novel the narrative episodes are devoted to a search for evidence. Leaphorn's checking of watering places, for example, is followed by his review of case notes, and then by his listening to the tape of Margaret Cigaret's comments on the murder of Hosteen Tso and Anna Atcitty. He talks with McGinnis. He goes to Tso's hogan and back to McGinnis, and then to talk with Margaret Cigaret, and so on. The episodes form a sequence of investigation held together by the fact that, as his thoughts inform us, Leaphorn is processing information. Until Chapter Fourteen Leaphorn's procedure dominates the novel, subordinating external action to the mind of the detective executing his method.

To that point in the novel, the narrative about Leaphorn bears a family resemblance to other police procedurals such as Dell Shannon's stories of Lieutenant Luis Mendoza or Ed McBain's accounts of the cops in the 87th Precinct. As the novel moves into its final section, however, it becomes transformed into an action thriller more akin to the fiction of Dick Francis whose heroes commonly endure a physical test like the one Leaphorn faces in the lost cave.

The appeal of action thrillers may lie in their fantasy value for readers. Our dreams, if not enough of our lives, are filled with occasions when we confront and overcome danger, by physical agility or simply endurance, by our wits or by blessed chance. Action stories seem to resonate with these dreams, drawing us into narratives that allow us a vicarious test of our mettle and eventual triumph. However that may be, action plots in detective fiction generate suspense by subordinating the intellectual puzzle for a time to the physical problem of survival. That is the case and is Hillerman's evident intention in the final chapters of *Listening Woman.*

Lost in unfamiliar canyons and pursued by Goldrims, Leaphorn escapes with his life from a fiery trap only to get caught in the cave for three days and nights without food or water and with no sense of the direction of an exit. Each discovery he makes in the cave heightens the tension. When he finds a cache of food, he also discovers the makings for bombs. After he encounters Father Tso, he also learns the extent of the nefarious design of Goldrims—that it includes threats to the lives of the hostages and Theodora Adams and plans to kill his own brother and his loyal co-conspirators.

In a brilliant management of his model plots—the procedural and the action story—Hillerman accompanies each tense physical step with revelation of more information useful to solving the criminal puzzle, so that the possibility of revealing the solution to the puzzle becomes identical to Leaphorn's attempt to stop Goldrims before he brings his lethal plan to its explosive conclusion.

The novel ends with Leaphorn's successful frustration of Goldrims' plan, but it stops short of the resolution that might be expected in the logic of a procedural. Leaphorn leaves the ransom money in the cave; he does not return it to the owners. He evacuates the survivors from the cave to watch the explosion and leave the sand paintings behind an impenetrable wall, lost to the Navajos forever. He works out the final details of the puzzle in his mind, linking all of the once independent cases in a single solution. But he makes no report to anyone about it, and he sits close-lipped, keeping everything to himself, when Theodora tries to talk about Father Tso.

In other words, Leaphorn adopts the manner of a private detective in the finale. Where police procedurals often show detectives working realistically on cases that bear no direct connection to each other, all of Leaphorn's cases come together as they conventionally do in private-eye stories. Where police officers can be expected to present their solutions of criminal problems for further use by the prosecution or to close the files, Leaphorn behaves as though he were a loner following his own personal code and resisting intimate conversation in a self-protective reflex of withdrawal. He might as well be a detective from the mean streets of L.A., like Raymond Chandler's Philip Marlowe.

The parts Leaphorn plays in the plot of *Listening Woman*—private eye, police officer, action hero—are functional at different points in the narrative. Leaphorn's appearance in those guises manifests Tony Hillerman's inventive approach to plot in this novel. Accepting the framework of the detective genre as his given territory, he has taken the means for innovation from within the boundaries of the territory, amalgamated three types of genre story, and produced a fresh look at the detective figure.

Rather than combining story types and conventions, *The Ghostway* holds to a single way of presenting its plot while opening up the narrative to accommodate a subsidiary story. The seed that grew into *The Ghostway* germinated in the short story "Chee's Witch." It influenced the shape of *Dark Wind* and now can be seen again in the circumstances of the plot for the third Chee novel. The short story had Jim Chee telling an FBI agent about witch killings in response to the agent's query as to what Chee knew about a stranger newly arrived in the area. It develops that the stranger must be a City Navajo named Simon Begay hidden away in the Witness Protection Program until he is returned to Los Angeles to testify in a federal car theft case. The stranger has attracted gossip that he is a witch, and, in fact, there is a recent witch killing attributed to him. In the denouement of the brief story, Chee establishes that the circumstances of the killing were faked to appear to be a witchcraft murder, and he realizes that the Navajo newcomer is not Simon Begay at all, but an impostor whose testimony will more than likely taint the prosecution's case.

Because the Witness Protection Program is built upon changed identities and secrecy, it lends itself well to a puzzle plot. In the short story Hillerman hardly had room to do more than introduce the idea of replacing a witness with a plant to weaken the government's case, but, in *The Ghostway* he exploits it to the fullest by making a photograph of the witness a key piece of evidence, location of his trailer the object of a search, and confusion about his real identity the cause of Jim Chee's changing his mind several times about who Grayson/Gorman/Beno might be and how he figures in events surrounding Ashie Begay. Hillerman also picks up the car theft crime from the earlier short story to use as background for the protected witness, and in an inventive twist on the false witch killing motif, he introduces the death of Gorman at Ashie Begay's hogan as a perfectly ordinary result of his wounds. Only at the end of the novel does it become clear that death came to the hogan in the quite extraordinary mode of murder.

By expanding the material of his short story, Hillerman makes it available for a fully developed puzzle story. In keeping with the form, the novel supplies Chee with a puzzle that will loom over all of the actions he takes in the narrative. Moving deliberately in the fashion of a police officer following procedure, Chee pursues leads about the death of Gorman, diverts his attention to the missing girl Margaret Sosi, and discovers that she fits somehow into the original problem, too. The puzzle takes him to Los Angeles where he questions a witness to Gorman's activities, learns about the car theft case, and visits relatives of Begay. However far he travels, and no matter how complex the lines of evidence become, Chee is always led back to the original case on the Reservation. Like elastic, the puzzle extends outward with new inquiries, but only to show that new discoveries just betray additional information to redefine and restate the problem originally introduced by the shooting at the Wash-o-Mat.

While the plot of the novel takes its essential form from the classic puzzle pattern that is so often repeated in detective fiction, Hillerman's narrative accompanies the puzzle with a line of suspense about Jim Chee's relationship with Mary Landon. The relationship is a personal matter that pertains not at all to the detection process, except that Hillerman embeds thoughts of Mary into his indirect discourse reportage of Chee's progress.

The technique called indirect discourse associates the third-person narrative viewpoint with a particular character, making the exposition of the narration a report of a character's thoughts and feelings. It is discourse because it tells of the feelings and thoughts, and it is indirect because it is not the character but the voice of the novel speaking of those thoughts and feelings. The value of indirect discourse lies in the access it offers to the subjectivity of character. In detective fiction it can introduce the reader to the detective's reasoning process, convey glimpses of a killer's mentality, and provide readers a suspenseful experience of participation with the detective.

Indirect discourse acts to make a bond between readers and the subject of the discourse. We can identify with a character we know so completely. At the same time, we are aware that the subjectivity revealed by the narrative lays bare the character's identity. The subjectivity of a detective detecting exposes the sources of the detective's method and the values that motivate the investigation. If, then, the indirect discourse of narrative introduces extraneous matter, the reader has no choice but to consider it a significant insight into character. And so the passages in *The Ghostway* about Mary Landon expand the characterization of Chee. Jim Chee is no robot mechanically applying police procedure to a problem. He is a complex, feeling human being. His Navajo heritage affects his behavior and molds his self-image. There is every reason to think that his affectional life also has its influence, that it is finally not extraneous matter at all but part of his being a detective.

To dramatize the solution of the puzzle, Hillerman makes it occur during the sing for Margaret Sosi. In that traditional setting, amidst a ceremony performed to restore Margaret to harmony, Chee tugs at the puzzle, seeking to reduce it to order. With an epiphany of realization that there had been a switch of the protected witness, he fits the pieces together (278). In a drive to closure that will tie everything together, Hillerman, then, sets up a faceoff between Chee and Vaggan that ends with Margaret's shots. The puzzle is solved, the action concluded. All that remains to be done is close the subsidiary story of Mary Landon, which Hillerman does with a letter that leaves Chee uncertain of the future.

The tidiness of the novel's ending is characteristic of its lineage in puzzle stories. The symbolic detail of the setting, however, derives from Hillerman's wish to enrich the texture of the genre with the unique elements of Navajo culture and character. And the insertion of the subsidiary, if inconclusive, story of Mary Landon and Jim Chee into the plot of the narrative expresses Hillerman's conception of the indivisibility of character. One is not a detective *and* a Navajo, not a puzzle solver *and* a loving human being. As the plot of *The Ghostway* makes clear, one is everything at once.

THEMATIC ISSUES

A practiced reader of Hillerman's fiction knows that he seasons his texts with cultural information. Repeatedly, he shows that Navajo and

Anglo conversational habits differ: a Navajo will wait for someone to finish speaking and not interrupt, whereas an Anglo expects reassuring verbal evidence from the other party that someone is listening. In several novels, Navajos gesture with small movements of their lips. In none of the novels will custom or belief allow a Navajo to speak the name of a dead person. In *Listening Woman* we learn that Joe Leaphorn considers it rude to gaze directly into his face (85). The same novel informs readers about the Navajo taste for puns with an illustrative example (137).

Much more functional are such uses of Navajo culture as the sings that afford setting to Joe Leaphorn and Jim Chee in these two novels, while even more significant than the use of Navajo cultural detail to give density to the novels is Hillerman's use of cultural insight as integral to the plot of criminal problems. The unwashed hair of the corpse in *The Ghostway* is one example. Jim Chee's hesitation about entering a hogan inhabited by a *chindi* is another example. In both examples, the cultural beliefs delay progress of the story, adding mystery to the puzzle in the first instance and retarding discovery of evidence of Ashie Begay's murder in the second instance. At other times cultural information spurs the investigation. That is true of the story of Standing Medicine's sand paintings in *Listening Woman* and of the history behind Los Angeles Navajos in *The Ghostway*.

The pervasive presence of Navajo cultural beliefs in the characterization of Hillerman's detectives and the unrolling of his plots has inescapable thematic importance—namely, to demonstrate the influence of culture in constructing personality and sustaining community. The lesson of that requires restatement in a society where the name American encompasses so much and for some people omits so much. People are not products of abstractions but the living issue of the learned behaviors of selected communities. They can accommodate to more than one community; yet, they take their identity and nourishment from the particulars of life closest to them.

Recognition of the particulars—the *pluribus* in the national *unum*—recommended by the design of Hillerman's narratives yields the further observation that in the novels crime is often associated with characters whose roots in a community have been severed: by the teachings of the Commander and his later repudiation of his son in the case of Vaggans, or by forced relocation in the instance of City Navajos. A version of willful severing of roots is encompassed by the Navajo teachings about harmony and adaptation to nature and circumstances. A person living in disharmony, refusing to adapt, becomes a threat to the community; he or she is possibly a witch and certainly evil.

The reverse of the negative example of rootlessness occurs in the positive efforts of Joe Leaphorn and Jim Chee to act in accordance with their community heritage. Despite his dismissal of the prevalent beliefs in witchcraft, Leaphorn remains dedicated to his people, feeling deep pride in them and directing his talents and profession to their service. Similarly, the dilemma facing Jim Chee in regard to his future occupation and his marriage to a woman from outside the Reservation centers on the issue of cultural integrity: how he can be true to his core of identity.

In some of Hillerman's narratives the issue of culture directs readers toward specific questions of ethics, but in all of them, as in *Listening Woman* and *The Ghostway*, Navajo culture forms the fabric of place and society, affecting the craft of plotting and characterization and thereby wedding theme to every significant movement of the story.

READING *LISTENING WOMAN* AND *THE GHOSTWAY* AGAINST THE GENRE

What we see as the infusion of narrative craft with themes of Navajo culture in *Listening Woman* and *The Ghostway* has relevance to the master conventions of the detective fiction genre. In Chapter 2 of this book, it was observed that history produced the genre, and that it developed from the needs and values of Western urban society. The presence of a great detective, the method ascribed to the detective, the focus on the problem of crime—all of that can be traced to origins in ideology about property and individualism, as well as science and the superior place of males.

The form of a genre constructed from such material has room for variation within it, but surely there must be limits to revision. Can characters be accommodated in the genre if they belong to a group that has little reason to respect the law as it is applied in the majority society? What if an author chooses to write about life in neighborhoods where Western values, such as the Judeo-Christian tradition, seem alien, where acquisition of property is scorned?

The question of accommodation to a genre frequently comes up in the study of ethnic literature and in feminist criticism. An African-American author such as Richard Wright, for example, could write a novel in which the "hero" is a killer, his values are at odds with white society's, his identity is scorned, and the murders he commits form the route to self-fulfillment, which is the pattern of Wright's *Native Son* (1940). How should that work be viewed within the genre of the novel? Does it represent such a departure from the expectations embodied in conventions of the novel that it must be called something else, or could it be that Wright has deliberately transgressed the prevailing values of the middle-class novel in order to write *against* the genre? If the latter case is true, readers have to be alerted to what the novel typically expects at the same time as Wright violates the expectations. Rather than becoming another form altogether, the novel acts transgressively.

Feminist criticism also addresses the possibility of transgressive texts, since most literary genres have been dominated by the writing of male authors and, consequently, by male-centered views. Detective fiction is one such genre, and Kathleen Gregory Klein's *The Woman Detective* is an example of criticism that explores the likelihood of there being transgressive feminist texts.

With the novels of Tony Hillerman we are presented a case similar to that of ethnic writing and feminist writing. Hillerman innovates upon the form he receives from past writers by creating entirely different detectives and, as we have seen, by insinuating into his craft themes about the integrity of Native American culture.

His detectives are males, but after that similarity the differences stand out. Leaphorn and Chee are not white and are, not from the majority caste in the United States; rather, they are descendants of a despised and racially segregated people, inspired by a belief system that is at odds with the individualistic and property-centered views of Anglo-American culture. Objectively, they seem to have no reason to adhere to the law of white men, because the law has been employed over the years to oppress and harass the Native American population. An accomplishment venerated in their culture, like hunting, is a sport and not a ritual to the whites. The roles of importance to their culture—singers of ceremonial ways, listeners, crystal gazers—have no direct counterpart in the observances of whites.

It would be natural, one might think, for Hillerman to make his detectives players in transgressive texts where they defy white law and stand for their community in opposition to the white society. Some actions fitting the description of transgression can be found in the novels. In *Dark Wind* Chee cites a higher law to side with Hopis against placing a windmill on disputed ground. In *Dance Hall of the Dead*, Leaphorn walks away from an ethical situation that is more important to white anthropologists who study Indians than to the people who live as Indians. Possibly what he does at the end of *Listening Woman* might be construed the same way.

Certainly, too, the detectives time and again state their differences with white ways, as do secondary characters. When active, militant opposition to the Anglo government occurs in retribution for the lamentable past history of culture conflict, it is the work, however, of villains in *Listening Woman*, and Leaphorn's commitment to his professional work casts him as antagonistic to the Buffalo Society.

In that plot it can be said that Leaphorn's code of conduct, the ethics of behavior following from his professional position, is indistinguishable from the code of most detectives in the genre. The same must be said of Chee. Not only do the plots of the narratives dedicated to Chee conform to the pattern of genre puzzles, but also Chee's conduct follows the directions predictable from the established conventions.

This is not to say that Hillerman's characters are superficially ethnic in the way that Earl Derr Biggers's Charlie Chan impresses readers. Chan talks "funny" and spouts sayings he claims are Confucian, but otherwise he brings nothing into his texts that significantly relates to the culture of overseas Chinese in Hawaii. In contrast, Hillerman's Navajos are immersed in the culture that gives them identity. Still, their texts are not transgressive. They stay firmly within the traditions of the detective fiction genre, adapting conventions to the outline of Navajo life but not repudiating them. Anti-generic criticism fails to find subversion in these novels, but study with the lens of such criticism nevertheless tells us much about how extensive Hillerman's innovations are.

9

Skinwalkers
(1986)

In the publishing trade, a breakthrough book is one that gets taken up by readers who might not be expected to be its normal purchasers. Detective fiction sells well among the devoted fans of the genre and to the libraries frequented by them, well enough to make it a rare occurrence when a publisher loses money on a title. On the other hand, its audience remains limited to those with a developed taste for the stories of detection and mystery. Sometimes, however, a detection novel does become a best-seller, indicating that it has "broken through" the limits of its predictable readership. Synonymously, the publishing trade may call the phenomenon of a detective genre work landing on the best-seller lists a "crossover." This term has the same meaning for the book business that it has in the popular music game—that a new issue selling more than the predictable numbers has appeal across the boundaries of the niche where it at first seemed marketable.

For Tony Hillerman the gratifying breakthrough occurred with his 1986 novel *Skinwalkers* featuring the detective team of Lieutenant Joe Leaphorn and Sergeant Jim Chee. Besides earning him a place on best-seller lists for the first time, the book also won the award called a Spur from the Western Writers of America, which, in its way, also demonstrated appeal beyond the detective genre.

ETHNOGRAPHIC CONTEXT

Hillerman developed the subject material of *Skinwalkers*, as he does other novels in his series, from the cluster of Navajo beliefs surrounding witchcraft. In an essay also titled "Skinwalkers," he explains that, according to tribal tradition, a person becomes a witch by performing an action that reverses Navajo values, such as those regarding the family or the principle of harmony. Incest, murder of a relative, or handling a corpse can make one a witch, as can a penchant for excessive wealth. Navajo lore about witches includes tales about them trying to stop drivers, attacking livestock, and rattling around on the roof of a hogan. Witches, called *mai tso* (wolf man) in the Navajo language, can take animal forms, fly, or, as their alternate name *yenaldlooshi* (he who trots on all fours with it) suggests, they also can run incredibly fast on their mission of bringing sickness and evil to hapless Navajos. As Hillerman explains in an essay, witches serve in Navajo culture as they can in the Anglo American "as scapegoats, blamed when people get sick, cattle die, or accidents happen" (*Companion* 322–24).

Yet witchcraft appears in a much more particularized and elaborated way in the fictional Navajo world of Hillerman's novels than it does in contemporary Anglo-American culture where scapegoating is employed loosely at a distance that makes the scapegoat almost abstract, as when an alleged decline in moral probity is attributed to "those people," any group currently available for majority disapproval. In Hillerman's contemporary Navajo world, however, the witches are so specific that they assume the individual forms of known persons, even though they develop the ability to change their shape. They require ritual defense against their evil, like the literal removal of the bone bead a witch lodges in a victim's chest and the use of an intimate article from the witch for a ceremony to reverse the spell and kill the witch. Thus, witchcraft on the Reservation presents repeated instances where the distinction between good or proper behavior and evil may be personified for Navajos in a life-and-death contest with someone guilty of violating specific moral prohibitions. Discussion of the terms and stakes of the contest occupies pages of the studies written by the professional social scientists specializing in anthropological description of cultures or ethnography. After recording cases of witchcraft gathered through interviews, perhaps classifying them in relation to similar tales from other cultures, and tracing their distribution among people on the Reservation and their survival from generation to generation, the ethnographer attempts to draw conclusions about the function of witchcraft, and beliefs about it, in a society.

Some likely conclusions about the internal function of witchcraft may be illustrated from Hillerman's stories. Bergen McKee, the professor of anthropology in *The Blessing Way*, is at work on a book that develops the most common thesis about witchcraft, and the one Hillerman advances in his nonfiction essay, namely, that witchcraft among Navajos represents the scapegoat procedure of simplifying calamity by locating its source in a willful agent. In the novel *Skinwalkers*, Hillerman ascribes explanatory views about witchcraft to both Joe Leaphorn and Jim Chee. As Navajos who have studied ethnography in universities, Leaphorn and Chee are participant-observers; that is, they are native to the culture that creates the witchcraft beliefs and lore, but are trained also in the methods of objective investigation. Chee, the narrative says, has an agnostic attitude toward witchcraft. "Perhaps they did have the power, as the legends claimed and the rumors insisted, to become were-animals, to fly, to run faster than any car. On that score, Chee was a skeptic willing to accept any proof. But he knew witchcraft in its basic form stalked the Dinee." That basic form, Chee believes, can be seen "in people who had turned deliberately and with malice from the beauty of the Navajo way and embraced the evil that was its opposite." Among the examples in Chee's mind are people he has met in police work, those who sell whiskey to children or buy expensive consumer goods while their relatives are hungry (252–53). For Chee, then, witchcraft images evil, but it might be more than that. It could be an active force, such as would be embodied by the shape changers in the folk stories. The proof isn't conclusive yet for Chee. Leaphorn, by contrast with Chee, gives witchcraft no credence at all, considering it "a sick tradition . . . a cruel business" (152). An ethnographer would not treat witchcraft as emotionally as either Chee or Leaphorn does, at least not in their professional scientific writing, but the range of views to be found from McKee to the police officers are plausible suggestions of attitudes about the function of witchcraft.

The function of witchcraft in an actual society, however, is a different matter than the function witchcraft can perform in a portrayal of a society in fiction. Some of those possibilities for characterization are evident in the way witchcraft becomes a touchstone of distinctions among the "objective" Anglo professor McKee, probing for the universal pattern behind the particulars of Navajo beliefs; the reflective Navajo Jim Chee, searching in his inherited belief system for a model of the destructive behaviors he encounters in police work; and the angry Joe Leaphorn, identifying the vestigial belief in witchcraft, rather than the actions the belief purports to explain, as a source of social disorder.

For the writer of fictional detective mystery, played against a background of right and wrong, the setting of a society where belief in witchcraft remains viable provides richly dramatic possibilities regardless of the literal truth of the belief. A fictional story becomes a stand-in for reality, a representation of behavior and a simulation of events linked in such a way as to constitute an equivalent of reality. To develop the equivalent reality of fiction, the writer must find convenient and effective images to help readers interpret the meaning of the written word. Nothing is more convenient for the purpose than a metaphor, something that stands for itself and for something else at the same time. When the genre concerns good and evil, and the cultural setting includes belief in good and evil dramatized in the appearance of witchcraft, economical metaphor springs forth. Tony Hillerman exploits the possibilities of that metaphor so regularly in *Skinwalkers,* and his other Navajo novels, that he transforms the material of ethnographic writing into the substance for richly figured writing.

CHARACTER DEVELOPMENT

Before *Skinwalkers,* Hillerman had written, first, three novels about the adventures of Joe Leaphorn and, then, three novels featuring Jim Chee. Appropriately, his seventh Navajo novel brings the two sleuths together. Actually, happenstance explains the coupling more than planning, for, as we have seen in Chapter 1 of this book Hillerman does not plan his books in advance of writing them. He starts *Skinwalkers* with an attempt on Chee's life, but he needed to give the Sergeant a superior officer "and there was good old Joe Leaphorn on the shelf" (*Companion* 61). Alternatively, Hillerman explains that Leaphorn and Chee appear together because, earlier, a woman at a book signing told him that she couldn't tell his two detectives apart. In the spirit of showing his critical fan that there are indeed differences between the two, he put them together in *Skinwalkers* (Goodman 77).

In support of the differences between the two lead characters, Hillerman depicts an uneasiness between them. Chee's uneasiness derives from their incompatible attitudes toward religious belief. "Like a nonfundamentalist Christian, Chee believed in the poetic metaphor of the Navajo story of human genesis. Without believing in the specific Adam's rib, or the size of the reed through which the Holy People emerged into the Earth Surface World, he believed in the lessons such imagery was intended to teach" (75). To Chee at least, Leaphorn has no appreciation of the poetic value of Navajo cosmology. He had seemed contemptuous of Chee's explanation of why and how a bone bead had been shot at Chee. Depending on who you asked among the Navajo police, there were two explanations for Leaphorn's well-known intolerance of witch-craft belief, as we have noted: either he inherited the attitude from a great ancestor who railed against the belief in witchcraft as a cultural infection from the time of the Navajo captivity by the U.S. Army, or as a young officer he had misinterpreted rumors about witchcraft with the result that several people were killed. In any case, Leaphorn sharply separates religious views from the civil functions of the police. For that reason, he also warns Chee against any interference in the affairs of Dr. Bahe Yellowhorse, specifically Chee's telling people that Yellowhorse's crystal gazing is fakery (76).

The contrast between the two men can be seen as a contrast between the romantic and the realist. In his ambition to be a ceremonial singer, Chee hopes to sustain the traditional Navajo ways in a world now dom-inated by Anglo culture. In fact, his "nonfundamentalist" religious out-look that makes the old teachings into metaphors marks him as a person who frames his life poetically. Alternatively, Joe Leaphorn's medium is the prose of everyday life for which the most important lesson of Navajo history comes through the well-known ability of the Dinee (the People) to adapt to changed circumstances. Those circumstances include the rou-tines developed in police experience and practice. Such experience tells Leaphorn that despite Chee's denial of any known reason for someone shooting up his trailer in an attempt on his life, when a police officer is attacked, there is always a reason, and the officer must know it. This experience produced in Leaphorn the air of distrust that Chee sensed when they met about the attempted killing of Chee, and their interview did nothing to dissipate that sense. Possibly, though, there is even more to Chee's uneasiness than that. Possibly Chee is awkward before a man, who "in the small universe of the Navajo Police, total membership less than 120 sworn officers . . . was a Fairly Important Person, and somewhat of a legend" (73–74). Moreover, their respective places in the hierarchy of police organization present them with different responsibilities. Being a supervisor, Leaphorn oversees the progress of any number of cases in his territory. There are three homicides pending when he enters the novel in Chapter Two. Chee's assignments are more exclusive and, as a noncommissioned officer, he assumes responsibility at the direction of superior officers.

Allowing for the uneasiness between the two characters, resulting from their differing views about the order of Navajo society and their differing levels of command due to rank and length of service, they still work cooperatively to control the crimes that imperil order in the Navajo world.

A principle of identity-and-difference links the work of two men in their stories. Their identity arises both from the fact that each is a professional police officer and from the shape of their shared narrative as a police procedural. This type of story gains its name from the prominent part occupied by the learned routine of police work. Law enforcement officers are trained to interrogate witnesses, investigate the background of possible suspects, assemble evidence, and build a case. They learn by instruction and study the typical elements of crimes, and they acquire an ability to reason about crime from material and circumstantial evidence. Through repeated work on cases, they enlist a store of acquaintances available for interrogation and build a memory bank for the records of crime in their territories. With experience they also develop a repertory of techniques with which they perform their job: specialties in certain types of evidence, intuitive ways of thinking through cases, styles of research, and questioning. Collectively, all of these elements form the knowledge base for the discipline of law enforcement by professional police forces. What police procedure amounts to is practiced application of the knowledge base to specific crimes. Police procedural fiction relates a fictional version of that application, and is written largely from the perspective of police officers engaged in the routine of their work. Issues that appear larger from another perspective are subordinated to the account of the procedure, as are biographical details about the police characters indirectly involved with their work. Leaphorn's concern about his wife Emma's illness enters the story, because it affects his state of mind during the case. Emma herself, however, is not a character because she is neither a police officer nor implicated in the case of *Skinwalkers*.

Within the framework of a police procedural, room for difference appears in the repertory of the officers, the ways they express themselves in following the routine protocol. At one point in Chapter Eight, Leaphorn mildly corrects Jim Chee's manner of reporting. He has "a funny way of working," he explains to Chee. He doesn't want a selective report of what another officer thinks are the important details. He wants all of the details, so he can sort them out himself. Feeling slightly resentful,

Chee amplifies his report, with the result that Leaphorn can see a connection between one case of homicide and another (106–107). Leaphorn, it seems, is not simply an executive supervisor of police. He is a detective, too, with a methodical way of working all his own.

In a passage late in the book, in Chapter Twenty, Hillerman gives Chee's own distinctive style of proceeding on a case a featured place. Stepping out of his truck at a spot where a calculated ruse has brought him, we are told that he senses a smell missing from the damp air. Using the absence of an odor as the occasion for expanding the characterization of Chee, Hillerman takes advantage of the third-person narrative point of view to tally the strengths and weaknesses of his intelligence. He has "a superb memory," but "a tendency to exclude new input while [his intelligence] focused too narrowly on a single thought, a tendency to be distracted by beauty, and so forth." Yet, the dreamer's disposition is accompanied by "an ability to process new information and collate it with old unusually fast. In a millisecond," we are told, Chee "identified the missing odor, extracted its meaning, and homogenized it with what he had already noticed," so that his "brain identified an assortment of explanations," which "changed him, midstride" from a contented man to a very apprehensive one (246–47).

Chee's intuitive quickness in this episode saves his life at the same time that it discovers the explanation of the earlier attempt on his life in Chapter One. The whole demonstration sets him off as a unique police officer, but not necessarily a more effective one than Joe Leaphorn. Leaphorn's more comprehensive processing of information about the homicides also yields a moment when he sees "how it all had worked" as "a single cluster at the Badwater Clinic," and he races in his car to conclude the case before it leads to further death (267).

In confirming the idea that, despite their different approaches to their police work, Leaphorn and Chee share an identity through their mutual participation on the cases, Hillerman provides Chee an independent solution of the interconnected cases. Because he had antagonized Dr. Yellowhorse by warning clients away from the clinic, the angry doctor seeks vengeance on Chee, which in the event leads him to make a self-justifying confession of the murders to Chee before drugging him. Completing the formula of identity between the officers, Hillerman brings Leaphorn on the scene in Chee's hospital room, just as the aggrieved mother, who had originally shot at Chee in Chapter One because she had been told by Yellowhorse that he was a witch, finally gets it right and uses her shotgun to execute the "real" witch and stop Dr. Yellowhorse's string of homicides. For the novel *Skinwalkers* at least, the character development of Lieutenant Joe Leaphorn and Sergeant Jim Chee is also summarized in this episode of convergence.

While attitude and style of procedure contribute the most to the characterization of Joe Leaphorn and Jim Chee, other details are worth noting for their elucidation of Hillerman's craft. One such detail is the physical appearance of the two men. Leaphorn has the physique typical of the "Checkerboard type" of Navajo, a genetic mix with Pueblo people that gets its designation from origin on that portion of the Reservation where tribes were settled on alternate squares of land. By contrast, Chee physically belongs to the unmixed category of "Tuba City Navajo": tall, long torso, broad shoulders (53). The men may think of themselves in these categories derived from anthropological classification, because the Reservation lands have long been hunting grounds for ethnologists and both of them studied anthropology in their university days. But Hillerman's application of the shorthand designations is of a piece with their presentation as characters straddling the Anglo and Navajo cultures with the effect of gaining the ability to see their people as both objects of study—Indians—and as subjects capable of study for themselves.

Other personal details of characterization serve quite other functions. References to Leaphorn's wife Emma appear in the narrative in an entirely instrumental way. Fear that she may have Alzheimer's disease (208) and a ray of hope when she turns out to have a tumor instead (262–63) intrude upon Leaphorn's mind. Without doubt, he feels deeply about Emma, but since she is otherwise missing from the narrative, her exclusive role as a character is to provide Leaphorn with a biography and to humanize him. His use of the California AAA map of "Indian Country" is apparently another personal detail of Leaphorn's to meet other purposes. Leaphorn's devotion to his map, much like Hillerman's own approval of it, is well known among the police as one of his trademarks. More than a matter of taste, however, the map, marked with Leaphorn's coded pins, gives readers an exposition of outstanding cases as he scans the homicide sites. Is there a connection among the killings? The fact that they can be charted on a single map denoting the landscape of the territory foreshadows the eventual discovery that, indeed, they are connected. In the meanwhile, Leaphorn's use of the map provides a telling indicator that he approaches criminal cases with an eye for the big picture.

Most of the personal, secondary details of Chee's character appear in the opening chapter. There his spartan living arrangements in a trailer and his fondness for an abandoned cat show his desire for a life of harmony with his physical surroundings. Chee's style of living appears as incidental detail in the opening chapter, subordinate to the narration of an attack on his life. But when the reader learns the crucial information about his ambition to be a singer of the Blessing Way and other ceremonials, his choice of living quarters turns out to be entirely consistent and thus reinforces the portrayal of his unique character. Similarly, the mail Chee receives in Chapter Eleven, incidental as it may seem, helps to personalize him. One letter is from Alice Yazzie asking him to perform a sing, which would be his second job in that role. This is good reason for him to feel elated and to dress up for the occasion when he goes to meet Alice. His second letter comes from Mary Landon, an Anglo school teacher he became fond of in the earlier novel *People of Darkness*. Readers familiar with that work will appreciate Chee's disappointment when he reads that Mary, who had returned home to Wisconsin promising to keep up her relationship with him, has started graduate school and won't be able to visit for months yet. But even those readers whose acquaintance with Mary is limited to her brief letter (145–46) will find its arrival useful to their understanding the man who participates in two cultures. He maintains emotional ties in both the Navajo world, where Chee wishes to assume a traditional ceremonial position, and the Anglo world that includes a woman whose use of the salutation "Dearest Jim," rather than "Darling" brings him sorrow.

Like other Hillerman novels, *Skinwalkers* is populated with a group of second- and third-string characters whose appearance results from functional necessity, but whose portrayal also presents the complex and peculiar mix of people history has brought to Indian Country. Iron Woman, the daughter of Lizzie Tonale and Isaac Ginsberg, runs her parents' trading post, which they built at great distance from Lizzie's family in Backwater Wash after she converted to Judaism. Iron Woman appears in the novel facilitating Chee's investigations when he comes for information about one of the killings (79ff). John McGinnis, proprietor of the Short Mountain Trading Post, performs the same task for Joe Leaphorn (210ff). Iron Woman and McGinnis make up part of the information circle that police procedure requires of every officer. Proving their worth in that function, both give the visiting detectives useful leads.

Characters such as the Councilwoman from Canoncito and Dr. Jenks play smaller but important roles. The Councilwoman registers complaints that typify the mundane routine of Leaphorn's police work and is otherwise in the novel to present an example of a tribal politician (15–

17). Dr. Randall Jenks is known to Leaphorn as an "Indian Lover," by which Leaphorn means a patronizing do-gooder, and his functional role, other than representing his type, is to provide clinical information (93–102). As in any detective novel, such characters, so to speak, fulfill the author's contract of realism with readers. To gain our credence, a writer simulates reality: the setting of a story is particularized by reference to its physical layout, dialogue is rendered in a version recognizable as the way people actually speak, and the detective will encounter other characters who are plausibly like unique human beings, however briefly they appear. The skill with which a writer executes the contract of realism in regard to character can be measured, first, by the economy with which the encounter is accomplished and, second, by what may be termed the "surplus value" of the character—that is, what the secondary character contributes to the narrative by way of typifying the world of the novel or through the inherent interest of the minor character. By these measures, Tony Hillerman usually comes up a winner.

Two other secondary characters deserve mention here. Dr. Yellowhorse, charlatan and the eventual villain of the piece, earns attention because his career presents the ethical theme of the novel. Janet Pete, who appears very briefly as a lawyer for Roosevelt Bistie in Chapter Nine, is of interest because of her resemblance to Jim Chee. She, too, faces the problem of sustaining loyalty to the People while undertaking a profession sponsored by the world outside. Intuitive readers might anticipate the possibility of Janet Pete replacing Mary Landon in Jim Chee's affections. They will be correct to do so, but for conclusive evidence readers must read a few more Hillerman novels.

PLOT DEVELOPMENT

Authors of police procedurals in the detective fiction genre practically have the plots of their narratives predetermined. The skeleton of the plot is taken from the fund of established police operations and move step by step to a conclusion. Distinctive styles of detection, within the outline of familiar procedure, and the novelty of the crimes flesh out the story. Still, there remains opportunity for creativity, enough so that sometimes it makes sense to abandon the image of a skeleton being dressed for different scenes in favor of an image arising from the author's peculiar vision of procedure in the novel.

That's the case with *Skinwalkers* where, in place of a skeleton, we might imagine the plot as parallel tracks. Hillerman's use of two detectives to carry his story explains the parallelism. The layout of the tracks over varying terrain explains the different rates of motion. And the readers' location above or between the tracks, able to turn attention from one track to the other until they jointly terminate at the same station, suggests how we experience the plot.

First, Jim Chee appears in the narrative, awakening slowly from his night's sleep when he hears the cat clatter through the pet door, and becoming alert when suddenly shots through his trailer startle him, making his mind race. A contrasting tempo marks Joe Leaphorn's appearance on his track of the plot. Ready to start but held up by bureaucratic requirements to meet with visitors to the bureau, and stymied by homicides that cannot yet be charted as a single case, he is slow to begin on the central case and feels that he is wasting motion.

Through his use of a third-person narrative voice, Hillerman puts his audience in position to follow both detectives and to discover that, while Chee and Leaphorn take individual routes through the detection procedure, the information they uncover separately pertains in the long run to both investigations. In that respect, the plot may be said to increase the efficacy of the investigation in exactly the way the assignment of a police force to a case, rather than a single agent, intends to do. The duality of a plot devoted to two detectives doubles the efficiency of investigation.

Yet, that sort of description of the plot of *Skinwalkers* is still not entirely adequate, for the evidence needed to solve the criminal problem does not lie quietly awaiting discovery, like information in reference books. In that case, two readers searching for data would be vastly more efficient than one. Police work is active investigation, however, for the reason that it involves acquiring evidence about the behavior of human beings capable of intelligent changes in their course and deceptive movement in response to the detectives. We find this to be true when Hillerman employs the third-person narrative briefly, in Chapter Four, to relate the thoughts of the aggrieved mother who shot at Chee. Someone has told her that he is the witch responsible for her child's anencephaly. Thus, it seems that, despite Chee's ignorance of a motive for the attack on him, he somehow has provoked it, and, because he did not die in the first attack, will provoke more assaults. Once the point has been made, the rest of the text consistently supports the fact that criminal investigation is akin to hunting, as the Navajo detectives see it in Hillerman's novels. Indeed, the detectives' object is to capture a cunningly animate creature who can respond to threatened discovery by diversion and counter-threat. This quality of detective investigation adds suspense to the plot of reasoning and police procedure as the stakes involved in solving the crime rise with the danger the detectives encounter.

That suspense and the parallel tracks of detection constitute the creative alteration Hillerman makes in the predetermined plot of the police procedural. Step-by-step progress may still be found in the plot, but by dispersing the evidence between two detectives, who sometimes work more independently than as a team, Hillerman slows down movement toward a conclusion that might otherwise seem too swift. This detective has some of the evidence, that one the rest of it; this one follows one set of leads, that one another set of leads. Only the reader has access to all the available information all of the time, and it is the reader, therefore, who experiences the satisfying tension of hoping and waiting for it all to come together within the detectives' consciousness, too.

THEMATIC ISSUES

The leading thematic concern of *Skinwalkers* is ethical. Hillerman prepares for the emergence of the theme by presenting Leaphorn and Chee as characters whose identities have been created through examination of the values they believe ought to motivate their lives. While they differ, for example, in their interpretations of witchcraft, each man discerns the meaning of witchcraft in moral terms: for Chee witchcraft signifies the appearance of evil in Navajo life, and for Leaphorn witchcraft, as a vestige of captivity, distorts the Navajo's capacity to deal with calamity in a realistic way.

The eventual implications of morality as a theme remain suspended, however, until the full exposure of Dr. Yellowhorse. Upon his first appearance when he lodges complaints about Chee with Leaphorn in Chapter Two, Yellowhorse seems to be a slippery customer. Leaphorn and Chee take differing positions about how to deal with him, but again each man bases his position on a moral outlook. Leaphorn derives his perspective from a constitutional principle of separation of responsibility for religious activity into a category distinct from responsibilities of government agencies such as the police, whereas Chee's position arises from a sense of duty to the People, to protect them against charlatans.

While the detectives are straightforward in their morality, Yellowhorse moralizes in his speech of self-justification to Chee in a way that deserves the term *sophistry*. Like the ingenious and misleading practice of the Sophists, Yellowhorse's reasoning twists and turns the relationship between means and ends so that he justifies killing as a way of protecting life and fraud as a way of securing legitimate financial support.

Yellowhorse's self-justification cannot be judged by logic, rhetoric, or morality alone. Hillerman makes sure of that by having Yellowhorse display in his act of confession the same arrogance that motivated him to commit murder. Thoughts are tested by the actions they produce; that's the message of this "skinwalker" case. For the villain, exaggerated thoughts about his service to the community result in his betraying Navajo beliefs, by misuse of crystal gazing and abuse of witchcraft, and finally in the taking of life. For the detective heroes, however, their reasoning about values motivates them to the genuine service of maintaining peace and order within the Navajo community.

A FEMINIST READING OF *SKINWALKERS*

Skinwalkers can be read from the perspective of a feminist critic, even though it features so few women as major characters. Feminist criticism, however, encompasses more than just characterization and the genders attributed to characters. Feminist readers also look to the implied values of narrative, the possible stress on a male way of life which typically is taken to mean a life of aggressive dominance, and the emphasis on male, but not female, participation in public arenas exercising power. They note, too, as Carolyn Heilbrun puts it in her book *Writing a Woman's Life*, that women's stories in our culture are framed as narratives of private emotion ending in marriage, just where men's stories can be expected to begin. In our reading, then, we often fail to find female participants when the narrative becomes one of adventure or public deeds. In other words, in our efforts at literary criticism, what is absent can be as important as what is present. And female absence becomes all the more striking when we think of the novels of Tony Hillerman who has done so much to replace absence with presence when it comes to the subject of Native Americans and their culture.

Much of American writing makes no mention at all of Native Americans, much less Navajos, but that hardly constitutes evidence that Native Americans do not figure in American culture. Rather, the absence of Native Americans from most of the widely promoted works of American literature, including those in the detective fiction genre, tells us that,

by and large, people of color are "other" than important. They are the
losers in a history of struggle over settlement of the North American
land. They are confined on Reservations, or perhaps they predominate
in the underclass of poor people. They live apart from the majority, or
so it seems; they are the other. Hillerman's detective fiction has done a
lot to make up for the exclusion of Native Americans from crime and
police stories and to make them integral subjects of the genre. But
women who are also treated as "others" do not fare as well.

As we have seen in the analysis of characterization in *Skinwalkers,*
women play secondary roles. References to Emma Leaphorn work to
characterize her husband more than to present her plight. Iron Woman
and the Councilwoman appear only very briefly and in roles instrumental to purposes apart from their own characters. Only Janet Pete takes
an active role in the story. While that holds promise for subsequent novels when the relationship between Pete and Chee becomes developed,
her place in *Skinwalkers* remains decidedly secondary.

Some of the women characters are admirable. Janet Pete is a confident
professional who serves her client well. Iron Woman has become a
source of community in her isolated part of the Reservation, and the
Councilwoman does a capable job of advocacy, even while Leaphorn
dismisses her complaint as old news. Still, there are so few women in
Skinwalkers that its world seems almost entirely male. Where is the other
half of the population?

An explanation, though not an excuse, might be found in the history
of the detective fiction genre. A feminist critic, concerned that we understand how history has been shaped by the politics of gender, might
give an exposition such as the following: in societies sharply divided
along gender lines, as American and European societies were when the
detective genre first appeared, law enforcement and science were male
preserves; philosophical training and advanced study in the sciences
were accessible much more to males than females. Thus, women would
have been rare in the fields that helped create fictional detectives.

Nevertheless, women authors have not been entirely passive about
their exclusion from the popular detective genre. The American writer
Anna Katherine Green, publishing from 1878 until 1923, and her contemporary, the British novelist Mary Elizabeth Braddon, publishing from
1862 until 1899, created some of the most popular detective novels of
their time. Louisa May Alcott, perhaps the epitome of the female author
in works such as *Little Women*, also made a respectable showing in the
popular market for thriller stories. Despite this accomplishment, the

genre found its template in stories where a male detective presides, and its kin in worldly adventure stories rather than in the domestic tales of the Brontes.

Kathleen Gregory Klein, one of the most perceptive analysts of the genre, makes clear in *The Woman Detective* that the deep structure of detective genre stories has until recently embodied an approach to reality that reflects ideas about masculinity. In other words, as the male dominance in Western society created the conception of disparate genders, one superior and the other subordinate to it, and the derivative ideas of appropriate work, behavior, expression, and realms of activity for each gender, the historically created genders also expressed attitudes that enforce gender separation.

Given such a background for the detective fiction genre, it takes unusual effort for a male author to produce detective fiction that comfortably accommodates women characters and the cultural experiences of women. Increasingly, male authors should find new possibilities for the genre in portrayal of female characters, but many works remain, *Skinwalkers* among them, displaying the vestiges of a masculine history of the genre.

10

A Thief of Time
(1988)

Asked in a recent interview if he has a personal favorite among his books, Hillerman without hesitation named *A Thief of Time*. "That would be my pet," he said (*Companion* 63). His publishers showed their own enthusiasm for the book by printing 75,000 first-edition hardcover copies (*Publisher's Weekly*, 27 May 1988) compared to the 30,000 copies they issued for the first edition of the "breakthrough" *Skinwalkers* (*Publisher's Weekly*, 28 November 1986). Distribution of *A Thief of Time* as a Book-of-the-Month Club offering and a Quality Paperback Book Club selection further broadened the book's popular appeal.

Eighth in publishing order within the series about the Navajo Tribal Police, *A Thief of Time* for the second time brings together in a single narrative Hillerman's sleuths, Lieutenant Joe Leaphorn and Sergeant Jim Chee. Each of them is at a critical moment in his personal life but nonetheless displays his distinctive detective abilities at their height. Adding to its intrinsic attraction, the novel also provides one of Hillerman's most accessible statements about Native American culture. As the book's title resonates in our reading, we come to see that the illicit trade in ancient pots and other artifacts, which forms the subject of the criminal plot, also signifies a thematic issue of the appropriation of the materialized record of a people's time on the North American continent, a theft of their history.

GENRE INVENTION AND CONVENTION

The memorable scene in Chapter Twelve when Joe Leaphorn interviews the rich New York City collector Richard DuMont, who owns a
classically perfect example of Anasazi ceramics, makes an intriguing
comment on the appeal of mystery stories. Leaphorn has arranged for
his meeting with DuMont after great difficulty persuading Nelson's,
dealers in Fine American Indian Art, to suspend their practice of keeping
the identity of clients confidential. Only his insistence that it is a matter
of Dr. Friedman-Bernal's life or death has gotten him an appointment.
Arriving at DuMont's Seventy-eighth Street address, Leaphorn finds that
he will yield the information Leaphorn seeks to document the origin of
his pot only in return for the whole story of the events surrounding
Friedman-Bernal's disappearance, the death of the two pot hunters,
everything.

Leaphorn had already found DuMont unpleasant. He seems all the
more so after explaining that he is in the market for grim stories of
sacrifice as well the objects that line his shelves. There is something
ghoulish about DuMont's professed wish to tell his friends about "murder and a missing woman" when he shows them his pot. He must have
a story to go with the pot, "details, details, details . . . all the bloody
details. The details to pass along" (198). When Leaphorn concludes that
the document showing the origin of the pot is false, DuMont's peculiar
humor remains unaltered. He had heard already from Dr. Friedman-
Bernal that the document was false, and continued "grinning his small
white grin." When Leaphorn leaves, DuMont sadistically asks him to
call "with all the details. When you find her body" (202).

If Hillerman meant by his portrayal of Richard DuMont to make readers who thrill to the stories of violence in mysteries uneasy, he suc-
ceeded. That effect is incidental, however, a kind of insider's joke about
the addiction to crime narratives. Much more important is Hillerman's
intention to develop a cameo role for an evil villain. DuMont is not
directly responsible for crimes in the novel, nor is he especially illicit in
building his artifact collection. He is, however, a man of wealth, which
accords him the power to make the pain of others the subject of his
entertainment. Behaving with inhuman detachment, he appropriates objects of culture for his amusement, severing them from their roots in a
civilization. As DuMont says, material possession does not satisfy his
acquisitiveness. The items he buys must become objects of his ego.

DuMont belongs to a lineage of villains that stretches from Arthur Conan Doyle's Professor Moriarty forward. Psychologically abnormal, he serves like other members of his family of villains to demonstrate behavior that is nearly inexplicable in terms of ordinary motivation, behavior that therefore becomes a manifestation of old-fashioned evil. In that regard, DuMont represents Hillerman's use of an indispensable convention of detective fiction.

DuMont's residence in New York City reminds us that crime fiction is ordinarily associated with metropolitan locations—the impersonal and densely peopled streets where anything might happen and the famed cities where whatever does happen is usually engaging. Crime is an urban phenomenon, as revealed by most of the examples we know. Despite stories about marshals pacifying Western towns, we also consider protection of the social order to be the more likely challenge in places where life seems most disorderly and thereby sometimes glamorous. Richard DuMont from Seventy-eighth Street, New York, fits the expectations of readers of the genre, but only as an exception in the body of Hillerman's fiction set on the Navajo Reservations.

Routine and sometimes stunning crime on Indian Reservations, and crime sufficient in occurrence to provide careers for professional Navajo detectives—could that prove possible? It hardly seems likely based on casual thought about the conventions of locale in detective fiction. The essence of stories about crime and its solution, however, derives from portrayals of disrupted order. Crime represents a break in the routine of expectation. Crime is a shock demanding explanation or solution, which once accomplished returns conditions to their original normative state. Any setting might do for that.

In fact, traditional societies such as the Navajo, characterized by elaborate clan relationships that determine identity and govern personal interaction through a system of prohibitions and obligations, deeply value social stability. Violations, even those not accorded designation as crimes in legal statute, are serious business requiring ritual healing to restore harmony. Such emphasis on order makes the Navajo homeland a natural setting for narratives of order broken, order restored. The open spaces of Arizona and New Mexico are sparsely populated and starkly contrasting with the familiar urban locale of crime fiction, but from Hillerman we discover that no setting has greater dependence upon the inherent pattern of crime literature. Hillerman's recognition of this idea is a mark of his brilliant fictional conceptions, and the fact that his inventive variation on the convention of setting has proven so singular makes its impact all the greater.

A similar naturalness and invention characterizes Hillerman's creation of his detectives in the Navajo world where the decorum of relationships requires care for propriety and where the geography demands a refined capacity for "reading" signs. Many Navajos, Leaphorn and Chee among them, are bilingual in their spoken discourse. All the Navajo, however, for their own survival must know the language of weather and topography and movement in the landscape. They are always decoding and tracking clues. The officers employed by the tribal police are unusually skillful in the methods mandated by Navajo life, as well by the conventions of the detective fiction genre.

In *A Thief of Time*, Hillerman innovates still further in the genre by including the development of problems associated with the sciences of anthropology and archaeology. Scientists in these disciplines are common figures in Indian Country, and, of course, they are themselves detectives, forming and testing hypotheses about the causes of events and assembling evidence to produce the order of an historical explanation. Starting his narrative with an archaeological quest and resolving the disappearance of Eleanor Friedman-Bernal through explanation of the significance for Randall Elliott of the genetic evidence he gathered by betrayal of Eleanor, Hillerman creates a parallel story of investigations to accompany and reinforce the detectives' central investigation into crime. It is an obvious convention of detective fiction to stress the methodical application of investigative procedure. Detectives are known as much for their methods of detection as for their personal attributes. With his parallel investigations in *A Thief of Time*, Hillerman trumps the convention, for Leaphorn and Chee are not only police detectives. They also have been trained in universities in the detection methods of anthropology, so that they are equally at home in and equally in command of each investigation.

CHARACTER DEVELOPMENT

In the manner typical of the formal detection story, *A Thief of Time* focuses on the explanation of the crime by the agents of order and thus presents the detectives as its featured players. Leaphorn and Chee are, first of all, representative of community will and values. They are the long arm(s) of the law. At the same time, however, Leaphorn and Chee are individualized characters much more than they are allegories for good versus evil.

In Leaphorn's case, the death of his wife from a brain tumor has taken the savor from life and satisfaction out of police work. For nearly thirty years he had been married to Emma, whom he met at Arizona State University, and had happily lived with her as she followed the traditional Navajo Way. The intimacy of her companionship had anchored him, even though he found less satisfaction in living tradition than she did. For example, his formal education, which includes the beginning of work on a Ph.D. in cultural anthropology, has disposed him to take an observer's attitude toward culture, such as the Navajo lore about witches, rather than the participant's accepting belief. Indeed, the scholarly approach to life he has found suitable to his disposition makes him deeply interested in religion in the way a comparative social scientist would be. He has also become an advocate of Navajo people in the fashion of an intellectual who senses his developed differences from folk ways.

In *A Thief of Time*, Leaphorn follows an arc of recovery from grief. Emma's death has disoriented him. He could not stay for the complete period of mourning prescribed by tradition and may come to regret that. The house is empty and lonely without Emma, reminding him of the wisdom in the Navajo practice of vacating a home once occupied by the dead. He becomes sensitive to the ways other men live alone, either obsessively tidy or in a mess. Lamenting his loss of Emma, he plans at the opening of the novel to retire from police work—he is so tired. It is as though he must uproot himself. As the narrative progresses, however, Leaphorn passes from despair through grief and mourning. Recollection of his past with Emma assists his passage, as does resolve to make some small changes, such as sleeping on the other side of the bed so that he will not awaken and look for Emma each morning. Therapy arrives for him as he becomes engaged in the puzzle of the disappearance of Dr. Friedman-Bernal and, then, as he reacquaints himself with Harrison Houk whom he had met twenty years before on the lurid case when Harrison's son Brigham had murdered his siblings. Once again police work has come to the center of his consciousness.

For the reader who has met Leaphorn in earlier novels, the unfortunate experience of his grief offers a view of him in continuing development. For the reader meeting Leaphorn for the first time, however, there is little sense that crucial information about his character has to be discovered in other texts. He is a fully realized character in the present novel. Through a functional use of Leaphorn's state of mind, Hillerman elicits

memories of student days with Emma and Leaphorn's earlier police career. For instance, while talking with Mrs. Luna in Chapter Ten about
Eleanor Friedman-Bernal's theory of the Ansazi potter, Leaphorn feels a
sense of pleasure ignited by Mrs. Luna's comment that, although she has
not yet published her findings, Ellie "has it pinned." It reminds Leaphorn of his graduate student days when he must have heard classmates
using the same words. He generalizes in his mind about "the human
animal's urge to know. To leave no mysteries. 'To understand the human
species,' [as] his thesis chairman liked to say." That was the same year,
he recalls, that he decided he could understand the species "better
among the living," had met Emma, and left graduate school (166).

The passage about method is quite illustrative. Tying memory of the
past to the present, revealing character, and character's feeling along
with it, it also shows the linkage of scientific and police investigations
we noted earlier in discussing the novel and genre convention. All of
that supplies the foundation of the detection method Leaphorn uses in
the remainder of the novel. By disposition and training he is a rationalist,
we see, who works by reasoning his way through possibilities to prob-
abilities. Disciplined and patient enough to visit and revisit crime scenes
in search of evidence, he methodically traces leads—all the way to New
York in one instance and down San Juan River in a kayak in another—
to gather evidence for conclusive inferences in solution of the criminal
puzzle. In short, Leaphorn's detection method is as much an expression
of self as it is the routine of police work. Inserting information about
that method into scenes originating as presentations of Leaphorn's memory, plausibly evoked by his feelings for Emma, shows how extraordinarily functional Hillerman's writing can be. By no means is the
biographical matter of Leaphorn's life appended to the narrative, as
though it appears just because verisimilitude seems to require it. Instead,
it is entirely integral to establishing the premises of character and story.

Jim Chee's detection method contrasts with Leaphorn's in this novel
as in the others but is just as integral. Chee is studying to be a singer,
that is, a person who performs traditional healing ceremonies. His study
requires that he memorize chants, learn rituals, practice the art of sand
painting—all the artful techniques of Navajo culture. His study originates in his devotion to the traditional beliefs from which Leaphorn
seems to have departed. In Chapter Seven Chee takes a sweat bath. At
the site of the killings in Chapter Nine, he is uneasy about the presence
of chinle (spirits of the dead). Neither scene would be appropriate for
Leaphorn. Chee, like his colleague, is university educated, but study in

the Anglo world has not distanced him entirely from sympathetic involvement in Navajo belief. Aptly, Chee's personality manifests itself in a detection method dependent on sympathetic involvement in human ways and culture. He can imagine himself a part of the events he investigates.

The critical point Chee has reached in his personal life relates to love and marriage. He had loved Mary Landon, an elementary school teacher from Wisconsin, and wanted her to marry him and live on the Reservation. Her contrary hope was that he would become an FBI agent and join her in the mainstream (i.e., white) world. As has been true in previous novels, the relationship with Mary reflects Chee's problem of identity. In *A Thief of Time,* he is deciding that he cannot go with Mary, partly because her absence weakens his tie to her and partly because she is adamant about following her own path in life. But he is also thinking of Janet Pete, the Navajo woman lawyer who displays a sympathetic interest similar to his own in cultural roots.

Readers soon notice that most of the characters in *A Thief of Time* can be analyzed in terms of their relationship to cultural roots. In the case of Richard DuMont we have the absence of roots, and in the case of the presiding detectives we have individuals whose connections to their past inform their present lives and detection methods. In addition, there is a range of secondary characters whose lives in the novel are involved with an active interest in the past. Jimmy Etcitty and Joe B. Nails, victims of murder at an illegal dig, are characters for whom heritage is available for exploitation, perhaps because Etcitty is a so-called City Navajo who was not raised in the Dinetah (among the People) and because Nails is not characterized at all. Slick Nakai, the evangelist and dealer in salvaged and possibly stolen pots, lives, as it were, between worlds. He is a Christian preaching on the Reservation, taking remuneration in pots but selling the historical objects as commodities.

Then there are the anthropologists. Dr. Friedman-Bernal whose disappearance begins the novel enters the narrative in person while in a coma, but by reputation she is a character respectful of the past. She is, in fact, actively working to recover the past and to make it vitally alive. The junior anthropologists, Randall Elliot and Maxie Davis, are considerably more developed in the novel, although like most secondary characters, they are presented with singular rather than multiple traits. Elliot's rivalry and affection are founded in social class. Mrs. Luna explains this at the same time as she tells Leaphorn about Eleanor's project. Elliot is a child of privilege, and Maxie, a self-made woman, won't let him forget it. Other passages of the novel, notably Chapter Six where Elliot and Maxie assist Leaphorn's examination of Friedman-Bernal's apartment and talk about their relationship to her, make it clear that both of these scientists are very capable in their respective work as population specialist and cultural anthropologist. Chapter Six also establishes the motive for Elliot's crime, his desperate hope to accomplish something that neither Maxie nor anyone else could explain as the gift of his privileged station.

Hillerman's skill in rendering secondary characters is at its best in the presentations of Harrison Houk and his son Brigham Houk. They appear only briefly in the narrative, even though both play important roles in leading to the discovery of Eleanor, but they occupy their scenes unforgettably. Brigham the schizophrenic has become arrested in his development by a near lifetime as a hermit that has made him an entirely unsocial creature of the wild, a kind of Tarzan as a mental case. Harrison has remained in the world, but his concealment of the fact that his son survived an apparent drowning after killing his siblings has given him a split personality in a way, too. There is Harrison's facade: honest, a pillar of the Mormon Church. Then there is his secretive self as the support of his fugitive son.

PLOT DEVELOPMENT

In Chapter Nine of *A Thief of Time*, Hillerman assigns a speech to Joe Leaphorn that neatly comments on plot. The detectives are at the site of the killing of Etcitty and Nails, the backhoe bandit. The site had been invaded by someone who knew about the Anasazi, that they buried their dead in the trash midden or against the wall. Thus, the thief had dug in those places in search of the pottery usually interred with the bodies. Leaphorn picks up a shard of pottery at the site which is of "the type called St. John's Polychrome" about which he has been reading.

The physical evidence of the shard demonstrates an overlap of the cases Leaphorn and Chee have been working on. "You were looking for a couple of men who stole our backhoe," says Leaphorn. "I'm looking for an anthropologist." The overlap is so important that Hillerman has Leaphorn comment on the connections, so that readers can grasp it along with Chee:

> We have Jimmy Etcitty killed here digging up this sort of pot. This same Etcitty worked over at Chaco where Friedman-

Bernal worked. This same Jimmy Etcitty found a pot some-where near Bluff which he sold to a collector who sold it to an auction house. This pot got Friedman-Bernal excited enough a month ago to send her driving to Bluff looking for Etcitty. And on top of that we have Friedman-Bernal buying from Slick Nakai, the evangelist, and Nails selling to Slick, and Etcitty playing guitar for Nakai. *Nice little tangle of strings, and right here is the knot.* (Emphasis added, 152–53)

The tangle that must be unknotted refers us to two features of struc-ture in the novel. One of these is the puzzle confronting Leaphorn and Chee. Originally, it seemed that there were different puzzles—who took the backhoe and where did Eleanor Friedman-Bernal get to. Now they are revealed as parts of a single comprehensive puzzle. The second fea-ture of structure indicated in Leaphorn's speech is the process of inves-tigation, which is what brought the two detectives to the point of discovering that their seemingly separate problems are actually one mas-ter problem.

Eventually, Harrison Houk's murder will be revealed as part of the master puzzle, too, and so will Randall Elliot's ambitions, but it must be remembered that the investigations constitute the action of the narrative. Randall Elliot's elaborate execution of a plan to harm Friedman-Bernal's reputation, his illegal digging, his murders—all of that takes place out-side the focus of the narrative. In that sense, it is the source of the puzzle that occupies the detectives' efforts within the focus of the narrative. It makes sense, therefore, to distinguish between the "plotting" by Elliot and the plot of the narrative, which is the untangling of the knotted strings.

From the point in Chapter Nine when Leaphorn delivers his speech about the tangle of knotted strings, the investigative lines of the two detectives become interwoven. Sometimes they go together to a scene such as Chaco Center where Mrs. Luna fills them in about Eleanor and Randall and Maxie. Other times they divide their labor as when Chee pursues Slim Nakai and Leaphorn heads off to New York City and then to find Dr. Arnold. Always, however, their searches are coordinated as a mutual hunt for evidence.

The freedom of movement Hillerman finds in the third-person omnis-cient narrative point of view aids greatly in rendering the cooperative nature of the detectives' independent work. A third-person narrative as-sumes a distance from the leading characters who are treated, as the

name of the viewpoint indicates, through their proper names of Leaphorn and Chee, or third-person pronouns telling readers that "he" did
this or that. That distance lets the writer move from character to character, first showing the evidence one acquires, such as Chee's observation
of the lined-up jaws at the site of the killing in Chapter Five, and, then,
information gathered by the other, such as the fact that Jimmy Etcitty
was the name of the Navajo pot hunter who sold the pot in Nelson's
catalog to Harrison Houk (141). The associative relationship of the evidence next becomes clear when the narrative viewpoint brings the detectives together, for example, at the site of Jimmy Etcitty's murder
where the detectives also observe the bones arranged in a categorical
way, indicating that "somebody seemed to be interested in jawbones"
(157).

Ah hah, readers might say, along with Leaphorn and Chee, jawbones
are evidence to keep in mind. It turns out to be true that, indeed, they
are important when Chee and Janet learn that Elliot filed a statement of
interest in aberrant jaw formations in his applications for permission to
dig on protected sites and when they find a collection of jawbones in
Elliot's house. Eleanor's gun is another example of evidence that turns
up in successive incidents. The Anasazi pot is yet another illustration.
Together they show how progress in the plot of investigation is marked
by the detectives' acquisition of evidence and their discovery of its connection to other characters.

What is true in A Thief of Time, that the plot of the action is constructed
out of the progress of the investigation and that the investigative process
moves toward a conclusive demonstration of a solution to the puzzle, is
true of the genre in general. The inventiveness of Hillerman's development of the plot conventions lies in the neat fit he effects among the
parts of the plot. No better illustration of the fit exists than in the way
Hillerman makes the crimes arise naturally from their context.

Randall Elliot's desire for approbation and status as a scientific investigator motivates his crimes. In origin that desire is benign. Like Dr.
Friedman-Bernal and other scientists, he selected his profession in a
discipline devoted to creating knowledge of the Native American past.
More particularly, Elliot is concerned with the baffling problem of the
Anasazi, who have left artifact evidence of their tenure in the Southwest
but disappeared from the scene as though vaporized, leaving no descendants, no heirs, no later heritage. The social organization of scientific
enterprise permits the exercise of ambition such as Elliot's, but it tries to
control competition by surrounding it with requirements for proof and

application of an investigative method that can be replicated by others. As we have observed, the scientific pursuit is like police detection. In the case of Randall Elliot, the same ingenuity that makes him a promising scientist has become distorted by his wish for acclaim. Like Richard DuMont, Elliot sacrifices his commitment to the community of science to his personal aims. In a kind of evil parody of the method of building a case used by scientists and detectives, he has devised the puzzling plan that Leaphorn and Chee must unravel.

The conjunctions are very impressive. Detection method is akin to science. Possessed by his need for fame, Elliot inverts science in a way that creates a puzzle for detection. The fit works so well that while the detectives are shown in the narration at work in the plot of applying their methods to the gathering of evidence for a solution to the puzzle they have been presented, the object of their investigation—the puzzle Elliot has constructed—becomes revealed as a similarly ingenious counterplot.

THEMATIC ISSUES

The themes of *A Thief of Time* can be usefully distinguished by their sources in characterization and narration. In regard to themes originated in characterization, Jim Chee provides entry.

We call the United States a melting pot, unless we are instead calling it a mosaic or a plural society. Optimistic phrases such as these have not always squared with social reality, and nowhere has it seemed more contradictory to suggest that there is comfortable accommodation among the diverse people of America than in Indian Country. Navajos on the Reservations, and in most of Hillerman's novels, know the story of Kit Carson's raid on the people, their exile at Bosque Redondo, and their return to the land of their origin. Most know, too, that despite their separate living arrangements, which on the one hand are a result of Navajo choice and, on the other hand, an enactment of a national policy of apartheid, the pressure to acculturate to the mainstream white culture can be astonishingly powerful. At one time the federal government undertook to relocate Navajos to cities to encourage their assimilation. Janet Pete's father was one of those relocated Navajos. At other times, schools maintained on the Reservations by the federal Bureau of Indian Affairs worked on the principle that tradition is the enemy of progress.

In such circumstances one may become exceptionally self-conscious about group identity. That is the case with Jim Chee in particular and with Joe Leaphorn to a lesser extent. Chee's desire to become a singer reflects his interest in keeping the traditions of his people vital, while Leaphorn's request at the conclusion of *A Thief of Time* that Chee perform a Blessing Way ceremonial for him demonstrates his own interest in tradition. Everything about the lives of the two detectives expresses the significance to them of culture. Chee's confused feelings about Mary Landon have as much to do with staying rooted as with love. Leaphorn's recollections of Emma are infused with awareness of the importance of cultural tradition to her, and through her to him. As for secondary characters, we have already noted that nearly all of them can be studied in reference to how they relate to native culture. One of the most remarkable illustrations of the pervasive significance of culture conflict can be found, in fact, in the sermon Slick Nakai delivers in Chapter Four.

The narrative's continual insistence on the issue of inherited culture makes Hillerman's thematic point that the vital problem for Native Americans can be found in Jim Chee's struggle with being both modern and a Navajo. For that matter, it would be no great exaggeration to say that Hillerman suggests a similar problem faces most inhabitants of North America, and perhaps of the world. How can one manage the past, his novel asks, within present circumstances?

Mention of the past leads to a theme that might be rendered in a pair of questions: What are the uses of the past, and who has title to it? The consummate villain Richard DuMont treats the past as a commodity of his ego. Objects once invested with the cultural significance of ancient civilization are now his to use in exchange for the approval and amusement of his friends. Pot dealers, Navajo or Anglo, exhibit little difference from DuMont. They also convert the items of domestic and cultural use into items useful only in exchange for money. Notably absent from the picture are the creators of the objects. The scientists at least make some effort to restore the objects to their original significance as they develop theory that will re-place pots and people in their historical context. Still, however, the objects of the past lose their original purpose in the hands of the scientists who convert them from items of daily use into signs for interpretation by their scientific method.

Hillerman clearly condemns the subjugation of aesthetic and cultural objects to cash value. Even so, he leaves a problem for his readers to ponder—namely, how to find a modern use for the past that preserves the integrity of tradition and culture. This is what relates his plot of the pots to his characterization of detectives. For that matter, it is also how these themes find a place within the genre of detective fiction. Detective fiction, too, is about making some practical present use of the past. After following their trails of evidence and exercising their powers of reason, detectives are in a position to explain events that took place in the past. They are historians of crimes who present a solution to indicate to the reader how and why a disruption of order occurred, even as the relating of the solution restores that order. Thus, the genre of detective fiction enacts an adaptation of the past for present utility.

Detective fiction can be conclusive about a particular crime and make specific use of its solution. The general question of the uses of the past, however, remains to be answered in the more contingent realm of daily reality. We can probably assert, however, that for Hillerman to raise the issue, and to show that the use of the past is an inherent concern of the genre of detective fiction, may well be enough. He has given us food for thought.

A POSTCOLONIAL READING OF *A THIEF OF TIME*

Chapter 7 in this book presents a definition of postcolonial literary theory and an example of how it can be applied to a work by Tony Hillerman. Here it will be helpful to discuss the general point of view among postcolonial critics before examining *A Thief of Time* with its help.

Almost no area of human habitation is isolated from the effects of industrialism, the distribution of manufactured commodities, and tele-communication emanating from Hollywood, London, or Paris. That's part of what is meant when political commentators talk about a global economy and a world community. No new thing, the amalgamation of the world's people and culture can be described as an outcome of the European exploration that was followed by the foundation of settler colonies in the Americas and the Antipodes, and finally the creation of colonial empires throughout the world.

For the new school of postcolonial criticism, empire or the subjugation of populations to the external power of a metropolitan nation is the crucial modern experience. In Africa and Asia indigenous people and their homelands became political possessions of European countries, with the result that their natural resources and labor energy, markets, and culture were subordinated to overseas rule and use. In some cases, such as the United States, Canada, Australia, and New Zealand, settlers from Europe became dominant in the population and achieved independence as new English nations. No longer colonies of the overseas government, they

nevertheless retained cultural and economic affinity for Europe and du-
plicated the practice of subjugating indigenous people. In the United
States, for example, the population of enslaved Africans and displaced
natives can be regarded as internal colonies.

More subtly, empire and colonization can be viewed as a process of
acculturation and collective psychology. A convenient presentation of
postcolonial theory appears in the book *The Empire Writes Back*, written
by Bill Ashcroft, Gareth Griffiths, and Helen Tiffin. Developing the view
of the new school, these authors discuss how the extension of political
power into colonies has its counterpart in the colonization of people's
minds with outlooks and values supporting the claims of European superiority. Literature becomes part of this cultural colonization to the extent that it, too, incorporates views about the superiority of the European
"race" and culture. In this regard, then, a postcolonial literary text is one
influenced by the experience of empire. That is to say, it is formed in
response to colonialization either because it repeats the intellectual and
emotional positions fostered by colonialism or because it reacts against
such positions.

Colonialism marginalizes subject people, making them producers of
raw materials or commodities for use in metropolitan societies, or colonial powers may simply use the territory of subject people for strategic
military bases. In any circumstance, colonialism also marginalizes native
culture, making it subordinate and less valuable than the culture of the
colonial power. The colonized citizens are excluded not only from the
circles of power, but also from the category of civilized and advanced
peoples. They are made into "others"—that is, people other than those
who are viewed as responsible for high civilization. This was the treatment accorded enslaved Africans in the United States and the so-called
Red Man, too. The process does not end with the construction of ideas
among the colonizers who hold power, however. The "others" are also
subjected to conditioning intended to make them internalize the values
that declare their standards of beauty, their religion, their art, and, most
decisively, their race inferior.

In *A Thief of Time*, the workings of colonialism lie behind the behavior
of the Navajos who deal in Indian pots at the service of absent white
collectors. Although the Anasazi might be thought to have some importance to Navajos as predecessors on the land, for Etcitty and Nails, and
maybe for Slick Nakai as well, the Anasazi are instead an opportunity
for monetary profit and, therefore, a chance for participation in the
exchange system imposed on Native Americans by their subjugators. In

an even clearer way, the Indian cultures of the Southwest are treated as "other" than important by DuMont, and eventually by Elliot.

But postcolonial criticism also encourages us to see the conflicts besetting Chee, Leaphorn, and their communities as struggles about psychic liberation from the imposition of alien values. This is not obviously about political independence or separatism. Even less is it a version of racialism when Chee wonders whether he can be both Navajo and modern. The idea of race, after all, is a construction of the West that is meant to justify its superiority over Africans, Asians, and Native Americans. Rather, it is about Chee's efforts, and others, to reconstruct their ideas of self free of presumptions that Indians are uncommonly strange, romantic, primitive, or exotic, free indeed of the notion that they are Indians at all. It was a European thought that they were to be classed with people from the East. To Navajos still, they are the *dine.*

The lens of postcolonial theory helps us to think of the Navajo experience as part of the general history of conquest and modernization conducted by Europeans in the world. It directs our gaze on characters such as Chee and Leaphorn as products of that history struggling with its legacy.

11

Talking God
(1989) and
Coyote Waits
(1990)

Putting the detectives he had developed in independent series together, Hillerman created a popular combination. Their first collaboration in *Skinwalkers* won a spot for Hillerman on the 1986 best-seller lists. Publication in 1988 of *A Thief of Time* made Leaphorn and Chee instrumental to Hillerman's deepening portrayal of Native American life through a plot that leads them into investigations of archaeological traces of the Anasazi past of Arizona and New Mexico and explores the tensions in the present culture of the Dinetah.

Hillerman had good reason to feel content with his decision to pair his two characters. After three novels in which he presented Leaphorn alone as the presiding detective, and three in which Chee was the dominant sleuth, Hillerman had had ample opportunity to provide each with a singular personality, an individual background, and a distinctive approach to police procedures. Their individual differences and their independent development made it improbable for them to merge into a flawless super detection team, and impossible that they could fit into the conventional mold of a master detective and sidekick. Instead of duplicating a convention of the detective fiction genre, Leaphorn and Chee in combination brought intriguing complexity to Hillerman's narratives. Working on cases that at first are seemingly unrelated, they give their audience two lines, not just one line, of investigation to follow vicariously with the detectives, and two credible and informative points of view on events. Within the comparatively small social world of the Reservations, the investigations of two detectives can realistically cross as often as they follow parallel paths, with intricate plot the result.

Hillerman quickly followed up the opportunities evident in the first two novels linking Leaphorn and Chee and within two years published two additional novels about the pair: *Talking God* in 1989 and *Coyote Waits* in 1990. Sales of these novels and the growth of Hillerman's reputation in recent years testify to public satisfaction with his decision to place the two detectives together. Because they represent in Hillerman's career a period when he is using well-established characters and materials that are becoming familiar to the large readership he has built, *Talking God* and *Coyote Waits* may be thought of as a peak, though not the highest peak his talent promises to attain. For that reason, the two novels may be critically considered together.

SETTING

Every writer who lays a claim to realism must describe the ground where characters walk, the roadways and buildings of the locale where they reside. Authors of detective fiction, however, often exceed the requirements of plausibility and create settings that evoke a typifying atmosphere for their scenes of crime and detection. We know that nineteenth-century London was foggy and poorly lit by its street lamps simply because we have read detective stories about the place in that time. Even before we get there, we know that Los Angeles is sprawling and Hollywood garish, because the private detectives have informed us, just as they have shown us that Miami is a vice town and Chicago is gangland. For people who know the sites because they live there, the real places are much more various than they appear in fiction, but that doesn't matter. Fiction only requires that a setting *seem to be real.* When a writer manages that, the setting can become an animate part of the narrative. It is no longer just ground beneath the characters' feet, but rather a sign to convey added meaning in the narrative.

The landscape of the Navajo, Zuni, Hopi, Pueblo, and Checkerboard Reservations in Tony Hillerman's novels work like that. The discussion of writing style in the chapter on *Dance Hall of the Dead* illustrates how the author brings the landscape before Joe Leaphorn's eyes in order to integrate the description with narrative action.

The frequency with which cloud formations, topographical patterns, weather, the soil, and all of nature are described in Hillerman's novels indicates the further importance of the setting. In a personal essay called "Dinetah, If I Forget You" he explains how General Tecumseh Sherman saw the Navajos' native territory as "totally worthless" and, therefore, unlikely to be attractive for anyone other than the Navajos. But for them the land has abiding appeal. With his friend Alex Etcitty, whose trip with Hillerman to meet a shaman is the subject of recollection in the essay, he drove on Navajo Route 8 to the southwest slopes of the Chuska Mountains that run along the border between Arizona and New Mexico. Atop a hill they saw before them "the ultimate in how erosion can ravage a land." The scene was "a wilderness of sun-baked stone, gray caliche, wind-cut clay red as barn paint, great bluish outcroppings of shale, the pockmarked dingy white of old volcanic ash, and the cracked expanse of salt flats where the mud formed by the male rains [hard-driving rains] of summer tastes as bitter as alum." It showed no signs of life. "A white mapmaker would call it Desolation Flats," but, said Etcitty, "our name for this is Beautiful Valley" (*Companion* 304).

The arid, inhospitable land obtains its importance from being the site of the mythological origins of the People and the continuing locale of spiritual drama. Rural westerners like the Navajo accommodate to the land so that they may live and farm and hunt on it. Yet, the land is more than just native environment, for after their return from exile and captivity, memorialized in nineteenth-century history as the Long Walk, the Navajos returned to territory bequeathed them by the Holy People. Since that time, they have remained at home in the Promised Land.

Even when reference to the natural setting of the Reservation seems incidental, as it may in *Coyote Waits,* the landscape hovers in the background of the Hillerman novels to make the terrain of spiritual reality concretely present. And even when the Navajo detectives are away from their native place, they remain intensely sensitive to suggestions in their surroundings. Witness, for example, Jim Chee in Chapter Eighteen of *The Ghostway* where this "connoisseur of sunsets . . . collector of memories of gaudy cloudscape and glowing western horizons that the Colorado Plateau produces" observes the "copper-colored sky" of Los Angeles "with the slanting evening light filtering through an atmosphere of oceanside humidity and chemical fumes." He feels that when he arrives at the top of the hill he is driving he will "look down upon . . . God knows what" (194).

Considering the powerful role taken by setting in most of the novels, *Talking God* presents a surprise, because it takes Joe Leaphorn and Jim

Chee to Washington, D.C., for most of the scenes and most of the time making up the novel. Descriptions of the Museum of Natural History, glimpses of the Capitol Hill neighborhood, and the location of embassies, street names, and hotel references are accurate enough to satisfy most readers, but the setting is notably lacking in atmosphere and any suggestion that it has more significance than as the site of the Smithsonian Institution. Instead, the setting gives an abstract historical relevance to the story, since Washington is the home office for agencies, such as the Bureau of Indian Affairs and the Federal Bureau of Investigation, that regulate Reservation life and the museums housing the trophies and artifacts accumulated in the federal campaigns to pacify the Native American population. While a plot about Indian museum treasures makes the Washington setting necessary, and likely inevitable, the texture of the Washington scenes is always thinner than that in the chapters where Leaphorn inspects the body of the aristocratic looking man, or when Chee and Cowboy see Highhawk and Bad Hands at the Night Way ceremony.

Returning to Reservation country in *Coyote Waits*, Hillerman revives the importance of landscape, with his plot focusing on the puzzle of the basalt formation and the lost history to be found in the seemingly numberless canyons and caves. The grandeur of western scenes is never lost on the tourists driving through, because the scale is so large, but emptiness and absence make their impression, too. The land is sparsely populated and in many places appears yet to be crossed or settled by human beings. It takes a Navajo or a naturalized resident to see the presence in the land of natural forces mythologized by Native Americans in stories of the Creation, the continuing presence of spiritual values in the variable shape of the topography, and the site of a history that continues to wield influence. When Hillerman's novels are set on the Reservations, they allow readers to experience naturalized residence in Indian Country for the duration of the book. When they are not, they may make readers feel they are missing something.

NARRATIVE VIEWPOINT

Perhaps humility lies behind Hillerman's consistent use of third-person narration in his detective fiction. Even though first-person narration, with the detective or an intimate associate speaking in the dominant voice of the novel, has long been an acceptable convention for the genre, Hillerman will not presume to know enough to inhabit the consciousness of a Navajo police officer in the way first-person narration would require.

Effectively, the issues involved in selecting a narrative point of view are distance and control. The first-person narration leaves no gap between the telling and the experiencing of events. It accords readers as much knowledge of self and surroundings as the character possesses, but the first person relinquishes control of everything else because it equips readers with only the "eye" of the narrative's "I." The third-person narrative viewpoint accepts a distance from the characters in return for the ability to see further than the character can. If the writer elects to make the third person also an omniscient narrative viewpoint that potentially sees everything, it can be moved at will among characters and be used to introduce any material about background, past, or future that the author considers relevant, even if a character might not be aware of the relevance. Plainly, first-person narration, with its identity of voice and viewpoint, creates the greater sense of intimacy but allows for less variety in the telling of a story. The third person, foregoing complete intimacy, permits varied perspectives.

If an Anglo writer's guardedness about using a Navajo outlook has contributed to Hillerman's selection of the narrative point of view he uses consistently, then he has been well served. The third-person narrative viewpoint establishes an initial bond between him and the majority of his readers who most likely are outsiders to Navajo life.

Once that bond has been established, technical advantages are yielded for intricately structuring the books. For example, in *Talking God* seven of the twenty-two chapters omit any reference at all to either Leaphorn or Chee. The first two of these chapters, which are also the first chapters of the novel, establish conditions for the plot—first, Henry Highhawk's media-conscious campaign to get the Smithsonian Institution to divest its holdings of ancestral bones, and, second, Agnes Tsosie's need for a ceremonial Night Chant. In time, the ceremonial will create an encounter between Chee and the conspirators, including Highhawk, and will lead all the major characters to the scene of Highhawk's theatrics in Washington. The five other chapters where Leaphorn and Chee are absent all center on another of Hillerman's psychotic hit men. Colton Wolf filled such a role in *People of Darkness* and Eric Vaggan in *The Ghostway*. Here it is Leroy Fleck whose inherently evil consciousness is profiled by the chapters that follow his murderous progress toward a showdown with the detectives in the Museum of Natural History.

These seven chapters set the plot in motion and, in the case of Fleck, add a frightening unpredictability to the complex puzzle at the heart of the plot because of Hillerman's freedom to know all and see all as a result of the third-person narrative viewpoint. With regard to managing the pursuit of solutions to the puzzle by the two detectives, Hillerman uses the narrative viewpoint to create a symmetry in investigation. Once the story has been set in motion by the opening two chapters, and except for intervening chapters about Fleck, Hillerman turns alternatively from Leaphorn to Chee and back again, until six chapters have been devoted to Leaphorn and five to Chee, and they join forces to complete their investigation in three chapters. Then, as though to even things up, Chee gets the final chapter, making it six for him, too.

A chart arranging the novel's chapters according to their attention to characters would look very planned: two chapters setting the tale in motion, five chapters for the serious villain, six for each of the detectives, and three for the detectives' appearance together, with Fleck on the scene in one of them. But that would suggest more design to start with than Hillerman would acknowledge. Hillerman claims that he does not write his novels from blueprints, but rather waits for them to evolve from an initial thematic idea and the revising he does as he goes along (Winks 139–40). However, lack of an overall plan at the start of writing does not mean the absence of any sense of order. The logic of investigation has an intuitive feel to it for writers as much as for real-life detectives and a cadence or swing as well. When the logic of the puzzle and the rhythm of the investigation synchronize, the narrative takes on a form that can very well result in the symmetry of *Talking God.*

For the record, it can be noted that in *Coyote Waits,* Leaphorn occupies center stage for seven chapters and Chee for fifteen. Readers are unlikely to feel the narrative is unbalanced, however, because while the guilt and trauma Chee experiences after the killing of Delbert Nez becomes his claim on a large enough portion of the narrative to resolve his feelings, Leaphorn assumes a presiding role in the investigations appropriate to his superior rank in the police force. Neither character takes a subordinate position in the narrative. In fact, Hillerman develops a different kind of symmetry than obtained in the previous novel by introducing Louisa Bourebonette into Leaphorn's life as a friend who becomes a companion in detection much in the way Mary Landon had been for Jim Chee in *People of Darkness* and Janet Pete is becoming for him in *Coyote Waits.* Giving the characters personal lives that the third-person narration construes as parallel underscores the professional parallels that the third-person narration is enabled to develop by its capacity to move freely from character to character, consciousness to consciousness.

PLOT DEVELOPMENT

The examination of narrative viewpoint in *Talking God* and *Coyote Waits* has already demonstrated its overall symmetrical design. What must be considered next is the way Hillerman insinuates his puzzle plot into that design. For this it will be helpful to recall that in the analysis of *Darkwind* the puzzle story is described as a convention of the detective fiction genre that presents a sequence of evidence that must meet the tests of plausibility and fairness to the reader. Plausibility rules out improbability but leaves room for all the ingenuity a writer can muster to motivate a crime, give it an appropriate means of execution, and provide a likely opportunity to occur within the framework of realistic portrayal. The test of fair play is that readers stay abreast of the detectives in the information they receive about clues and the results of investigative procedures. No secrets are allowed, because the purpose of the exercise is to devise a plot that satisfies the readers' interest in detection at the same time that it empowers the detectives to restore their world to order.

Hillerman creates his puzzling plot in *Talking God* with wit and cleverness. Lieutenant Joe Leaphorn comes upon the first element of the puzzle when his friend, FBI agent Jay Kennedy, tells him about an unidentified body found by the railroad tracks. Upon inspection, it turns out that all identification has been removed from the body except for a cryptic note apparently overlooked by the killer. The note names Agnes Tsosie "near Windowrock" and includes trial spellings of *yeibichai* (the Night Chant ceremonial). Otherwise, the body with an aristocratic cast to its face, dressed in expensive clothes, and lacking any teeth reveals nothing to explain its presence along the railroad in Arizona. In fact, physical evidence demonstrates that the dead man, skillfully slain in a professional way, is an evident stranger to the area, and that the killer disposed of his body in Reservation territory through the workings of chance. When Leaphorn follows up the circumstantial evidence of the note mentioning Agnes Tsosie, he gets nowhere. She does not recognize a photograph of the dead man and has no idea why he would be coming to her ceremonial.

Coincidentally, chance also appears to be at work when Sergeant Jim Chee (in the novel *Sacred Clowns* we learn that Chee has been "acting"

Sergeant all this time) picks up his part of the puzzle. Captain Largo has dispatched him to Agnes Tsosie's Night Chant ceremonial to look out for Henry Highhawk, who is wanted for desecration of graves as a result of his mailing Agnes' Anglo ancestors' bones to Catherine Morris Perry, a public affairs officer at the Smithsonian Museum. Chee finds and arrests Highhawk, observing the man he calls "Bad Hands" in the process. Highhawk claims partial Navajo ancestry, but in Largo's experienced view, he is a nut and is typical of those who "decide to turn Indian." He is even more laughable, because his Anglo grave-robbing stunt on behalf of a campaign to return Native American bones to tribal lands is so averse to the Navajo way of shunning death and corpses rather than venerating the ancestral remains (35–36). In this practical sense, then, Highhawk is as much a stranger to the Reservation as the unidentified dead man, an intruder by the chance of having seen a photograph of Agnes Tsosie in an old copy of *National Geographic* (30).

In considering plot in any detection narrative, but especially in the so-called puzzle story, it is important to distinguish between the solution of the criminal puzzle which forms the object of the detectives' investigation and the actions of characters while they work toward solving the puzzle. There is a logic for each. Chee goes to Washington partly to think again about joining the FBI, partly because he has leave time, and probably largely because Janet Pete is there with whom he shares an association with the Highhawk case. Thus, the decision to travel puts him in the scene to work on the puzzle he has been presented in the novel. Leaphorn gets to Washington, and the scene where he can follow up his portion of the criminal puzzle, because his exhaustive inquiry into the case of the expensively dressed corpse leads to the baggage office in Union Station. That's the action of the novel, and, the logic of these active events continues throughout the narrative, bringing the two detectives together to collaborate on the master puzzle encompassing both of the problems they started with and much more besides.

The hope of discovering the final comprehensive explanation urges the detectives on. Meanwhile, however, they must investigate, speculate, and reason, for it is this *process* of investigation that makes up the plot and subject of their narrative. Leaphorn shows a decided preference as he conducts the process for pursuit of motive in criminal puzzles. "Why was always the question that lay at the heart of things" (26). Discovery of motive, however, requires assembly of data and the patience to follow all leads. Examining the victim's luggage and reading his notebook, interviewing an eyewitness, and making a shrewd deduction that one item in the notebook refers to a pharmaceutical prescription give Leaphorn the victim's identity, Elogio Santillanes y Jimenez. One form of puzzle is solved, only to create a newer one—who is Elogio? (170). And motive is still unclear.

In contrast to Leaphorn, Chee seems to pursue circumstances more than motive, circumstances such as the mysterious man tailing Janet Pete and the curious fact that Highhawk has made a replica of a fetish. Nevertheless, Chee's investigative method assembles data as effectively as Leaphorn's, so that when they meet in a Washington hotel coffee shop, both are equally prepared to advance the solving of the puzzle. Their meeting, which brings their independent actions in the plot to an end and joins them in collaboration, also puts their separate puzzles in a new light. The dead man's notebook contains a reference to Highhawk. Now there are too many connections between the Highhawk case and the dead body for coincidence. Where it once seemed that chance had brought the two strangers to the attention of the Navajo police officers, now there is evidence for an essential relationship between them and a master puzzle driving the detectives on. The point has already been confirmed by the narrative's account in Chapter Sixteen of Fleck's thoughts on how he committed the murder of Santillanes. As the killer of the victim in Leaphorn's case and Janet Pete's tail in the Highhawk case, Leroy Fleck holds the key to the puzzle.

At one point late in the novel, Leaphorn describes Chee and himself as two hunting dogs "who followed two different sets of tracks to the same brush pile. One dog thinks there's a rabbit under the brush, the other thinks it's a bobcat. Same brush pile, different information" (296–97). The image perfectly summarizes the plot, making the point clear, by the way, that the narrative's plot as distinct from criminal plot, consists of the process of solving the puzzle. Appropriately, the remainder of the novel is given over to the two detectives rehearsing their thoughts on the case, recounting their investigations to each other, and cooperating in action that prevents assassination and disaster in the Museum of Natural History.

The metaphor of hunting dogs works equally well to describe the plot of action in *Coyote Waits*. There the two detectives have different incentives for investigating Ashie Pinto, but after treading the same ground and examining the evidence from their own perspectives, they arrive at the same solution of the puzzle. *Coyote Waits* is less complexly constructed than *Talking God*, and for that reason it seems less witty and clever, but it employs a similar pattern of confluence of several puzzles.

Interestingly, however, *Coyote Waits* inverts the pattern so that the puzzles appear finally as contingent rather than dependently linked.

Jim Chee becomes aware of the death of Officer Delbert Nez, the complicity of Ashie Pinto in the crime, and the reappearance of the rock painter all as a single episode, as though they have some still inexplicable but essential connection. Seeking an explanation of that connection, Chee, and Leaphorn from his angle on the case, find instead that circumstances rather than deliberate planning brought them all together.

The process of investigation consists in sorting out those circumstances to lay bare Professor Tagert's use and abuse of Ashie Pinto; Odell Redd's resentment and avarice; Taka Ji's romantic gesture that placed him at the scene of Nez's death; Redd's mistaken belief that it was Huan Ji who witnessed the killing of Tagert; and the whiskey possessing Ashie Pinto's soul. The chance arrangement of circumstances, some kind of generalized coincidence, brought everything together—just as the title reference says, "Coyote . . . always . . . waiting" (310). But remember that invocation of fate is the solution to the puzzle, not the novel's plot. *Coyote Waits* may be slighter and less interestingly developed than *Talking God*, and it is perhaps less satisfying to read because it becomes a demonstration of coincidence rather than dependent order. In plot, however, the two novels are closely related examples of the detection puzzle.

CHARACTER DEVELOPMENT

Although a tense exchange takes place between Chee and Leaphorn in *Coyote Waits* about how they came to be working on the same case (249–50), as befits their roles on the police force they keep up a respectful professional relationship in these two novels. In *Coyote Waits* Leaphorn appraises Chee as unusually bright and clever but with "what might be a fatal flaw for a policeman. He was an individualist, following the rules if and when they agreed with him. On top of that, he was a romantic. He even wanted to be a medicine man." We notice that Leaphorn smiled at the idea of "a Tribal Policeman-Shaman" (30). He did not frown, and at the conclusion of the novel he thinks it a good idea to get Chee in the criminal investigations unit, "where screwing up didn't matter much if you had a creative thought now and then" (349). A genial relationship is developing there.

The characters have been fleshed out in their previous appearances in novels, and occasional references work to remind readers of the series about what they have seen before. For example, Leaphorn, depressed by his wife Emma's death in *The Thief of Time*, was ready to retire, but in *Talking God* he admits to Jay Kennedy that he has decided to stay with the force. The same novel reviews Leaphorn's religious outlook with a reminder that he had asked Chee to sing a Blessing Way for him (180) and with a sketchy note that his metaphysics "had evolved from the Navajo Way into a belief in a sort of universal harmony of cause and effect caused by God when He started it all" (153). The same idea of order informs his detection process, along with the preference for finding motive. This is illustrated by a narrative comment about his approach to the unidentified body: "while in many ways Joe Leaphorn had moved into the world of the whites, his Navajo requirement for order and harmony remained. . . . And now it seemed that nothing violating this natural order had happened in the sagebrush plain east of Gallup" (88). Chee also receives a share of refresher references. For example, *Coyote Waits* reviews Chee and Leaphorn's different views of Navajo witchcraft (319).

In contrast to the presentation of them as individuals, Leaphorn and Chee's personal relationships to other characters show considerable development in these two novels. For long periods in Washington, Chee spends uninterrupted time with Janet Pete. They ride the Metro together, sharing the experience of being tourists. He and Janet talk at length about her disappointment with her job in Washington and a little bit about Mary Landon, who is rapidly receding into Chee's memory as someone he once loved. This growing congeniality and their mutual engagement in Highhawk's case bring them closer and closer until they act like a team of investigators.

That companionship continues in *Coyote Waits* when Janet becomes a comfort and support to Chee in his pain and remorse from the death of Nez. There is a satisfying openness about the relationship—"the thing about Janet Pete was that he could talk to her about things that were hard to talk about" (63). They also share a sense of significance about Navajo identity, even though Janet's mother was a Scot and Janet was raised away from the Reservation, that encourages intimacy and sets Chee's mind free to begin imagining a life with Janet.

An advance in intimate relationship also marks Leaphorn's story in these novels. The man whom Janet Pete calls "Grouchy Joe" in *Talking God*, the man never satisfied with anything (180), becomes captivated by Louisa Bourebonette in *Coyote Waits*. At least he is so pleased with her company that they had talked volubly about her field of comparative mythology and at the end of the novel planned a trip to China together. The association with Louisa makes Leaphorn a warmer, more flexible man than he has been in previous novels, perhaps it even makes him more appreciative of Chee. In any case, in *Coyote Waits* scenes with Leaphorn show for the first time in his fictional career the humorous indulgence of self-parodic reference. Driving with Louisa to examine the rock formations painted by Nez's vandal, he offers the thought that they will turn out to be the same rocks photographed by Taka Ji. Asked why he thinks so, he says it's because he's learned from television "that's the way the plot ought to work out" (270). When they arrive at the rock formation and see that the painting spells out I LOVE JEN, Louisa congratulates him, calling his deduction something "right out of Sherlock Holmes." Sealing the moment, he confesses, "I'm sort of proud of it myself" (276). Self-reflexive references like these always point back to their subject. In a minor convention of detective stories, they also point back to the formalities of the genre, exposing their artifice. Usually, they are mildly humorous, but for the usually serious Leaphorn even mild humor is considerable.

Given the importance of the detectives' personal relationships in the character development of these two novels, the women involved acquire significance as supporting characters. For Janet Pete this means we learn about how she responds to the discovery that she is the token Indian in her Washington law firm and how abashed she is by her naive love for John McDermott, the Anglo specialist in Indians, because this information helps explain her needs and her ambitions. For Louisa Bournebonette it means we become acquainted with the will that makes her a champion of Ashie Pinto, the dedication to research that has motivated her working with Pinto for twenty years, and the intellectual acuity that has taken her to Asia and a professional position at Northern Arizona University, because these details fill in the profile of her strengths. The care Tony Hillerman devotes to developing Pete and Bournebonette in these two novels suggests that he intends to give them a long run in his fiction.

THEMATIC ISSUES

The same conversation in *Talking God* that ends with Janet Pete taking Jim Chee to the airport and announcing that she, too, is coming home also includes a short exchange about Henry Highhawk's motivation. "I'd like to think I wasn't a complete fool," says Janet, "wanting to help him when he was helping to murder a lot of innocent people . . . I guess I needed to keep believing Henry just wanted to do good." Chee replies, "I think that's right . . . It took me a while, but I've decided that too" (330). The tentativeness of the conversation points up the unresolved ethical issue inherent in the story of Highhawk.

It is easy enough to ridicule Highhawk and his dreams of becoming Indian. The sensationalism of his tactics is familiar enough to earn him the label of a media-hound militant. Set aside the tactics of shock, however, and disengage him from the conspirators who used him, and he had a point. The Indian artifacts in the national attic of the Smithsonian are the spoils of war, demonstrating the truth of the adage that the winners write history. America is haunted by bad conscience about the treatment of Native American populations by the European settlers and their descendants. What Highhawk meant to do was stir that conscience to make amends in some tangible way.

On the other hand, the museum spokesperson quoted in the *Washington Post* observed that the institution has a research mission. Those bones and artifacts, however they may have come to the museum, are now scrutinized and studied with the instruments of objective science for the purpose of advancing knowledge. They no longer have subjective importance in themselves; they have been objectified. But, it can be complained, converting something one people feel about subjectively into value-free objects shows the working of power no different than the application of military force to "pacify" the indigenous populations so that the land they inhabited could be objectified as acreage for Anglos.

Of course, the cavalry displayed power, but there was progress too, with the land developed to support more people than Indians ever supported on it. And there was progress in the advancement of knowledge, progress for everyone.

And so the argument goes. It is unresolved by debate because that is not how issues like ownership of museum artifacts are decided. But there is the ethical issue, which can be decided in the arena of language. *Talking God* is a construction of language directed to an examination of the issue. The author gives Highhawk a good case and by the time the novel ends makes him a much more attractive figure than he was at the opening. He is artistically talented, sensitive, well-meaning—an ethical character. The author also gives him dubious politics and a pliability of character that lets him be used by others for their own ends.

So, what is to be made of the ethical issue in *Talking God*? First of all, what is to be made of it is that the novel sets its theme in the form of a question rather than a didactic declaration. The novel asks its readers to ponder the question, What is ethical behavior in regard to the cultural inheritance of the Native Americans? No doubt the theme is presented in a question rather than a detachable statement partly because the book is a mystery for detection, and the mixture of means, motives, and ends attendant upon the ethical issue makes for a good puzzle. And if that isn't the reason for formulating the theme as a question for further consideration by readers, then Tony Hillerman's reluctance to pontificate either like Highhawk or like Anglo apologists is sufficient cause.

Readers will find the theme of guilt and shame in *Coyote Waits* considerably easier to handle than the thematic question of *Talking God.* The solution to the puzzle in *Coyote Waits*, as we have seen, dissolves apparent connections into coincidences, allotting the shock of the story to the revelation in Ashie Pinto's courtroom confession that this honorable man, the holder of oral treasures of his people, committed murder. In a manner characteristic of a society with a strong sense of shared values, he experiences shame or humiliation in the eyes of his peers for his violation of their joint code. That is in contrast to the more personal feeling of guilt or self-loathing, such as Chee feels temporarily about not being on hand to help Nez. With shame, motivation can be disconnected from the deed. With guilt, worry about motive is all. Still, for whatever reason you do something shameful, you have offended your community.

For Pinto, whiskey, "the water of darkness," took over his being; whiskey that Tagert had given him destroyed his controls and he killed. Despite the extenuating circumstances a defense lawyer might introduce, that is cause for confession of shame. Thus, Pinto leaves it to others, to Chee, and Pete, and Leaphorn, and readers to consider the destructive force of alcohol. When they do so, they will determine that the worst thing about the abuse of alcohol is that it removes people from the human condition, putting them momentarily beyond the reach of shame or guilt to behave as unmediated impulse demands.

Contemplating the story of Ashie Pinto in *Coyote Waits*, the characters in the novel and readers of the novel must conclude that to be human is to be subject to the socially created values that foster community. Such values take different forms. They can be expressed in the myths studied by Louisa Bourebonette, the chants Jim Chee aspires to sing for his people, or the pride Joe Leaphorn has in Navajos, but always they are the force of culture and the constant topic of Tony Hillerman's novels.

AN HISTORICIST READING OF *TALKING GOD* AND *COYOTE WAITS*

Historical study may be the most common approach exercised by critics and scholars of literature, unless it is careful dedicated attention to a text, so that one is conducting what is called "close reading." Historical studies summon up information about the past, possibly Kit Carson's raid on the Navajos in 1864 and their subsequent captivity at Bosque Redondo for the next four years. In other words, the general use to which history is put for the study of literature is to assume that in some way or another the text will refer to the past, and it is the task of criticism to discover how the structure in language manifests the events of the past.

Historicist criticism, however, is quite different from historical study. Whereas historical study looks for the background of a literary work, historicism considers the literary text itself to be an historical product like all other cultural phenomena. The field of religion presents an interesting analogy to the study of literature. When scholars write about the spread of a religion, they are doing an historical study that could, for example, explain why some biblical texts were written in Greek or how Islam reached Indonesia. When a scholar attributes characteristics of religious belief to social origins, as Sigmund Freud does in *Moses and Monotheism*, then the study has become historicist. Similar types of investigations can be made of literary genres and their circulation. For example, an historical scholar might write about poetic elegies, pointing out that they presented models not only to European authors but to American poets as well. When, however, the scholarly investigator begins to consider why it was that Phillis Wheatley, Senegalese by birth and American by enslavement, vied with English authors in composing elegies, then the study is becoming historicist, because Wheatley's verses are being treated as products of the way she gained her literacy and the social order in which she aspired to find a place through her writing.

In Chapter 2 of this book, the discussion of the detective fiction genre as an embodiment of middle-class values and anxiety can be taken as historicist. So, then, how can *Talking God* and *Coyote Waits* be subjected to such an historicist study?

Looking at the unresolved ethical dilemma constituting the theme of *Talking God*, we noted that America has a preoccupation with Native Americans. Athletic teams sport Indian names and logos. Maps of the

United States are sprinkled with geographical designations originally made by the Native Americans. Museums display tribal art and artifacts. Every school child studies American Indian units in class, and perhaps still plays Cowboys and Indians after school. Fiction based on the legends of Indian wars has a loyal readership. Films about Indians, such as *Dancing with Wolves*, are widely celebrated. It might be that for the descendants of immigrants to the United States, stories of Indians substitute for the antiquity the Old World of Europe uses as its classical time of grandeur.

Yet the tissue of discourse that has developed in North American popular culture about the indigenous population of the continent betrays mixed feelings. Native Americans are described in advertising and school rooms as reverent in their use of the environment, although the appropriation of their lands permitted the comfortable development of towns and cities that receive the advertising and the classroom lessons and where the only Indians visible today are on teenagers' warm-up jackets. Indians are thought of as noble people, provided that they are dead and gone like Joseph Brant, Geronimo, or Sitting Bull, but national policy has been to subjugate the culture that bred those heroes and push their descendants to assimilate Anglo-American language and culture, assimilate, that is, while living in the style made infamous in South Africa as apartheid.

As we noted earlier in this chapter, Americans have good reason to be haunted by thoughts about the natives. Those thoughts form the body of opinion bequeathed to the Americans who are not themselves Native. Obviously, that body of opinion, usable in day-to-day life and conversation, has been socially created and is as much a part of the culture that determines or influences a resident's Americanness as the values surrounding the ideas of democracy and representative government. The body of opinion reproduces itself in each new generation, creating new manifestations of the preoccupation with the past and fate of the American Indians. Among the manifestations are works of literature produced at least in part by the continuing power of the body of opinion to shape popular views of Native Americans.

That is what is meant by saying, as historicist criticism does, that Hillerman's novels can be read as products of history. From the angle of historicist criticism, the unresolved ethical problem in *Talking God* can be described in a way that points to both Hillerman's inclusion of the problem of the ownership and use of ancestral bones and to the way he structures the story. By including the problem in his novel, Hillerman taps into an expression of American bad conscience about the legacy of subjugation of the Indian populations. In structuring the story, however, an historicist critic might say that Hillerman construes Highhawk's case weakly, because Americans resist considering the problem in terms of relative political and social power. If ownership and use of a population's inheritance were dealt with as a clear issue of appropriation, the inevitable conclusion that believers in justice would reach is that the minority has been maltreated. Their cultural legacy should be freed for them to use in the ways they choose, just as Americans say that the Tibetan sacred places should be ceded by the occupying Chinese government back to Tibetans for their free use, or that Jerusalem should be a city open to all people who revere it as holy. A conclusion drawn from an analysis of power, however, would be extremely uncomfortable for Americans dealing with Indians. The claims of the Indian sovereign nations on land and resources supported by past treaties or the principle of original occupancy could make incredibly extensive practical demands on the wealth of states and municipalities. It would be much wiser then, to cast the problem of treatment of the Native American minority as a cultural issue. Effectively, the historicist critics might say, Tony Hillerman does just that in his fiction: he recasts a legacy of political and military domination of Native Americans as the issue of cultural survival. To be sure, it is a matter of cultural survival, because, in fact, there is no longer any point to combat between the majority and minority sovereignties, between Washington and the Indian nations. Still, casting the issue in cultural terms alone leaves politics and power conveniently unnoted.

This particular commentary on the Hillerman novels is not to say that historicist critics place no value on cultural vibrancy, reducing all events to matters of power, or that all historicist critics would employ the illustrative argument laid out here. Rather, the intention of this demonstration is to show that application of the historicist premise—that literature is an historical product—can enlarge our sense of literature's sources.

12

Sacred Clowns
(1993)

In the three years that passed between the account of Leaphorn and Chee working on the Ashie Pinto case in *Coyote Waits* (1990) and the reappearance of the detectives in *Sacred Clowns* (1993), Tony Hillerman made some interesting changes in his fictional project. In the first of the changes, he has assigned Chee to work with Leaphorn in the Special Investigations Office of the Navajo Tribal Police (7–8). For all we know, Hillerman may have discovered that the specialization in law enforcement characteristic of larger police forces has influenced the organization of the Law and Order Division of the Bureau of Indian Affairs. Then, again, perhaps he took the model for the special office from crime fiction itself, where detectives are commonly assigned to the homicide squad, the vice squad, and so on. Regardless of how he came up with the idea, Hillerman's creation of the new two-man unit for the Navajo Tribal Police underscores the premise of *Sacred Clowns* as a police procedural narrative. In previous novels, the detectives evidently took up particular cases because the crimes occurred near their regional offices, or because Captain Largo assigned the cases. Now, however, a special unit seems to be justified for particularly challenging cases, and, naturally, the crack detectives on the force are to be given those puzzles requiring their exceptional skill in detective investigation.

The creation of a unique Special Investigations Office demands cooperation and a degree of intimacy between Leaphorn and Chee that the

earlier novels produced through the design of plots that made one character's investigation of a case overlap with the investigation conducted
by the other character. As a consequence of Hillerman's new organization of the police force, he has created an institutional reason for the
detectives working together and, thus, has also found an opportunity for
their continuing interaction in the narrative.

An "Author's Note" to *Sacred Clowns* signals another change affecting
the premises of Hillerman's fiction, at least for this novel. Most of the
note consists of conventional disclaimers. The characters are fictional,
Hillerman states, and represent no one. But then he goes on to say that
while he has had advice from an expert on ritual clowns, "the descriptions in this book do not represent Hopi religious activities" any more
than Tano represents a Hopi village. Rather, he explains, the Tano cer-
emonialism in the novel "is a melding of the author's experience at other
pueblos." Since there can be no doubt that for many readers the ethnographic detail in Hillerman's novels adds to their appeal, it seems a remarkable statement for the author to say, in effect, "Don't you believe
it. These facts are fiction."

On the other hand, we must always be at least a little wary of taking
the accounts of religious performance and beliefs in the novels as reportage rather than the work of imagination. At this point in his series
of Native American detective stories, Hillerman takes pains to confirm
the fictitiousness of his project, which is not to say that the information
his novels provide about the indigenous people of the Southwest bears
no relationship to reality. Indeed, Hillerman directs us from time to time
in other authorial notes to published sources that will show that the
information does pertain to reality. Instead, Hillerman is declaring that
his narratives imitate, but do not constitute, reality.

This is not so much a change in the way that creation of an office for
special investigations amounts to a change, as it is an affirmation that
all along Hillerman has been writing, and will continue in this novel,
too, to be writing literature. In his own way, Hillerman is repeating the
"Notice" Mark Twain placed at the beginning of *The Adventures of Huck-
leberry Finn*: "Persons attempting to find a motive in this narrative will
be prosecuted; persons attempting to find a moral in it will be banished;
persons attempting to find a plot in it will be shot." That last bit about
plot is something of a joke, since fiction likely has more apparent plot
than reality does, but the tone of Twain's "Notice" anticipates Hillerman's "Author's Note." Both of these novelists of American experience

and character wanted to be certain that readers wouldn't overlook the inventions of their craft.

CHARACTER DEVELOPMENT

Part of the exposition of Leaphorn and Chee's new relationship in *Sacred Clowns* addresses the official ranks they hold in the police force. Prior novels have uniformly given Leaphorn the rank of lieutenant, except for an apparent slip in the book that introduces Chee, *People of Darkness*, when he finds a note on his desk to call *Captain* Leaphorn at the Chinle substation (48). Chee has the rank of corporal in the two short stories, "Chee's Witch" and "The Witch, Yazzie, and the Nine of Clubs," but is referred to intermittently in the full-length narratives as a sergeant. *Sacred Clowns* clarifies that Chee has been an *acting* Sergeant, but "he hadn't liked it much and it hadn't lasted" (32). If Chee succeeds in solving a hit-and-run case of vehicular homicide, Leaphorn figures he will deserve to be permanently a sergeant. This time Chee could like it, because the pay and status might advance his tentative hopes of marrying Janet Pete.

Ambivalence follows Chee through all of his relationships. After he had met Mary Landon in *People of Darkness*, he had become preoccupied with the personal conflict about the alternative directions in which his love for her could take him. He had been torn between thoughts of merging into the mainstream world by joining the FBI and marrying Mary, which would result in his leaving the Reservation, and the unrealistic idea of her acculturating to Navajo life. Chee had drifted between the poles of choice until Mary resolved the issue by reentering graduate school in Wisconsin and effectively ending any prospect of their marriage. With Janet Pete, the part-Navajo lawyer whom Chee had met in *Skinwalkers*, his ambivalence takes the form of "a soaring joy at the beauty of this young woman, and . . . a leaden sense of doubt that she would ever, ever, ever settle for him" (66).

Just as their mutual affection seems sufficient to unite Janet and Chee, Hillerman finds another factor that will frustrate the progress of love—the incest taboo proscribing marriage between people of the same clan. It seems to be in keeping with the character of a man devoted to Navajo tradition to feel he has to consult elders on the history of the Navajo clans in order to guarantee that he and Janet will not violate the taboo.

On the other hand, Janet Pete's mother is a Scot, not a Navajo, and her father was one of the Navajos relocated by government policy to the city to foster their assimilation into general American society. Like other City Navajos, Janet's father had only the slightest trace of a memory of his clan affiliations. One might think a less zealous person than Chee would rest content in that lack of knowledge.

Chapter Twenty-four of *Sacred Clowns* relates the results of Chee's investigation of clan connections to an account of the oral informants summoned by his uncle telling the stories of clans at great and inconclusive length until an old woman says that, after all, only the mother's clan matters. In Janet's case, that's MacDougal (279). There's some reason to believe that the experience of this personal investigation could modify Chee's attachment to tradition, for he tells Janet that he has discovered he is nowhere near traditional enough to suit the male elders of another generation (275).

Chee's relationship to tradition, however, must always remain complex. When police business takes him to the site of the Navajo Agricultural Industries (NAI) in Chapter Nineteen, he displays mixed feelings about its success in irrigating the land for crops. In a "patriotic" mood, he is proud of the development, but when he is feeling religious, he is bothered by the way the NAI has altered the landscape, tearing away the original plant life and "reducing nature to great irrigated circles." (194). In a conversation with Janet Pete, Joe Leaphorn captures the oddness of Chee. "He wants to be a bona fide traditionalist. . . . Not just to be a shaman, but to be a really effective one," which is hard to manage, if you are a modern man, too. But "Officer Chee," says Leaphorn, wants somehow to subject modernity to tradition; he "wants to save his people from the future" (242).

The "odd sort of idealist" (242) Chee is makes it inevitable that he and Leaphorn will not make a neat fit in their new association. As Leaphorn sees him, Chee cannot comfortably abide by rules. He is an individualist going his own way. He is sometimes boneheaded, as when he leaves the tape of Councilman Chester's conversation with Ed Zeck in Leaphorn's office and creates the circumstances for Leaphorn's temporary suspension from the police force. Discussions of cases between the two detectives, as in Chapter Two, are often tense, but even though Chee feels cowed at times, he cannot stop going his own way. *Sacred Clowns* makes that romantic independence clearest in Chee's resolution of the hit-and-run case. Legally speaking, in terms of *bilagaan* (white society's) justice, the case is solved but not resolved. Chee discovers who committed the crime and all of the circumstances surrounding it, but viewing the actions of Clement Hoski through the lens of Navajo belief in *hozho,* or harmonious adjustment, rather than punishment, he determines that Hoski's reparations to the family of his victim and his sense of shame are sufficient conclusion. He suppresses his solution of the case, leaving it "unsolved." In aid of his detective character, Hillerman uncharacteristically detaches the hit-and-run case from other lines of inquiry in the novel. Almost always his plots work to tie together all of the cases the detectives pursue into a comprehensive puzzle. This time, however, the dramatic opportunity of showing Chee adapting tradition to contemporary conditions moves Hillerman to peel away the Hoski case from the other cases in this novel.

Hillerman presents an illuminating treatment of his characters' dual cultural consciousness in Chapter Eleven of *Sacred Clowns.* Sergeant Harold Blizzard, a Cheyenne from Chicago who has been sent from his office in Albuquerque to join the hunt for Delmar Kanitewa, accepts Janet Pete's invitation to go with her and Chee to see the John Ford movie *Cheyenne Autumn.* Evidently, on the principle that all Indians look alike to the Anglos, lots of Navajos were hired as extras in the film to impersonate Cheyennes. Chee's oldest sister Irma is one of those extras singing a modified song from a Navajo ceremonial "slowed . . . down to make it sound solemn." The extras' intrusion of other Navajo elements into the putatively Cheyenne film makes for an insiders' joke that the Navajo audience at the Gallup Drive-In finds irresistibly and repeatedly hilarious. Serious-looking Cheyenne impersonators in the movie respond to questions from Richard Widmark and other white actors in sobersounding Navajo, which is translated in the movie into something sensible for the plot. But what they really said "tended to have something to do with the size of the colonel's penis, or some other earthy and humorous irrelevancy" (120–21). The whole affair elicits celebratory horn honking and gales of laughter from the cars full of Navajos at the drive-in.

Chee notices, however, that Blizzard's response is quite different. The Navajos would be laughing at the private joke; Blizzard "would be looking sad. Same scene, exactly. He'd be watching the destruction of his culture. We'd be watching our kinfolks making fun of the white folks in the movie" (130). The private joke equals a small victory for Navajo living culture, but Blizzard has no viable Native American culture. Raised in a city far from the Cheyenne Reservation that he visited only once, he is a stranger even to his own culture. Perhaps he feels personally the significance of the absence of the legendary tribe of Cheyennes from the movie meant to be about them. But Blizzard is not the only one in the position of relative ignorance. Janet Pete also has trouble understanding her Native American identity. Realizing that, Chee grasps the poignance of Janet's position on "this Big-Reservation-Full-of-Strangers." Habitually, he has seen "only the shrewd attorney who looked great in expensive clothing, who wore the armor of wit, humor, education, intelligence. He hadn't seen the girl who was trying to find a home" (131). Janet Pete and Harold Blizzard surely become representative characters in this chapter of *Sacred Clowns*. They are representative not only of a population of Native Americans lifted from the nurture of their ethnic culture, but also of many thousands, and millions of other people in the modern world who have been physically uprooted by migration or exile and experience psychological rootlessness and indecision about identity. Seen in association with Blizzard's and Pete's deracinated circumstances, Jim Chee's constant sense of an identity crisis will strike readers more as a deliberate quest for psychic survival in the modern world that has made his people a so-called minority than as the expression of obstinate romanticizing of tradition that it seems to be when he belabors the problem of Janet Pete's parental clans.

Joe Leaphorn has always played a more stable, less conflicted part in their novels than Chee. In *Sacred Clowns* he runs true to form in his devotion to the rules of police procedure and professional responsibility. What has changed about Leaphorn's development since his original appearance in Hillerman's first Navajo novel *The Blessing Way* is the relative attention given in the narrative to his personal life. From the start, Hillerman included biographical information about Leaphorn, but much of that could be taken as fulfilling the minimum requirements of verisimilitude or the simulation of reality. Leaphorn had a wife, but instead of appearing directly in the novels, she entered them in Joe's memory, particularly when she became ill and died. Even when her death motivated him to retire from the police force in *A Thief of Time*, he continued to live his personal life out of the focus of the novel, so that Joe Leaphorn's biography consisted exclusively in scenes of his police practice. That began to change with the entry of Louisa Bourebonette on the scene in *Coyote Waits*. Given a significant relationship to the leading suspect in that novel, Louisa gradually became an informal colleague of Leaphorn's in the investigation, someone whose involvement in Leaphorn's case is shown in the book rather than merely reported as his wife Emma's had been in brief passages of the early books. In *Sacred Clowns* Louisa is a fully realized participant in his life, talking over the central puzzle of the book with Leaphorn in Chapter Seven and, more importantly, injecting into the narrative a degree of suspense over whether or not they will be able to make their trip to China.

In addition to providing Leaphorn with an affectionate companionship in the novel, Hillerman gives him a congenial long-term friend in the FBI agent "Dilly" Streib. Actually, Streib had appeared in the novel *Skinwalkers* where he was identified as Delbert (Dilly) Streib. In *Sacred Clowns* he is called David (Dilly) Streib and becomes a figure who replaces the genre convention of caginess between a clearly superior leading detective and an intellectually limited "official," such as can be found when Inspector Lestrade appears in stories about Sherlock Holmes, or when other FBI agents play parts in Hillerman's fiction, with genuine comradeship. Dilly ribs Leaphorn about his interest in Louisa, accompanies him on visits to crime scenes, and during his scenes with Leaphorn softens the stark appearance of a mastermind plodding onward through the procedure required by the case.

With these additions to the characterization of Leaphorn, the notable love of detail that makes him something of a pain to Chee (25), while also something of a model (290), and the passages where Leaphorn fits clues together—for example, the dark wood shavings in Dorsey's shop (156) and the Lincoln Cane (180)—gain a humanizing context that makes Leaphorn more interesting than the methodologist of police procedure the plot of a novel requires him to become. In this respect, in *Sacred Clowns* Leaphorn becomes a more equal partner with Chee than he has ever been before.

Of course, method must have a central place in the characterization of any reflective detective. That is why readers learn most of what they know about Leaphorn and Chee from scenes where they are actively working on their cases. It is these scenes (such as the one in Chapter Twenty-six when Chee rehearses with Janet the issues of justice relating to Clement Hoski, or the one in Chapter Twenty-eight when Leaphorn's Navajo conditioning to search for harmony results in his discovery of the puzzle's solution [295]), that delineate the contours of their quizzical minds and the sources of ways they have chosen to express themselves in work.

Characterization in fiction seems to follow a linear order. Chee moves one way on his cases. The order is suspended for a while, and Leaphorn moves forward to take the story in another direction. The two progressions cross at various times, as when Chee inadvertently becomes the cause of Leaphorn's suspension. These patterns, however, are matters more of plot than characterization. For knowledge of the human cast of the narrative, the sort of knowledge that in real life equips us to feel that we can predict how a person will behave and what is really important to the person, we must look instead to the interrelationships of characters and how they act and react to the simulations of activity in the world. This is why Janet Pete and Louisa and Dilly and Blizzard are so significant and why the seemingly secondary course of affections in a detective novel tells us so much of importance.

PLOT DEVELOPMENT

Earlier discussions in this book of the structure of Hillerman's detective novels have focused on a distinction between criminal plot and narrative plot. Criminal plot corresponds to a common denotation of plot recorded in most dictionary entries as the first meaning of the term, namely, a secret scheme to accomplish some purpose, especially a hostile or evil purpose. By contrast, narrative plot denotes the systematic arrangement relating the detectives' progress in the narrative toward explanation or solution of the criminal plot.

Samuel Taylor Coleridge proclaimed the audience's "willing suspension of disbelief" in a fictitious construction to be an essential requirement of literature. Hillerman seems to have had Coleridge in mind when he told Ernie Bulow that he intends his narratives to provide a base of reality that will encourage his readers to suppress their disbelief (Bulow 67). Certainly, Coleridge's durable formulation applies well to the popular genre of detective fiction. It is almost as if there were a tacit contract between author and readers. If the author will do this, then the readers will lend the author their credence. To help an audience "believe" in the criminal plot requires that the author construct it on a level of acceptable plausibility: motive must be sufficient to the crime, victims must be likely ones, and the crime, which is usually homicide in detective fiction, must occur in ways that are consistent and possible within the environment. Narrative plot also demands plausibility for audiences to believe in it. Narrative plot in detective fiction, however, follows the method of detectives assembling evidence, drawing inferences from it, constructing a scenario of explanation for the criminal plot, and bringing the events of the narrative to conclusion. As the emphasis on methodological procedure indicates, plausibility for narrative plot in detective fiction issues from what might be called the detectives' argument, which must have a semblance of logic to it. Neither plot, criminal or narrative, need be simple and routine in its execution. Within the scope of the contract with readers, there is room for ingenuity in the criminal plot and wit or elegance in the narrative's demonstration of the detectives' discovery of the criminal plot. Our previous discussions of plotting in Hillerman's fiction have uncovered plenty of ingenuity and wit.

The criminal plot of *Sacred Clowns* originates in Roger Applebee's character. In his early appearances, he seems to be anything but a villain, for he is an effective environmentalist lawyer and an entirely affable person. In keeping with a sturdy convention of detective fiction, Hillerman has drawn him as an unlikely suspect in the ensuing crimes. For that matter, Eugene Ahkeah, taken into custody when an anonymous tip leads police to a cache of items stolen from Eric Dorsey's shop hidden under his porch, also seems an unlikely suspect, but he is caught "with the goods on him." Evidence makes a big difference. Applebee assumes a "take no prisoners" role in his battle for the environment. Shortly after Applebee tells Janet Pete and Jim Chee that he believes there may be evidence that Council Member Jimmy Chester was paid by proponents of the waste dump to favor their project (78), the evidence surfaces in a clandestine tape that appears out of nowhere in Jim Chee's office (143–47). Who else could have made the tape but Applebee, thinks Chee, but the tape suggests nothing more to Chee than zeal, because he, too, is an outspoken opponent of the dump and, therefore, in sympathy with Applebee's cause.

The hint of deceptiveness in Applebee's acquisition of the tape, and his failure to confirm that it refers to cattle deals rather than the dump project, is but a small sign of his deeper implication in the cases of homicide the detectives are pursuing. Over a long period of time he has deceived Eric Dorsey, so that he would make replicas of the Lincoln canes. He has used his life-long friend Asher Davis in a design to impugn the reputation of the governor, and, of course, he is guilty of one murder his deception has been employed to cover and guilty of instigating another.

Applebee's character, on the surface so benign, beneath the surface so calculating, serves as the key article in Hillerman's contract of plausibility in the criminal plot. Chapter Twenty-one where Leaphorn encounters Davis at Applebee's motel (although the final chapter seems to confuse the principals by saying Chee interviewed Davis [299]) draws on Davis's long experience with Applebee to paint the picture of a man for whom other people exist to be used. The point becomes conclusive at the end of the novel when Leaphorn relates the entire criminal plot to the flawed character of Roger Applebee (301). Given the character structure Hillerman describes, a structure that identifies Applebee according to a familiar type in clinical psychology and everyone's practical experience, Applebee can be seen to have developed a plausible motive for his crimes. The incongruity between his superficial manner and the depths within him establishes the psychological means by which he carried out his crimes. His patient building of relationships with Dorsey and Davis, conducted in the manner of a chess player looking many moves ahead, his shrewd manipulation of Chee and Ahkeah, and the arrogant extent and complexity of his criminal plot signal, entirely plausibly, a psychotic ingenuity in Applebee. His victims are the likely objects of his manipulative scheme, and the means he employs are completely consistent with the small community of the Navajo Reservations. In sum, Tony Hillerman's draft of the criminal plot in *Sacred Clowns* easily and successfully meets his contractual obligation to make readers believe.

The same can be said of his narrative plot. The scenario Chee develops with Blizzard and Janet in Chapter Twenty-six about Dorsey being used, and the fuller scenario proposed by Leaphorn in the novel's final chapter, account for all the significant evidence in their exposition of the criminal plot. Along the way to the point of creating their scenarios of exposition, each detective is represented in the narrative developing his evidence by a combination of routine police work, such as interrogation, and careful thought. Indeed, the overarching drama in a novel full of events becomes the detectives' processes of thought. Chapter Seventeen well illustrates this approach. There Leaphorn questions Teddy Sayesva, the brother of the murdered koshare (a sacred clown in The Kachina dance ceremony) Francis, about the package their nephew Delmar was seen carrying. Learning its religious importance, Leaphorn has an answer to one of his puzzles. A replica of the Lincoln Cane was in the package and had its apparently intended effect when it was placed at the last minute in the wagon hauled by the koshares during their part in the traditional ceremony. As suddenly as he has the answer to one puzzle, Leaphorn finds it leading to new puzzles. They must be welcome ones, though, since the new queries about why Dorsey would have made the replica cane and why it ended up in the wagon direct the investigation along quite specific lines that bring Leaphorn closer to a solution of the master problems of murder.

The examples of Leaphorn's discovery of new puzzles in Chapter Seventeen and the trial scenarios each detective advances as they come closer to solving their detection problem should be sufficient to show that Hillerman fulfills his contract with his readers about the narrative plot as well as he does the contract about the criminal plot. The disruption of order which the novel introduced in its first chapter is plausibly explained by the evidence gathered in the ways the police conduct their inquiries and by the reasoning of highly intelligent officers whose Navajo culture has conditioned them to read signs and seek connections among all things. The narrative plot broadens to include two homicides and a collection of suspects and, then, through the working of the detectives' minds centers on increasingly specific elements of the puzzle. In this way, the plot again displays in *Sacred Clowns* the ingenuity that earns Hillerman's craft its high reputation.

THEMATIC ISSUES

Sometimes ethnic characters are introduced into fiction by an announcement that their complexion is dark or that their names reveal family origins somewhere other than in Northern Europe. When there is no more to it than that, the characters are accidental ethnics. That is never so with the characters in Hillerman's detective fiction. Leaphorn, Chee, and other Native Americans who play roles in the Hillerman novels are inherently Native American even as they undergo the trial of sustaining their identities in modern America. Consequently, the narratives presenting Hillerman's Native American characters inevitably carry meaning relevant to the Native American cultures. Despite the disclaimer found in the author's note to *Sacred Clowns,* there can be no doubt that Hillerman intends this novel to resonate with Navajo values in the same way that his other books do.

Jim Chee's resolution of the case of Clement Hoski's hit-and-run gives a strong example of the inherent importance of Navajo values. It is not existential heroism that moves Chee to suppress the evidence he has gathered linking Hoski to the death of Victor Todachene, nor is it adherence to an individual code. That sort of motivation frequently occurs, for example, in the novels about Spenser written by Robert L. Parker and in the narratives about Sam Spade and the Continental Op written by Dashiell Hammett. In those works, the individualistic actions of the protagonists signify that the detectives live in a society that lacks consensual value structures. Each person must create a value system for himself or herself in order to be innocent of the bad faith existentialists find is entailed in thoughtless application of moral systems that have lost relevance to modern life. Jim Chee, however, exists in a society that is not yet like that. Alcohol, misguided government policy, and poverty have weakened Navajo communal ties, but in Hillerman's novels these durable and adaptable people sustain their mutual belief that immanent meaning fills their world.

For that reason, Jim Chee worries about the conflict between the legal requirement of punishment and the spiritual presence of *hozho,* or harmony, and decides finally that the claims of a superior order should guide him. The same philosophical conception sustains Leaphorn in his estimate of the likelihood that Asher Davis can be convicted for killing the koshare. Leaphorn finds he really doesn't care about the legal case because "by the laws of Navajo metaphysics he would, inevitably, suffer for" turning evil. His reputation as an Honest Indian Trader would be ruined (302). It may seem alien to the duty of a sworn officer to care so little for the successful legal conclusion of a case and the wreaking of appropriate punishment, but the gap between expectations about police officers and Leaphorn's view in the matter is exactly Hillerman's point. Leaphorn, like Chee, is a *Navajo* police officer. In that sense, he serves his people with the double consciousness of cultures that makes him their kin.

Another, related theme of heavenly values informs the presence of the Hopi ceremony in *Sacred Clowns.* The koshares, apparently so disruptive of the solemn rite, actually enact the theological distinction between the human propensity to do everything wrong and the nature of spirits to do everything right (14). In their satiric skits, Teddy Sayesva explains to Leaphorn, the koshares function as "ethical police" showing how human beings drift from the ways they have been taught by the spirits (178). Hillerman creates an interesting twist on the practiced role of the koshares in *Sacred Clowns.* With their inclusion of the Lincoln Cane in their wagon and their greedy vending of artifacts to Indian traders, they convey a message about preserving native culture, but the shock of this specific pantomime follows upon Applebee's devious schemes. The theme of the koshares remains valid enough, but it gains an added significance, invisible to the audience, owing to the intrusion of Applebee's design upon the sacred ritual. His actions, in effect, underline the validity of the koshares' satire.

Each of the themes noted so far arises from the special conditions of the Navajo ethnic enclave where communal values retain efficacy. A more generalized theme about exploitation also appears. The novel tells us that Indian traders have a well-earned reputation for dishonesty growing out of the way they habitually cheat customers. From the prodding of the satiric koshares, it becomes possibly more important to observe that opportunity for cheating arises in the first place when artifacts are converted into commodities for cash exchange. In their original state, the artifacts now offered for sale and trade embodied a culture's history. Produced for ceremonial or domestic purposes, the artifacts were intended for functional use; thus, their utility was primary, their appearance or antiquity secondary. Trade in artifacts reverses the relationship to make the appearance or the age of an item the source of its value measured in monetary terms. Thinking of aesthetically pleasing art one can see in museum collections of Native American artifacts makes the idea of their reduction to commodities seem severe. Yet, there is something to ponder in the idea, and it is the intent of *Sacred Clowns* to encourage pondering.

Indeed, the theme of integrity of use informs all of Hillerman's detective fiction, whether the topic is the natural environment, as it is when Chee visits the Navajo Agricultural Industries project in *Sacred Clowns*; archaeological excavation presented in *A Thief of Time* and other works; or when it relates to the traditions of history, as when Chee or Leaphorn harken to Navajo legend and philosophy during their criminal investigations. By extension, the theme of integrity of use can also apply to human relationships, for the evil to be found in Applebee's behavior and the problems of identity that confront Jim Chee, Janet Pete, Harold Blizzard, and the imaginary Tano Pueblo are all and always about integrity. With that in mind, it seems accurate to say that besides the creation of effective narratives, Tony Hillerman devotes his craft to moral study.

A NARRATOLOGICAL READING OF *SACRED CLOWNS*

If this book about Hillerman's detective fiction were to pass into the hands of a relentlessly practical critic, we could expect the critic to complain that the discussions of characterization sometimes read as though they are supposed to be about real people, and that the Reservation pictured in the novels gets treated like a real place. What's the matter, don't you know it is all fictitious? Of course, in a way the critic is entirely correct. It *is* all fiction, and critics ought to control their disposition to give physical substance to characters or setting and to ascribe actuality to narrative events. In another way, the relentlessly practical critic would be taking a leaf from the writings of narratological critics who view fiction as entirely pretense. The words denoting the names of characters are simply written signs. The conversations characters are alleged to have, the thoughts assigned them by their creators—all of this is writing on a page. It may resonate in readers' minds, so that when they see the writing they think of feelings they have had or experiences they have met in other times; but all of that activity in the book? What it amounts to is acts of language—phrasings and statements and queries that may simulate actuality but are instead pretenses.

If we can entertain the perspective that written narratives of fiction are pretenses parading as reality, we may use that insight to construct a statement about the materials and craft of fiction. The reader's tendency to recognize the behavior of characters as relevant to their own experiences, when, for example, Roger Applebee's manipulative ways echo what we have seen of actual psychotic actions, indicates that to make up a character in fiction the author takes elements of reality and fictionalizes them. The same can be said of all the concrete details in a narrative: the landscape of the Reservations, the buildings, the police station. In addition, when we read a passage of fictional dialogue, we are observing how real speech practices are borrowed and fictionalized for the purposes of fiction.

These principles of narratology lead to the conclusion that a narrative's literary quality lies in its imitation of reality. The idea is as old as Aristotle whose *Poetics* argues that literary creation "becomes a vehicle of *mimesis*, that is, of representation, or rather of the *simulation* of imaginary actions and events" (Genette, 6–7). Much of the critical writing in narratology investigates the appropriate categories and terminology for describing the artifice of fiction. Still, such fundamental work helps us read in a practical way.

Consider, for example, that *Sacred Clowns* was published three years after *Coyote Waits*, but we have no reason at all to believe that Chee's relationship with Janet Pete and Leaphorn's relationship with Louisa Bourebonette has been going on that long. Maybe they have, maybe they haven't, but real chronology is not the same as fictional time. An elementary example fixes the matter of fictional time. Hillerman makes it a habit to try to confine the narrative time of his novels to a few days, but the passage of time in the fiction never becomes equivalent to a reader's real time. Reading, we can cover a few days in a few hours, or we might set the book aside and not pick it up again for weeks.

Narratology leads into further complexity when it is applied to the examination of plot(s), criminal and narrative. The criminal plot of Roger Applebee in *Sacred Clowns* extends over a long period of time before the novel begins and occurs offstage, so to speak, once the book is underway. Can we therefore view the criminal plot as less important than the narrative plot? Not at all. But Hillerman has pushed the criminal plot outside of the frame of his narrative, decentered it in order to stress instead the detection work, and he has done that because the fictitious way of imitating events that has come to be called the genre of detective fiction requires it.

One final notation on the insights accorded by narratology is in order. Among the materials of reality the author may choose to employ for fiction are the written forms in which facts are presented, sometimes newspaper articles or police reports, other times dialogue or journals or whatever. When the writer is skillful, the fictitious nature of the simulation of a factual form can be forgotten. That sounds, we may think, just like the way somebody might talk or just the way a bureaucratic discussion might proceed. Nevertheless, it is just as much invented as anything else in the narrative.

Armed with narratological insight, our critical interpretations of text will not necessarily become better, or even markedly different, than they would be anyway. Narratological insight, however, opens the way for readers to comprehend, for example, how an author meets the stipulations of the tacit contract with readers. In the long run, the effect of fiction depends on the author's craft. The term *craft* is well chosen, for craft means not just talent and skill but also artifice and cunning. No author of detective fiction can write without employing it all.

13

Finding Moon
(1995)

When the rumors and hints that Tony Hillerman was working on a novel set in Asia were fulfilled with publication of *Finding Moon,* he prefaced the new book with an apology to fellow desert rats "for wandering away from our beloved Navajo canyon country" and a promise that "the next book will bring Jim Chee and Joe Leaphorn of the Tribal Police back into action" (ix). This assurance that he was simply interrupting the steady issue of Navajo detective narratives makes a notable contrast to the writing plans Hillerman had entertained twenty-five years before at the start of his writing career. Then he had aimed to devote himself to writing the "big book" that is the dream of everyone with literary ambitions. Uncertain of his capacity to handle a major work on the subject of politics and journalism, Hillerman undertook what he expected to be only an apprentice work, which was eventually published as *The Blessing Way.* Turning then to his "important" subject he wrote and published *The Fly on the Wall,* but shortly afterwards returned to the subject of crime and detection in Navajo country. Whatever motivated Hillerman's reconsideration of his original aim for his fiction, he adapted with alacrity and skill so that he has become now almost completely identified with, and widely respected for, the cycle of Leaphorn and Chee novels exploring ethical and cultural themes in the vivid settings of Native American reservations. Surely the excursion to other territory for the narrative of *Find-*

ing Moon, in light of Hillerman's prefatory apology and promise, will not change the direction of a remarkably successful writing career.

All the more reason, then, for readers and critics familiar with the body of Hillerman's fiction to view *Finding Moon* against its background. How does it relate to the stories of Leaphorn and Chee? On the other hand, it is just as interesting to find ways that *Finding Moon* appears to be unique in Hillerman's canon. Inescapably comparative issues like these frame our reading and discussion of the narrative of Moon Mathias's journey to Southeast Asia.

GENERIC CONVENTIONS

Hillerman centers the narrative of *Finding Moon* on a nest of puzzles. The first of these is the odd news from the office of Philippine Airlines that Moon's mother, Victoria Mathias, is hospitalized in Los Angeles, thousands of miles from her home in Florida. When Moon arrives at the hospital and examines the documents in Victoria's purse, new surprises come forth. Moon's deceased brother Rick, it seems, had fathered a child, and Victoria was on her way to bring the infant girl back to the United States. But where is the child's mother, and why wasn't Moon told that he has a niece? Each query suggests additional mysteries. Each step Moon takes to seek answers carries him into more complex circumstances. Mr. Lum Lee and his grandson Charley Ming, strangers to Moon, evidently have had dealings with Rick and know about Victoria's mission. Arriving in the Philippines, Moon encounters Mrs. Osa van Winjgaarden, yet another acquaintance of Rick's and another person with expectations about the journey Moon has reluctantly begun.

Nesting mysteries are a familiar convention in the detective fiction genre, because they readily present an object of investigation and suggest a chain of causation that it is the purpose of the rational detective to reveal. Implicitly they indicate that everything may be found by the rational mind to have connection. Hillerman commonly employs a sequence of puzzles in his fiction and precisely for the reasons indicated— to provide a trail for the detection method.

In the case of *Finding Moon* the nesting mysteries also form a regression from present to past that leads deeper toward the roots of causation. Among modern authors of detective fiction, Ross Macdonald, creator of the Lew Archer stories, possibly exemplifies best the use of regressive mysteries, which lead beneath the appearance of present normality to reveal family pathology engendered by an earlier tragedy. Macdonald's representation of the nesting regressive mysteries takes its inspiration from the Freudian scheme of psychology, and while Hillerman does not share Macdonald's Freudian belief, he does use the nest of mysteries to enter issues of character. This is particularly so in *Finding Moon*, where the puzzle of the Asian child leads finally to exploration of the puzzling contradictions in Moon Mathias himself.

A much more unusual convention of detective fiction for Hillerman than the nesting puzzles occurs when Moon Mathias accidentally becomes the detective protagonist of the narrative. As the Managing Editor of the Durance, Colorado, *Press-Register*, Moon Mathias shares with John Cotton, the central character of *The Fly on the Wall*, the profession of journalism that requires its adherents to act on many occasions as investigators, but there is something else about Moon's becoming the detective that associates him with another familiar convention of the genre. Moon in no way seeks to become the investigator of the Asian background of his brother, nor is he originally especially disposed to investigate his own character. He is the accidental detective. Like such unprepared and innocent characters as Charles Latimer in Eric Ambler's pattern-setting novel *The Mask of Dimitrios*, Moon Mathias is overtaken by events and seems almost willfully resistant to becoming engaged by the problems of Mr. Lee, Mrs. van Winjgaarden, and maybe even Rick. To indicate this attribute Hillerman inserts passages in the novel where Moon yearns for the mundane life at home or minimizes the observations he is provided about the Pol Pot regime in Cambodia (154, 208).

It is not hard to see the attraction of the accidental detective. There is a tendency in all readers to seek a character who seems easily accessible, somebody neither outsized nor debased. Such a portrayal is designated normative by critics, meaning, of course, that the fictional figure represents the usual, the common, somebody like the readers in most ways. In detective fiction a sidekick, a Dr. Watson, may perform the role of normative character. When events of the narrative are extraordinary, however, and the tale set far away, a writer may choose to equip readers with the guidance of a normative figure in the guise of the central character. That is exactly what Hillerman has done in casting Moon Mathias as the accidental and reluctant detective.

Yet another pleasing convention of the genre appears in this novel through Osa van Winjgaarden—the love/companionship relationship. In keeping with his handling of the relationship of loving companions in his other novels, here Hillerman presents it developing slowly as the characters are brought together by events. Soon they become collegial participants in the investigation. In what seems a major departure for Hillerman, however, the relationship concludes within the confines of this single book with Moon and Osa's plan to marry. This is further evidence that *Finding Moon* is only a break in the established cycle of Navajo novels.

SETTING

Impelled as we are to look at *Finding Moon* against a backdrop of Hillerman's other novels, the greatest departure will be found in the setting of the narrative. First of all, Hillerman brings his characters overseas. Moving through the Philippines, Cambodia, and Vietnam, they remain within reach of American influence but experience their story in the vastly different circumstances of Asian societies in the crisis of war. With the taciturn Mr. Lum Lee, the Dutch national Osa van Winjgaarden, and expatriate American associates of Rick Mathias as the only "expert" participants in the cultures of Asia, the narrative lacks the intimate association of character and setting that marks Hillerman's Navajo novels. Consequently, the setting remains distant and indecipherable for non-Asian readers, but then comprehension of cultural difference is not as important to Hillerman in this novel as it is in his other works.

This is not to say, however, that setting is incidental to *Finding Moon.* The setting has been developed so that what gains our attention is the *war in Southeast Asia,* not the enduring reality of Southeast Asia. Hillerman accomplishes the development of his setting by the simple device of dating the chapters from April 12, 1975, to May 9, 1975, the twenty-seven days when Saigon fell, the United States abandoned its embassy in Cambodia, and America lost the war. Additionally, each chapter carries as an epigraph a dated press dispatch reporting another stage along the slide to military and political defeat. By foregrounding the end of the war, Hillerman makes setting cause and counterpoint within the narrative: cause in the sense that the war has generated the alliances, oppositions, and confusions that create the mysteries of the narrative; counterpoint in the sense that the close of the historical period that the war's end denotes serves as a contrast with the opening for new possibility, and happiness, that Moon achieves by the story's end.

PLOT

Previous chapters in this book have made a distinction between two meanings for the term plot. One of those meanings refers to the criminal design of the evildoers in the narrative, while the other meaning refers to the arrangement of events and episodes within the narrative so that the process of detection provides the movement for the novel. To treat plot in *Finding Moon* also requires us to observe a distinction between two levels of activity in the narrative, but they are not the same as in the other fictions.

The convention of nesting mysteries not only provides for regression into past happenings and tapping into causes for the circumstances of the present, but it also gives arrangement to chapters and scenes and, thereby, accounts for movement within the narrative. In this respect the convention provides the detection plot to the novel.

The second and accompanying plot is strongly signaled by the title of the novel, *Finding Moon*. Not finding the baby, not finding Rick, but finding Moon, who is cast by the narrative in the role of the searcher. He is finding himself, as the saying goes. And Moon's trail of self-discovery is blazed through encounters with the sympathetic priest Father Julian and Mrs. Osa van Winjgaarden. The priest, whom Moon meets on the fifth day of his journey and subsequently revisits, offers a sympathetic ear and a provocative tongue to Moon. At one point he tells Moon he must be "treasuring hatred" and getting used to his sin (78–79). Other times he provides leading questions to draw Moon out, not so much to reveal anything to the priest, as his presence in the church's confessional might at first lead us to expect, but to help Moon inspect himself. Clearly Father Julian is a pastoral therapist, but for all of his worldliness he is, after all, a priest, and that has considerable importance to the construction of Hillerman's narrative.

As we know from biographical information, Hillerman had a Roman Catholic upbringing. From his writings we know also that he holds faith in a spiritual cosmology, one in which evil and good do exist, where respect for the dignity of the world's creatures gives a purposeful order to life. That much is evident, even though the Navajo novels communicate spiritual values in terms of Native American culture. In *Finding Moon* the spiritual values regain what we may assume are their Christian origins for Hillerman. The significance of this lies in the provision to the novel of an inner journey, a second plot.

Hillerman works assiduously to intertwine the two plots of *Finding Moon,* the investigative procession and Moon's internal journey. Information gathered through the first plot about, for example, Rick's surprisingly high opinion of Moon, helps Moon drop his defensive self-denigration and, thus, makes the two plots interdependent. At other times Hillerman takes pains to indicate that while actively participating in the adventures of entering war-torn lands, Moon is simultaneously struggling with self-definition. An example occurs when Hillerman describes the exhausted Moon riding in the armored personnel carrier driven by Osa; he is slowly beginning to make sense of life (280–81).

Structural unity might properly be thought of as the function of this careful integration of Hillerman's two kinds of plot in *Finding Moon.* When we consider the narrow time frame (twenty-seven days) for the events, the continuous reinforcement of the atmosphere of historical crisis created by the setting, and the integration of plot, we must conclude that *Finding Moon* is one of the tightest, most closely fitted novels Hillerman has so far written.

CHARACTERIZATION

Moon Mathias is modeled on a template of familiar psychology. He has experienced tragedy in his life. As a child, he saw his mother's devotion during his father's incurable illness; as an adult, he feels unable to live up to the role models of strength they provided. A drunken accident that resulted in the death of his best friend has left him riddled with guilt; his guilt is exacerbated when his mother marries a man she doesn't love to gain the money to provide for Moon's legal defense. In adulthood he has become his own foe. He takes up relationships with women that will be undemanding. He works at what he considers to be a third-rate job. He suppresses feeling and resists adventure. In a real sense he is withdrawn from life, a spiritual zombie.

What gives this portrayal its interest is the drama Hillerman creates in the revelation and resolution of Moon's tortured psyche. Hillerman integrally relates Moon's inner experience to the investigation he reluctantly undertakes. The most striking technique for this linkage is Hillerman's layering of present and past in Moon's reported consciousness. The best examples of this are Moon's discussions with Father Julian; the priest's interrogation provokes Moon to talk about the past events that so bother him and, we imagine, to feel their pain again. Within those passages the narrative re-enacts past events complete with dialogue and exposition, so that the narrative present contains episodes from the past reported as though they are again in the present. This collapsing of time, thus, provides the formula by which we as readers know Moon, subjectively and objectively, by action and by thought.

In contrast to the manner of presenting Moon, other characters are portrayed as Moon relates to them. He perceives them and filters them into the narrative—such as when the reader is told that Osa "was the kind of woman Halsey [the friend Moon accidentally killed] always wanted him to chase . . . the tall ones wearing pearls. The ones with the long patrician faces, Bermuda tans, and the high-fashion jackets. The ones who handed the parking lot attendant the keys to the Porsche, who knew exactly how to walk, and hold their heads, and tell the world they owned it" (249). The decorative and mannered details of that description tell us a lot about how Moon expresses his self-loathing, but not so much about Osa. That we derive from her reported actions: the persistence of her desire to join in Moon's mission, her evident self-sufficiency, her intelligence, and her bravery. She is a character that Moon ought to aspire to equal, and when she accepts his declarations of affection, the reader takes it as a promising sign that he may redeem himself.

Other characters, such as Victoria Mathias and the deceased Rick, confirm the centrality of Moon in the narrative. Both mother and brother appear only in terms of their importance to Moon. A possible exception is Mr. Lum Lee, who functions in the mystery plot as a shadowy figure and in the general exposition of the narrative as representative of traditional cultural values. His search for the urn of ancestral bones and his dedication to finding them a suitable resting place make him something like the elders in the Navajo novels, that is, a keeper of culture and its protocols. In *Finding Moon*, however, Mr. Lum Lee stands alone, without the enriching and supportive culture that the Navajos have.

THEME

In 1990 when Tony Hillerman talked to interviewers about works-in-progress, he mentioned his interest in completing a coming-of-age novel as well as the work set in Asia that has now appeared as *Finding Moon*. At the time he described the coming-of-age manuscript in process as a Southwestern *Catcher in the Rye* set during the Great Depression (Bernell and Karni 49). Perhaps another departure from the Navajo cycle will appear to fulfill that description, but one has to wonder if in *Finding Moon* Hillerman has not completed both of the works-in-progress. Surely the thematic heart of this novel, nourished by structure, technique, and adaptation of the detective fiction genre, is tantamount to the arrival at maturity that climaxes coming-of-age novels. Moon Mathias may be older than the usual protagonist of such stories, but possibly finding an adequate way to live with the contingencies of experience in the family and the world seems for Hillerman to be a compelling philosophical and existential issue.

As we reflect upon the themes of Hillerman's novels, it seems easy to say that the cultural integrity in his earlier books is akin to Moon's spiritual resolution in *Finding Moon*. Hillerman's use of a popular literary genre concerned with the violation of social and ethical order indicates his wish to explore moral geography, not simply the mean streets and underworld. His use of characters who are aware of and understanding of the differences between cultures as his detectives show that Hillerman intends that his novels have a serious side. And the ongoing dialogue in his novels and between his novels about harmony, as Navajos describe the condition of being morally at ease, confirms that, despite all his machinations of characters and plots, Hillerman conceives of reality as a moral drama in which the goal is to become spiritually whole. This is true for *Finding Moon* as well as for Hillerman's Navajo books.

A LITERARY HISTORICAL READING OF *FINDING MOON*

Despite the attention given to critical approaches in the study of literature and to theory about literature, the essential activity for most literary scholars and the departments of English is literary history. The term has self-evident signification. It refers to the development of literary forms as it is understood by experts. In that regard it may be seen as parallel to other subdivisions of the historical enterprise, such as military history or economic history. Each of those studies singles out one element from the general accumulation of information and data about past events and seeks to organize a record of the passage of that element through time.

To do this effectively, scholars of the discipline devise categories that are inherent to the subject. For literature and its history the largest of the categories is usually the period. The simplest way to define periods is to select arbitrarily some dates thought to have significance; thus, many anthologies of American literature designed for use in historically based courses will present writing from colonial times until 1865 in one volume, and from 1865 until the near-present in a second volume. The point of division—the year 1865—appeals because it can be argued that the end of the Civil War in the United States was a time when a new society, and, therefore, new ways of writing, began.

The problem with that arbitrary selection, though, is that the date 1865 has political, military, and economic significance, but not necessarily literary importance. It is not inherently a demarcation for a *literary* period. Far more useful is some designation related to styles of writing or the appearance of dominant themes in literature. For that reason, scholars write about such periods as the Neo-Classical, when models derived from European antiquity became popular, or Romanticism, when the philosophy of individualism and devotion to nature came to prominence. The possibility for dispute remains in forging a precise definition of either Neo-Classicism or Romanticism, but at least the categories are founded in literary practice.

In a similar quest to create valid foundations for literary history, literary historians also devote their energies to tracing the appearance and variations of literary genres, indicating when each literary form arose and marking the alterations its form has undergone since the eighteenth century. Thematic interests constitute another basis for categorizing literature in an historical way. One of the subdivisions of literary history that *Finding Moon* fits into is the study of popular literature. *Finding Moon* fits neatly into this category because of the characteristics of detective fiction that it displays, and its large audience. It can also be classified thematically, as a coming-of-age novel.

Finding Moon can be seen to have roots in much earlier ideas when we investigate the presentation of its spiritual theme in the terminology of Christian tradition. Finally, that is the critical result of this pursuit of the novel into literary history—tradition. The novel relates to precedent works, and it resonates with the meanings that repeated use of the themes has created. Each new instance of the use of a tradition in literature declares its continuing relevance; thus, each new instance forges a connection to the past. This is by no means simply redundancy, for each new instance modifies its predecessors and successors. Having read *Find-*

ing Moon, we will inevitably adjust our ideas of other works of its kind, published earlier or later, so that when we encounter narratives of similarly conflicted characters, our experience with Malcolm "Moon" Mathias will hover in our minds, sharpening our perceptions.

Bibliography

Note: Page numbers referred to in the text are to the paperback editions of Tony Hillerman's novels, with the exception of *Sacred Clowns* and *Finding Moon.* These page references are to the hardcover editions of the novels.

WORKS BY TONY HILLERMAN

Detective Novels

The Blessing Way. New York: Harper & Row, 1970.
Coyote Waits. New York: Harper & Row, 1990.
Dance Hall of the Dead. New York: Harper & Row, 1973.
The Dark Wind. New York: Harper & Row, 1982.
Finding Moon. New York: HarperCollins, 1995.
The Fly on the Wall. New York: Harper & Row, 1971.
The Ghostway. New York: Harper & Row, 1984.
Listening Woman. New York: Harper & Row, 1978.
People of Darkness. New York: Harper & Row, 1980.
Sacred Clowns. New York: HarperCollins, 1993.
Skinwalkers. New York: Harper & Row, 1986.
Talking God. New York: Harper & Row, 1989.
A Thief of Time. New York: Harper & Row, 1988.

Detective Short Stories

"Chee's Witch." *The New Black Mask 7.* 1986. Reprinted in *The Tony Hillerman Companion.* Ed. Martin Greenberg, 366–75. New York: HarperCollins, 1994.
"First Lead Gasser." *Ellery Queen's Mystery Magazine.* April 1993. Reprinted in *The Tony Hillerman Companion.* Ed. Martin Greenberg, 355–65. New York: HarperCollins, 1994.
The Perfect Murder. By Jack Hitt with contributions by Lawrence Block, Sarah Caudwell, Tony Hillerman, Peter Lovesey, and Donald Westlake. New York: HarperCollins, 1991.
"The Witch, Yazzie, and the Nine of Clubs." *Crime Wave.* London: Collins. 1981. Reprinted in *The Tony Hillerman Companion.* Ed. Martin Greenberg, 341–54. New York: HarperCollins, 1984.

Other Works

Editor. *The Best of the West: An Anthology of Classic Writing from the American West.* New York: HarperCollins, 1991.
The Boy Who Made Dragonfly: A Zuni Myth Retold by Tony Hillerman. Albuquerque: University of New Mexico Press, 1972.
"Editorial Judgement or Censorship?" *The Writer* (May 1991): 21–22.
The Great Taos Bank Robbery and Other Indian Country Affairs. Albuquerque: University of New Mexico Press, 1973.
Hillerman Country: A Journey Through the Southwest with Tony Hillerman. With photography by Barney Hillerman. New York: HarperCollins, 1991.
Indian Country: America's Sacred Land. With photography by Bela Kalman. Flagstaff, Ariz.: Northland Press, 1987.
"Making Mysteries with Navajo Materials." *Literature and Anthropology.* Eds. Philip A. Dennis and Wendell Aycock, 5–13. Lubbock: Texas Tech University Press, 1989.
Editor. *The Mysterious West.* New York: HarperCollins, 1994.
"Mystery, Country Boys, and the Big Reservation." *Colloquium on Crime: Eleven Renowned Mystery Writers Discuss Their Work.* Ed. Robin W. Winks, 127–47. New York: Scribners, 1986.
New Mexico. With photography by David Muench. Portland, Oreg.: C. H. Belding, 1974.
New Mexico, Rio Grande, and Other Essays. Portland, Oreg.: Graphic Arts Center Press, 1992.
Rio Grande. With photography by Robert Reynolds. Portland, Oreg.: C. H. Belding, 1975.

Editor. *The Spell of New Mexico*. Albuquerque: University of New Mexico Press, 1976.

Talking Mysteries: A Conversation with Tony Hillerman. With Ernie Bulow. Albuquerque: University of New Mexico Press, 1991. Originally *Words, Weather, and Wolfman: Conversations with Tony Hillerman*. Limited Edition by Ernie Bulow.

WORKS ABOUT TONY HILLERMAN

General Criticism

"Anthropological Thrillers." *The Economist* (London), 14 August 1993: 83.

Bakerman, Jane S. "Cutting Both Ways: Race, Prejudice, and Motive in Tony Hillerman's Detective Fiction." *MELUS* 11 (Fall 1984): 17–25.

———. "Joe Leaphorn and the Navajo Way: Tony Hillerman's Indian Detective Fiction." *Clues* 2 (Spring/Summer 1981): 9–16.

———. "Tony Hillerman's Joe Leaphorn and Jim Chee." *Cops and Constables: American and British Fictional Policemen*. Eds. Earl F. Bargainnier and George N. Dove, 98–112. Bowling Green, Ohio: Bowling Green State University Popular Press, 1986.

Breen, Jon L. "The Detective Fiction of Tony Hillerman: A Book-by-Book Guide." *The Tony Hillerman Companion*. Ed. Martin Greenberg, 1–48. New York: HarperCollins, 1994.

Chapman, G. Clarke. "Crime and Blessing in Tony Hillerman's Fiction." *Christian Century* 108, 13 November 1991: 1063–65.

Cleveland, Carol. "Tony Hillerman." *Twentieth Century Crime and Mystery Writers*. Ed. John M. Reilly, 449–50. Second Edition. New York: St. Martin's Press, 1985.

Doerry, Karl W. "Literary Conquista: The Southwest as a Literary Emblem." *Journal of the Southwest* 32 (Winter 1990): 438–50.

Engel, Leonard. "Landscape and Place in Tony Hillerman's Mysteries." *Western American Literature* 28 (Summer 1993): 111–22.

Erisman, Fred. *Tony Hillerman*. Western Writers Series No. 87. Boise, Idaho: Boise State University, 1989.

———. "Tony Hillerman's Jim Chee and the Shaman's Dilemma." *Lamar Journal of the Humanities* 17 (Spring 1992): 5–16.

———. "Tony Hillerman's Southwest." *The Roundup Quarterly*, n.s. 1 (Summer 1989): 9–18.

Freese, Peter. *The Ethnic Detective: Chester Himes, Harry Kemelman, Tony Hillerman*. pp. 168–245. Essen: Verlag Die Blaue Eule, 1992.

Gaugenmaier, Judith Tabor. "The Mysteries of Tony Hillerman." *The American West* 26 (December 1989): 46, 56–58.

Hirshey, Gerri. "Murder, Mayhem, and Mythology." *GQ* (Gentlemen's Quarterly), September 1993: 133, 136–40.

Neary, John. "Dillettantes in the Game of Life." *Archaeology*, March/April 1995: 58–62.

Parfit, Michael. "I Think You Should Take Out the Indian Stuff: Weaving Mysteries That Tell of Life Among the Navajos." *Smithsonian*, December 1990: 92–105.

Pierson, James C. "Mystery Literature and Ethnography: Fictional Detectives as Anthropologists." *Literature and Anthropology*. Eds. Philip A. Dennis and Wendell Aycock, 15–30. Lubbock: Texas Tech University Press, 1989.

Quirk, Thomas. "Justice on the Reservation." *The Armchair Detective* 18 (Fall 1985): 364–70.

Roush, Jan. "The Developing Art of Tony Hillerman." *Western American Literature* 28 (Summer 1993): 99–110.

Schneider, Jack W. "Crime and Navajo Punishment: Tony Hillerman's Novels of Detection." *Southwest Review* 67 (Spring 1982): 151–60.

Stasio, Marilyn. "What's Happened to Heroes Is a Crime." *New York Times Book Review*, 14 October 1990: 1+.

Strenski, Ellen, and Robley Evans. "Ritual and Murder in Tony Hillerman's Indian Detective Novels." *Western American Literature* 16 (Fall 1981): 205–16.

Van Deventer, M. J. "Tony Hillerman's West." *Persimmon Hill* 21 (Summer 1993): 36–43.

Ward, Alex. "Navajo Cops on the Case." *New York Times Magazine*, 18 May 1989: 38–39.

Biographical Information

Bernell, Sue, and Michael Karni. "Interview with Tony Hillerman." *This Is about Vision: Interviews with Southwestern Writers*. Eds. William Balassi, John F. Crawford, and Annie O. Eysturoy, 41–51. Albuquerque: University of New Mexico Press, 1990.

"Big Deals: Tony Hillerman's Contract." *Entertainment Weekly*, 3 December 1993: 65.

Breen, Jon L. "Interview with Tony Hillerman." *The Tony Hillerman Companion*. Ed. Martin Greenberg, 49–70. New York: HarperCollins, 1994.

Breslin, Catherine. "Interview with Tony Hillerman." *Publisher's Weekly*, 10 June 1988: 57–58.

Bulow, Ernie. "Interview with Tony Hillerman." *Talking Mysteries: Conversations with Tony Hillerman*. pp. 46–91. Albuquerque: University of New Mexico Press, 1991.

Current Biography Yearbook 1992. pp. 258–60.

Goodman, Susan. "Interview with Tony Hillerman and Sue Grafton." *Modern Maturity* 38 (July–August 1995): 74–82.

Herbert, Rosemary. "Tony Hillerman." *The Fatal Art of Entertainment: Interviews with Mystery Writers.* pp. 85–111. New York: G. K. Hall, 1994.

Holt, Patricia. "Interview with Tony Hillerman." *Publisher's Weekly,* 24 October 1980: 6–7.

Parker, Betty, and Riley Parker. "Interview with Tony Hillerman." *The Armchair Detective* 20 (Winter 1987): 5–14.

"Publisher Signs Hillerman." *The New York Times,* 17 November 1993: B8.

Ross, Dale H., and Charles L. P. Silet. "Interview with Tony Hillerman." *Clue* 10 (Fall/Winter 1989): 119–38.

Sobol, John. *Tony Hillerman: A Public Life.* Toronto: ECW Press, 1994.

Stead, Deborah. "Crashing the Ceremony." *New York Times Book Review,* 3 July 1988: 6.

Taylor, Bruce. "Interview with Tony Hillerman." *The Armchair Detective* 14 (Winter 1981): 93–95.

REVIEWS

The Blessing Way

The Armchair Detective, Fall 1990, 426.
Booklist, 1 March 1970, 1079.
Booklist, 15 March 1970, 1154.
Booklist, 1 April 1971, 654.
Booklist, 15 November 1990, 600.
Book World (Washington Post), 10 May 1970, 14.
Catholic Library World, October 1971, 112.
Christian Century, 13 November 1990, 1063.
Critic, July 1970, 74.
English Journal, February 1992, 92.
Kirkus Reviews, 1 January 1970, 26.
Kirkus Reviews, 15 February 1970, 187.
Library Journal, 15 May 1970, 1860.
Library Journal, 15 June 1970, 2320.
Library Journal, 1 February 1991, 109.
Newsweek, 19 June 1989, 61.
New Yorker, 6 June 1970, 136.
New York Times Book Review, 19 April 1970, 36.
Publisher's Weekly, 29 December 1969, 61.
Roundup, Summer 1992, 25.

Saturday Review, 28 March 1970, 40.
Times Literary Supplement (London), April 1971, 308.
Western American Literature, November 1981, 206.
Western American Literature, Summer 1993, 99, 111.

The Fly on the Wall

The Armchair Detective, Winter 1991, 110.
Best Sellers, 1 November 1971, 363.
Booklist, 1 January 1972, 381.
Booklist, 15 January 1972, 430.
Booklist, August 1991, 2107.
Harpers, October 1971, 120.
Kirkus Reviews, 15 July 1971, 771.
Library Journal, 1 September 1971, 2674.
Library Journal, 15 December 1971, 4206.
New Leader, 13 December 1971.
New Yorker, 25 September 1971, 142.
Publisher's Weekly, 26 July 1971, 45.
Village Voice, 22 April 1989, 58.

Dance Hall of the Dead

The Armchair Detective, Fall 1990, 426.
Best Sellers, 1 November 1973, 339.
Booklist, 15 October 1973, 208, 222.
Books West, February 1978, 40.
Book World (*Washington Post*), 26 July 1992, 1, 50.
Catholic Library World, April 1974, 456.
Critic, March 1974, 75.
English Journal, Fall 1992, 92.
Kirkus Reviews, 15 August 1973, 839, 891.
Library Journal, 1 October 1973, 2884.
Library Journal, 15 January 1974, 225.
Library Journal, 15 May 1974, 1453.
Newsweek, 19 June 1989, 61.
New Yorker, 31 December 1973, 60.
New York Times Book Review, 25 November 1973, 49.
Publisher's Weekly, 27 August 1973, 272.
Roundup, Summer 1992, 25.

Times Literary Supplement (London), 5 April 1985, 394.
Western American Literature, November 1981, 206.
Western American Literature, Summer 1993, 99, 111.
Wilson Library Bulletin, February 1974, 465.

Listening Woman

The Armchair Detective, Fall 1990, 426.
Atlantic, June 1978, 100.
Booklist, 15 June 1978, 1610.
Books West, February 1978, 40.
Book World (*Washington Post*), 16 April 1978, E6.
Book World (*Washington Post*), 3 December 1978, E16.
Book World (*Washington Post*), 27 May 1990, 12.
English Journal, February 1979, 104.
English Journal, November 1979, 77.
Kirkus Reviews, 15 February 1978, 205.
Library Journal, 1 May 1978, 997.
Los Angeles Times Book Review, 27 May 1990, 10.
New York Times Book Review, 7 May 1978, 25.
New York Times Book Review, 22 April 1979, 39.
Observer, 28 January 1979, 35.
Publisher's Weekly, 13 March 1978, 107.
Roundup, Summer 1992, 25+.
School Library Journal, November 1978, 82.
Western American Literature, November 1981, 206.
Western American Literature, Summer 1993, 99+, 111+.

People of Darkness

Booklist, 15 October 1980, 308.
Book World (*Washington Post*), 16 November 1980, 7.
Christian Century, 13 November 1991, 1063.
Critic, January 1981, 8.
Kirkus Reviews, 15 August 1980, 1115.
Library Journal, 1 September 1980, 1754.
New Republic, 13 December 1980, 40.
New Yorker, 29 December 1980, 74.
New York Times Book Review, 4 January 1981, 16.
New York Times Book Review, 7 February 1982, 39.

Observer, 8 August 1982, 30.
Publisher's Weekly, 15 August 1980, 45.
Roundup, Summer 1953, 25+.
Science Fiction Review, November 1983, 47.
Spectator, 16 October 1982, 25.
Times Literary Supplement (London), 29 October 1982, 1196.
Village Voice, 22 August 1989, 58.
Western American Literature, Summer 1993, 99.
Wilson Library Bulletin, March 1981, 533.

The Dark Wind

Antioch Review, Summer 1982, 362.
Atlantic, June 1982, 102.
Christian Science Monitor, 5 March 1982, 17.
Kirkus Reviews, 1 February 1982, 167.
Kliatt (Young Adult Paperback Book Guide), Fall 1983, 11.
Los Angeles Times Book Review, 25 July 1982, 6.
Library Journal, 1 March 1982, 566.
Listener (London), 19 May 1983, 24.
New Republic, 20 September 1982, 43.
Newsweek, 19 June 1989, 61.
New York Times Book Review, 17 October 1982, 41.
New York Times Book Review, 5 December 1982, 22.
New York Times Book Review, 1 May 1983, 35.
Observer, 20 March 1983, 33.
Publisher's Weekly, 12 March 1982.
Quill & Quire (Canada), May 1982, 41.
Roundup, Summer 1992, 25+.
Spectator, 2 April 1983, 25.
Western American Literature, Summer 1993, 99+.

The Ghostway

Best Sellers, April 1985, 17.
Booklist, 1 January 1985, 620.
Book World (Washington Post), 17 March 1985, 10.
Kirkus Reviews, 15 December 1984, 1169.
Library Journal, 1 February 1985, 114.
New Yorker, 25 February 1985, 106.

New York Times Book Review, 2 June 1985, 38.
New York Times Book Review, 3 August 1986, 28.
Publisher's Weekly, 30 November 1984, 82.
Publisher's Weekly, 30 May 1986, 58.
Roundup, Summer 1992, 25+.
Spectator, 22 February 1986, 28.
Times Literary Supplement (London), 27 December 1985, 1478.
Western American Literature, Spring 1986, 63.
Wilson Library Bulletin, Summer 1993, 99+.

Skinwalkers

Atlantic, February 1987, 95.
Best Sellers, December 1986, 340.
Booklist, 15 November 1986, 450.
Book World (Washington Post), 15 February 1987, 4.
Book World (Washington Post), 26 December 1987, 13.
Kirkus Reviews, 1 December 1986, 1763.
Library Journal, January 1987, 111.
Listener, 9 February 1989, 24.
Newsweek, 19 June 1984, 61.
New Yorker, 2 February 1987, 102.
New York Times Book Review, 18 January 1987, 23.
New York Times Book Review, 22 November 1987, 50.
People, 9 February 1987, 16.
Publisher's Weekly, 28 November 1986, 67.
Times Literary Supplement (London), 2 December 1988, 1351.
Tribune Books (Chicago), 22 February 1987, 6.
Tribune Books (Chicago), 2 September 1990, 6.
USA Today, 27 January 1987, 4D.
Village Voice, 22 August 1989, 58.
West Coast Review of Books, August 1987, 29.
Western American Literature, Summer 1993, 99+.

A Thief of Time

The Armchair Detective, Winter 1989, 24.
The Armchair Detective, Spring 1989, 218.
Atlantic, August 1988, 80.
Booklist, 15 May 1988, 1553.

Book World (Washington Post), 19 June 1988, 8.
Book World (Washington Post), 26 July 1992, 1+.
Christian Century, 13 November 1991, 1063.
Christian Science Monitor, 4 August 1989, 13.
Cosmopolitan, June 1988, 40.
English Journal, February 1993, 63+.
Kirkus Reviews, 1 June 1988, 794.
Listener, 10 August 1989, 25.
Los Angeles Times Book Review, 3 July 1988, 7.
Los Angeles Times Book Review, 21 January 1990, 14.
Newsweek, 18 July 1988, 54.
Newsweek, 19 June 1989, 61.
New Yorker, 18 August 1988, 84.
New York Times Book Review, 13 July 1988, 6.
New York Times Book Review, 10 December 1989, 42.
Observer, 14 May 1989, 50.
People, 22 August 1988, 27.
Philadelphia Magazine, August 1988, 71.
Publisher's Weekly, 27 May 1988, 53.
Publisher's Weekly, 17 November 1989, 50.
Quill & Quire (Canada), September 1988, 79.
Roundup, December 1988, 32.
Roundup, Fall 1990, 45.
School Library Journal, March 1989, 209.
Spectator, 18 November 1989, 42.
Time, 4 July 1988, 71.
Tribune Books (Chicago), 26 June 1988, 6.
Village Voice, 22 August 1989, 58.
Voice of Youth Advocate, February 1989, 285.
West Coast Review of Books, June 1988, 31.
Western American Literature, Winter 1989, 376.
Western American Literature, Summer 1993, 99+.

Talking God

America, 18 November 1989, 389.
Antioch Review, Summer 1989, 374.
The Armchair Detective, Winter 1990, 122.
The Armchair Detective, Spring 1990, 171.
Atlantic, October 1989, 116.
Booklist, 1 March 1989, 1490.
Christian Century, 30 August 1989, 795.

Christian Science Monitor, 4 August 1989, 13.
Cosmopolitan, June 1989, 48.
English Journal, October 1990, 81.
English Journal, February 1992, 92.
Inside Books, June 1989, 60.
Kirkus Reviews, 1 May 1989, 660.
Library Journal, 15 May 1989, 89.
Los Angeles Times Book Review, 9 July 1989, 13.
Los Angeles Times Book Review, 16 December 1990, 10.
Newsweek, 14 August 1989, 60.
New Yorker, 14 August 1989, 92.
New York Times Book Review, 18 June 1989, 9.
New York Times Book Review, 23 December 1990, 15.
Observer, 6 May 1990, 61.
People, 14 August 1989, 26.
Playboy, March 1990, 30.
Publisher's Weekly, 21 April 1989, 83.
School Library Journal, November 1989, 137.
Time, 19 June 1989, 66.
Tribune Books (Chicago), 4 June 1989, 7.
Village Voice, 22 August 1989, 58.
Virginia Quarterly Review, Winter 1990, 23.
Voice of Youth Advocate, October 1989, 212.
Western American Literature, Fall 1990, 287.
Western American Literature, Summer 1993, 99+.

Coyote Waits

America, 17 November 1990.
The Armchair Detective, Winter 1991, 48.
The Armchair Detective, Summer 1991, 295.
Atlantic, September 1990, 121.
Bloomsbury Review, July 1990, 12.
Booklist, 15 March 1990, 1753.
Books, March 1991, 6.
Book World (Washington Post), 8 July 1990, 6.
Christian Science Monitor, 11 July 1990, 13.
Christian Science Monitor, 17 December 1990, 13.
English Journal, February 1992, 92.
Kliatt (Young Adult Paperback Book Guide), April 1992, 8.
Los Angeles Times Book Review, 8 July 1990, 8.
Los Angeles Times Book Review, 16 February 1992, 10.

New Yorker, 20 August 1990, 91.
New York Times Book Review, 24 June 1990, 12.
New York Times Book Review, 2 February 1992, 28.
Observer, 31 March 1991, 54.
People, 27 August 1990, 22.
Publisher's Weekly, 1 January 1992, 53.
Reference & Research Book News, October 1990, 25.
Tribune Books (Chicago), 8 July 1990, 6.
Tribune Books (Chicago), 2 December 1990, 28.
Vogue, July 1990, 108.
Voice of Youth Advocate, December 1990, 282.
Wall Street Journal, 13 July 1990, A7.
Western American Literature, Summer 1993, 99.
Wilderness, October 1990, 370.

Sacred Clowns

Atlantic, October 1993, 132.
Booklist, 1 September 1993, 4.
Book World (Washington Post), 5 September 1993, 4.
Christian Science Monitor, 22 October 1993, 11.
Entertainment Weekly, 17 September 1993, 82+.
Kirkus Reviews, 1 August 1993, 967.
Kliatt (Young Adult Paperback Book Guide), November 1994, 10.
Los Angeles Times Book Review, 3 October 1993, 12.
New Yorker, 23 August 1993, 165.
New York Times, 20 December 1993, C15.
New York Times Book Review, 17 October 1993, 36.
Playboy, November 1993, 33.
Publisher's Weekly, 26 July 1993, 60.
Tribune Books (Chicago), 26 September 1993, 6.
Wall Street Journal, 29 September 1993, A16.

Finding Moon

Booklist, 15 September 1995, 116.
Entertainment Weekly, 3 November 1995, 59.
GQ—Gentlemen's Quarterly, November 1995, 59.
Library Journal, 1 November 1995, 106.
New York Times Book Review, 22 October 1995, 29.

Publishers Weekly, 4 September 1995, 48.
Washington Post, 6 November 1995, D2.

OTHER SECONDARY SOURCES

Ashcroft, Bill, Gareth Griffiths, and Helen Tiffin. *The Empire Writes Back.* London: Routledge, 1990.

Du Bois, W.E.B. *The Souls of Black Folk.* Chicago: A. C. McClurg, 1903.

Freeman, R. Austin. "The Art of the Detective Story." *Nineteenth Century and After.* May 1924. Reprinted in *The Art of the Mystery Story.* Ed. Howard Haycraft, 7–17. New York: Biblo & Tannen, 1975.

Freud, Sigmund. *Moses and Monotheism.* New York: Knopf, 1939.

Genette, Gerard. *Fiction and Diction.* Ithaca, N.Y.: Cornell University Press, 1993.

Haycraft, Howard. *Murder for Pleasure: The Life and Times of the Detective Story.* Revised edition. New York: Biblo & Tannen, 1968.

Heilbrun, Carolyn. *Writing a Woman's Life.* New York: Norton, 1988.

Klein, Kathleen Gregory. *The Woman Detective: Gender and Genre.* Second edition. Urbana: University of Illinois Press, 1995.

Knox, Ronald A. "A Detective Story Decalogue." *Best Detective Stories of 1928.* London: Faber; New York: Livesight, 1929. Reprinted in *The Art of the Mystery* Story. Ed. Howard Haycraft, 194–96. New York: Biblo & Tannen, 1975.

Murch, A. E. *The Development of the Detective Novel.* New York: Philosophical Library, 1958.

Reilly, John M., ed. *Twentieth Century Crime and Mystery Writers.* 3rd ed. New York: St. Martin's Press, 1991.

Steinbrunner, Chris et al. *Detectionary: A Bibliographical Dictionary of the Leading Characters in Detective and Mystery Fiction.* Revised edition. New York: Overlook Press, 1977.

Steinbrunner, Chris, and Otto Penzler. *Encyclopedia of Mystery and Detection.* New York: McGraw-Hill, 1976.

Symons, Julian. *Bloody Murder.* New York: Viking Press, 1984.

Van Dine, S. S. "Twenty Rules for Writing Detective Stories." *American Magazine.* September 1928. Reprinted in *The Art of the Mystery Story.* Ed. Howard Haycraft, 189–93. New York: Biblo & Tannen, 1975.

Index

About the Author

JOHN M. REILLY won the Edgar Allan Poe award from the Mystery Writers of America for his reference work *Twentieth Century Crime and Mystery Writers* (1980). Before joining the faculty at Howard University, where he is a graduate professor of American literature, he taught at the State University of New York and served for six years as president of the 22,000-member faculty and professional union. He has written extensively on popular literature and detective fiction. For his critical work on African-American writing he received the MELUS award for distinguished study of multi-ethnic culture.